The Up Stairs Lounge Arson

Thirty-Two Deaths in a New Orleans Gay Bar, June 24, 1973

CLAYTON DELERY-EDWARDS

McFarland & Company, Inc., Publishers
Jefferson, North Carolina

LIBRARY OF CONGRESS CATALOGUING-IN-PUBLICATION DATA

Delery-Edwards, Clayton, 1957–
    The Up Stairs Lounge arson : thirty-two deaths in a New Orleans
gay bar, June 24, 1973 / Clayton Delery-Edwards.
        p.   cm.
    Includes bibliographical references and index.

    ISBN 978-0-7864-7953-5 (softcover : acid free paper) ∞
    ISBN 978-1-4766-1510-3 (ebook)

    1. Arson—Louisiana—New Orleans—Case studies.   2. Murder—
Louisiana—New Orleans—Case studies.   3. Gay bars—Louisiana—
New Orleans—Case studies.   4. Gays—Louisiana—New
Orleans—Social conditions—20th century.   5. Homophobia—
Louisiana—New Orleans—History—20th century.   I. Title.
HV6638.5.U6D45 2014
364.152'340976335—dc23   2014017736

BRITISH LIBRARY CATALOGUING DATA ARE AVAILABLE

On the cover: plaque now on the sidewalk outside the Up Stairs Lounge,
commemorating the fire (Clayton Delery-Edwards), background image
iStockphoto/Thinkstock

Printed in the United States of America

*McFarland & Company, Inc., Publishers
    Box 611, Jefferson, North Carolina 28640
    www.mcfarlandpub.com*

The Up Stairs
Lounge Arson

To all those who died,
especially three unidentified males,
and Ferris LeBlanc,
who was identified, but never claimed

Table of Contents

Acknowledgments

Writing can be an isolating enterprise, but it is also a surprisingly collaborative one, and I have many people to thank for their support and assistance.

I am extremely grateful to the people who agreed to interviews or who wrote to me, via mail or email, and shared their experiences. These people include former patrons of the Up Stairs Lounge, survivors of the fire, participants in the subsequent memorial services (particularly those on June 25 and July 1, 1973), as well as others whose experiences, research and expertise have become entwined with the story of the fire. Whether their words appear in the text or not, they have been instrumental in helping me make sense of what happened. My thanks to Regina Adams, Roberts Batson, the Rev. David Billings, the Rev. Dexter Brecht, the Rev. Paul Breton, Stewart Butler, Phillip Byrd, Jack Carrell, the Rev. Anita Dinwiddie, Clancy Dubos, Francis Dufrene, Steven Duplantis, Aaron Edwards, Skylar Fein, Vince Fornias, James Hartman, Carey Hendrix, Charles Kaiser, Henry Kenner, Paul Killgore, Crystal Little, Marcy Marcell, Jim Massaci, Jr., Toni Pizanie, the Rev. Troy Perry, Richard Pool, Lawrence Raybourne, Javier Sandoval, George Tresch, Steven Whittaker, and the Rev. Carol Cotton Winn. If I have left anyone out, I apologize for the oversight.

I owe a great debt to Johnny Townsend, author of the only other book on the Up Stairs Lounge, *Let the Faggots Burn*. Although Mr. Townsend and I have never met in person, we have emailed each other throughout the past five years, and he was kind enough to grant me permission to draw upon his book. He might logically have regarded me as a rival, but in an early email he wrote, "In regard to this fire, all I ever wanted was that the story be told." *Let the Faggots Burn* is based heavily on interviews with patrons and survivors of the Up Stairs Lounge conducted in the late eighties and early nineties. By the time I began my book in 2009, many of these people had died, and many others, tired of reliving such a traumatic experience, were no longer willing to speak.

Johnny Townsend was also good enough to send me a treasure trove of photographs he has collected, which help bring visual life to the story.

Aside from Johnny Townsend, there is a small but very collegial group of writers, composers, artists and filmmakers documenting the Up Stairs Lounge: Royd Anderson, Robert L. Camina, Jim Downs, Skylar Fein, Frank Perez, Wayne Self and Sheri L. Wright. They have all been generous in sharing thoughts, contacts, photographs and illustrations, documents, and support. Of special note is the Rev. Paul Breton, who was good enough to share with me the journal he kept in 1973 as he helped give comfort to the survivors and plan memorials for the dead.

I spent many hours investigating the news coverage and the paper trail from the various investigations into the fire, and doing so meant that I haunted several libraries for days or weeks at a time. My thanks to the Louisiana state fire marshal, H. "Butch" Browning, for giving me access to the records of the arson investigation, which are held in a special collection in the Louisiana State Archives in Baton Rouge, and my thanks to the staff at the Louisiana State Archives for helping me go through boxes of un-indexed files so that I could locate the records. Thanks also go to the reference, microforms and archival staffs of the following libraries: the Edith Garland Dupre Library at the University of Louisiana, Lafayette; the Troy H. Middleton Library at Louisiana State University, Baton Rouge; the Louisiana Collection of the New Orleans Public Library; the Howard-Tilton Library at Tulane University, New Orleans; Watson Library at Northwestern State University in Natchitoches, Louisiana; the Earl K. Long Library at the University of New Orleans; the Williams Research Center of the Historic New Orleans Collection; and the One National Gay and Lesbian Archives in Los Angeles, California.

Once I acquired hundreds of pages of notes, transcripts, photocopies, articles and emails, I had to put them in some kind of order. There were thousands of details to consider, each significant in its own way, leaving me with the difficult job of deciding which to include and which to omit so that I could present a fair and comprehensive narrative without confusing or overwhelming the reader. For their assistance in critiquing and editing my drafts, I thank the members of the Cane River Writers: Nahla and Bill Beier, Carolyn Breedlove, Joanna Cassidy, Carol Connor, Cedelas Hall, Julie Kane, Stephanie Masson, Margaret Pennington, Frank Schicketanz, and Mary Kay Waskom.

Finally, for listening to me talk about this project for several years before saying, "Just write the book already!" I thank my beloved husband, Aaron Delery-Edwards, who encouraged me at every step and who was poorly rewarded by having to endure many weeks when I was more fully alive in 1973 than in the present. Sweetie, you're the best.

Preface

The 1973 fire at the Up Stairs Lounge is the deadliest fire in the history of New Orleans. This is not an easy distinction to achieve. The city has had many notable fires in its nearly 300-year existence, including two in the eighteenth century that both came close to destroying the struggling young settlement. The Up Stairs fire was brief; firefighters extinguished the blaze only 16 minutes after getting the call. The damage was limited to a single building, which survived the fire and still exists. Even so, that quick blaze killed 29 people within minutes, and three more later died of their injuries. Arson was immediately suspected and, though a likely suspect was soon identified, there was never an arrest or a trial.

The fire received extensive newspaper and television coverage, both locally and nationally, but the story died down sooner than one would have expected. Sooner, frankly, than some people thought was appropriate, or even decent. Leaders from the government, church, and community were surprisingly silent regarding the event. To most people today, the reasons seem simple: the Up Stairs Lounge was a gay bar, and nearly all who died were gay men. In the early 1970s, journalists didn't really know how to treat issues regarding LGBT people, and public officials were often either hostile to this population, or embarrassed to support it too openly.

Because there was never an arrest or a trial, many questions have remained officially unanswered, creating a perfect environment for rumor, speculation, and conjecture. The fire is often reported as a hate crime. There are stories of a gasoline-soaked shirt being found at the site, and of Molotov cocktails being thrown in the windows as victims died inside. Because the suspect was never arrested, there are rumors of conspiracies, some involving a hostile police department that just couldn't be bothered solving a mass-murder of gay men, and some involving the Mafia wanting to protect the culprit from prosecution.

Some people argue that the fire became the New Orleans equivalent of the Stonewall riots in New York, which took place four years earlier, and say that the Up Stairs fire fostered the birth of gay activism in the city. Some people say that it had no effect on the social or political culture of New Orleans at all.

I have had an interest in the fire since first watching news coverage in 1973, but I did not start active research until 2009. In the course of writing this book, I read and took extensive notes on contemporary news coverage, as well as accounts of the fire that appeared in various books, magazines and journals published in the ensuing 40 years. My research also involved sources that graduate school in English literature had not trained me for. I read case files from the investigations conducted by the New Orleans Police Department, New Orleans Fire Department and the Arson Investigation Unit of the State Fire Marshal, using the investigators' own words to gain insight into how they approached the crime. I read the transcripts of official, sworn statements given by many of the people who survived the fire, not to mention the statements from people who knew the primary suspect and who might (investigators hoped) reveal information that would bring the case to a satisfactory conclusion. I even read the autopsy reports of the 32 victims. I interviewed former patrons of the Up Stairs Lounge, some of whom had actually survived the fire, and I interviewed many people involved in memorial efforts, especially the one on July 1, 1973. I was also fortunate to personally meet or otherwise come in contact with many people whose lives or professions had brought them into contact with the Up Stairs Lounge in some way.

An important member of this last group is Johnny Townsend, whose book *Let the Faggots Burn* is the only other published book on the Up Stairs Lounge. Townsend's book concentrates on telling individual stories of individual lives. Though he includes an extensive bibliography, Townsend does not provide internal documentation, limiting the usefulness of the book as a research tool, as Townsend himself admits. My own book is less concerned with individual stories (though it includes some). Instead, it is focused on recreating the overarching narrative and on providing a documentary trail.

My work has also allowed me to meet Royd Anderson, Sheri L. Wright and Robert L. Camina. Royd has a completed documentary about the fire, and Sheri and Robert each have separate ones in production. I have also been fortunate to become reacquainted with Wayne Self, a former neighbor and an alumnus of the school where I teach, whose musical *Upstairs* is a fictionalized account of the fire.

Research brought me to New Orleans frequently, and this was one of the more pleasant parts of the job, though not for the reasons one would expect.

I haven't lived in New Orleans for many years, but I was raised in the metropolitan area, and my work gave me an excuse to spend more time with family and old friends. In the early years, though, I was amazed by how many locals—many of whom had been living in the city in the 1970s—either had no knowledge of the fire at all, or only a very hazy recollection of it. I also encountered many people who knew about the fire, or rather, who "knew" about the fire, their knowledge shaped by the rumor, speculation, and conjecture that have come to define it. In some cases, I knew immediately that what they were telling me was false. In other cases, I learned that later. My own knowledge of the fire and the events it spawned was under constant re-evaluation.

The story of the Up Stairs Lounge is the story of an officially unsolved crime. It is the story of anti-gay animus. It is the story of a city that experienced multiple horrific events in the early 1970s, responding to some by showing its best qualities, and responding to one by showing, perhaps, its worst. At times it is a story of cruelty, expressed either through accident or design. At times it is the story of people and communities reaching out to each other in love and support.

What kind of place was the Up Stairs Lounge? Who went there and who died there? What took place on June 24, 1973? Were local leaders truly either negligent or hostile in their responses? What kind of press coverage did the fire receive? What course did the police investigation follow, and why wasn't an arrest made? And has the fire changed the city of New Orleans and its people in any tangible way? These are the questions that this book tries to answer.

A Note on Language

One of the earliest problems I encountered with respect to language was how to write the name of the lounge itself. In print sources, I have seen it written as Upstairs, UpStairs, Up-Stairs and Up Stairs. Phil Esteve, the owner of the lounge, is now dead, and Buddy Rasmussen, his bartender and manager, is no longer willing to speak about the fire. Several news photographs from 1973 show the canopy over the entrance, and on the canopy the name is clearly written as two separate capitalized words: Up Stairs.

In the twenty-first century, members of same-sex couples tend to refer to each other as partners, life-partners, spouses, or even as each other's husband or wife. In the 1970s, these terms largely did not exist. Among friends, members of same-sex couples were usually referred to as lovers, and I have chosen to retain use of that word. In settings involving government officials, strangers or acquaintances, gays and lesbians in the 1970s often dropped the term lover and replaced it with a euphemism such as "friend" or "roommate" to provide a socially acceptable label for their relationships. I have noted several such uses.

In some chapters I have used the verb "to out," meaning "to reveal someone's homosexuality," as in "several members of the Metropolitan Community Church were outed to their families by the news coverage." This is something of an anachronism, as the earliest written uses of the word I have found date from the 1990s. Although the term may have verbally circulated as slang in the 1980s, it does not seem to have been used in the early 1970s. Similarly, the term "hate crime," employed in several places, was coined in the 1980s.

I

Beer, Prayer and Nellydrama
The Story of the Up Stairs Lounge

Things would have been much different if there had been a balcony.

The appearance of the building suggests that it might once have had one. Occupying a corner of the intersection of Chartres and Iberville streets, the site of the Up Stairs Lounge is actually a complex of three buildings sharing common walls, and today they look very much as they did at the time of the fire. The ground floor of each is devoted to commercial use. The two upper floors may have been intended for living space, but by the 1960s, the second floor, too, had become commercial, and the third floor contained storage spaces and a few flophouse rooms.

The windows on the second floor are about nine feet tall, with the sills near floor level, and the sashes designed to rise high enough so that the openings are almost the size of doorways. A tall person stepping through the door might have to duck, but the French Quarter is full of buildings in which the line of distinction between window and door is similarly blurred. This was desirable in a hot, humid climate before the invention of the air conditioner. The large windows let in a breeze, and a balcony provided a secluded outdoor space for families living above a business.

Many French Quarter bars occupy second-floor spaces similar to this one, and most have balconies, usually enclosed with cast-iron railings of artistic design. The balcony is a place to escape the cigarette smoke and get a breath of fresh air. Since it is removed from the loud music inside, it provides a retreat that is ideal for private conversation and conducive to flirtation. And, although this is not its primary purpose, in the event of an emergency such as a fire, a balcony would be a useful means of escape. If the Up Stairs Lounge had a balcony, the loss of life would not have been so high.

The Up Stairs Lounge occupied the second floor of this building located at the corner of Chartres Street and Iberville Street, on the very edge of the French Quarter (author's photograph).

With a final death toll of 32 people, the fire at the Up Stairs Lounge still stands as the single deadliest fire in the history of New Orleans. Investigators for the State Fire Marshal determined it to be a case of arson, and there was a probable suspect, but no arrest was ever made. Any of these facts would probably serve to pique the interest of readers 40 years later, but the Up Stairs was a gay bar, and the fire has come to be known as the largest mass murder of gay men in American history.[1] The story of the bar and its destruction therefore provides a particularly painful way of viewing the place gays held in the latter half of the twentieth century.

The fire took place in 1973, but the bar first opened in 1970, and those three years were part of a socially tumultuous era in American history. A very limited list of events and movements from the period would include the war in Vietnam, and the protests against it, the Nixon presidency, the beginnings of the Watergate scandal, the Supreme Court's ruling on *Roe v. Wade*, the Women's Liberation movement, the Gay Liberation movement spurred by the 1969 Stonewall Riots, the Black Power movement, the rise of an open drug

Café Lafitte in Exile, the oldest continually operating gay bar in New Orleans, occupies both floors of this building at the corner of Bourbon Street and Dumaine. In the event of a fire, the balconies would help save anyone trapped on the second floor (author's photograph).

culture, and the appearance of hippies and Jesus freaks who, with their outrageously colorful clothing and unpredictable behaviors, had a short but vivid presence on the scene.

Many of these events and movements had their beginnings prior to 1970, but they were still very much a part of the national consciousness, and while some people (the young, the marginalized, the disenfranchised) welcomed all the changes in the air, there was, of course, a reaction against them, and a strong desire to preserve the status quo. Though we now tend to celebrate the revolutionaries and activists for their achievements, there was a strong feeling among those who were then termed "the establishment" that the post–World War II version of the American Dream should have been enough to satisfy anyone's needs. America, they felt, was already a great nation, and it would be even better if these agitators would just stop yelling about feminism, gay liberation and black power. Why couldn't these troublemakers just cut their hair, buy some sensible clothes, and find satisfaction with their homes, jobs and families? Why, in short, couldn't they be more like their parents?

Gays and lesbians have historically faced a great deal of pressure to conform in just that way: to be more like their parents. Bowing to the pressure often takes the form of a life in the closet, a loveless marriage to a person of the opposite sex, and a pretense of normalcy. Rejecting the pressure frequently leads to life in a big city, far away from curious friends and relatives. Someplace like San Francisco. Or New York. Or New Orleans.

The books *The Gay Metropolis* by Charles Kaiser and *Stonewall* by David Carter both devote extensive attention to how, in the pre–Stonewall years, the ever-present threat of police raids kept behavior in gay bars ridiculously circumspect; outward displays of same-sex affection—such as kissing or even brief affectionate hugs—were enough to bring down the wrath of any under-cover policeman in attendance. In *Stonewall*, David Carter tells the story of a young gay man in New York being instructed by a bartender not to make eye contact with other men. The rule was devised to prevent the bar from being closed because of police charges of solicitation on the premises. The young man was left wondering how he was ever going to meet people if he wasn't even allowed to look at them.[2]

The New Orleans of the mid-twentieth century had a reputation for treating gays with comparative tolerance. An anecdote used to circulate about a New Orleans man who visited Los Angles in the pre–Stonewall era. He was in a gay bar and was about to shake the hand of a new acquaintance when he was stopped by a horrified bartender. "Hey, now, cut that out," said the bartender, fearful of police raids. "No touching in here" (Townsend 9).

Handshakes, eye contact, and at least some forms of touching were allowed in New Orleans. At least most of the time. In 1958 the city made a concerted effort to rid the city of homosexuals, an effort that has been characterized as "a drive against the deviates" (Treadway "Gay Community" 13). Although those efforts faded, leading to a renewed sense that the city was (for then) fairly gay friendly,[3] the anti-gay efforts experienced periodic revival.[4] Sometimes late at night, or very early in the morning, police would raid gay bars for no real cause, beating up the patrons without fear of repercussion, and arresting people for infractions not much more serious than shaking hands. A man named Kerry Lyn, who was known around New Orleans by his nickname, Napoleon, once had the bad luck to be in a gay club when the police raided it and arrested all the patrons. Napoleon was booked on an obscenities charge, and his particular crime was "dancing with a member of the same sex in an intimate embrace" (Townsend 241).

Men also often met each other in cruising spots, generally for quick, anonymous encounters in the bushes, or in restrooms known as "tea rooms" which had reputations as being good spots for a hook-up. One of the best known of these spots in the French Quarter was Cabrini Park, a fenced green space which was, in the fifties and sixties, a playground for children by day and a cruising ground for gay men by night. In January of 1971 the police led a four-night raid on the park, arresting thirteen people in the process. Shortly thereafter most of the bushes and all of the playground equipment were removed to eliminate hiding places and make the place less well suited for sexual activities.[5] This seems to have been the last crackdown on gay activity for some time, because in July of 1973 a local journalist was able to report that the police had "made no arrests on any 'homosexual' or 'morals' charges ... in the last two years" (Rushton "Forgetting" 6). Cabrini Park is no longer known as a place to look for anonymous sex; instead it is used almost entirely by downtown residents, both straight and gay, as a popular and sociable place to exercise their dogs.

Outside of bars and tea rooms, gays didn't have a whole lot of options for finding each other socially in the 1950s, 1960s and early 1970s. Post–Stonewall, a few organizations formed for political purposes. New Orleans had chapters of the Daughters of Bilitis, the Gay Liberation Front, and the Gay Activist Alliance, but most of these early efforts lasted only a year or two before fading.[6] Filmmaker Tim Wolff's documentary *The Sons of Tennessee Williams* tells the story of gay Mardi Gras "krewes" that formed in the 1950s and 1960s. These organizations, which were chartered and admitted members by invitation only, existed for the putative purpose of staging elaborately costumed balls mimicking those staged by krewes such as Rex and Comus. Restricting themselves to a gay membership, they had no explicit political agenda, but instead provided a way to socialize in groups without the risk of being arrested. Their ball *tableaux* featured miles of satin, fortunes in faux jewels, and enough plumes to feather a thousand peacocks, all worn by men who were bending gender in ways that were almost unimaginable anywhere outside of New Orleans.

Because these krewes were open only by invitation, membership was comparatively small, leaving the majority of gay men to the bars, cruising areas and whatever other small pockets of sociability they could find. As is still the case among gay men today, the effeminate and the cross-dressers were usually the ones who suffered the most harassment from both civilians and police because they were the most obvious targets. A transgender woman who asked not to be identified in this book tells a story about being harassed by the police in about 1970.

> Back then, I was living as a man during the week when I was working, and I only went out as a woman during the weekend.
> One day I was walking down the street and a cop grabbed me. He spit in my face, and then wiped off my make-up. "Go on home and change, boy," he said. "You're required by law to be wearing two articles of men's clothing." I said, "I've

got tube socks in my bra cups, and I'm wearing B.V.D.'s. Those are my two articles." He said, "Don't give me any lip. Go on home and change." So I went home, and I changed my blonde wig for my brown one, and when I walked right past him ten minutes later, he didn't recognize me.

On the other hand, the police could sometimes act both fairly and with compassion. In 1970, a gay man named Frank Scorsone, Jr., picked up a man for a trick, only to be robbed by him. The robber, intentionally targeting gay men, took Frank's watch and wallet and told Frank that he would call and let him know how much it would take to get them back. He also threatened blackmail, telling Frank he would be asking for money in return for not calling Frank's family or employer and telling them that Frank was gay. Frank Scorsone telephoned a friend, Paul Killgore,[7] for assistance, and Killgore convinced him to go to the police. Much to the surprise of both, the police took Frank's experience seriously; the same assailant had apparently robbed and blackmailed several other men, all of whom were afraid of making an identification or filing a formal report, because they didn't want to be identified in police reports as gay. As Frank Scorsone and Paul Killgore left the department, the police actually thanked them for coming in. "Of course," says Paul Killgore in speaking about the experience today, "we have no idea what they said about us after we left."

The police force in any city is not necessarily representative of the population at large, and perhaps New Orleans' reputation for tolerance had more to do with the social atmosphere in the Quarter, where gays and lesbians were most visible. However, while the French Quarter is in New Orleans, New Orleans is not the French Quarter. Neighborhoods uptown and in the suburbs tend to be more conventional. Often, they are at least as conservative as the nation as a whole, and sometimes they are much more so. The suburb of Metairie, for example, elected the Klansman and white supremacist David Duke to the state legislature in the 1980s. During his one and only term in elective office, Duke authored one bill to give increased penalties for drug offenses to people living in housing projects, and another bill that would pay women on welfare to use contraception.[8] Duke also believed that gays and lesbians should be barred from teaching jobs so that they couldn't recruit students, and wanted to require people with AIDS and HIV to have their genitals tattooed with glow-in-the-dark ink to prevent them from infecting unsuspecting partners. He came to this last position after abandoning the idea of putting people with AIDS in "quarantine" (i.e., in camps), a solution that he thought worked well in Cuba, but which he felt would be cost-prohibitive in the United States.[9]

In contrast to the conservative suburb that elected Duke to office, New Orleans neighborhoods downtown (i.e., down-river) from Canal Street tend to be much more tolerant of individual and group differences, not to mention idiosyncrasies. The French Quarter as it is perceived today—a place of bohemian individuality—was able to achieve its character largely because during much of the twentieth century it was a slum.

Sometimes known as the Vieux Carré, literally the "Old Square," the Quarter is the oldest part of New Orleans, and it was established by the French and Spanish colonists, along with a sizeable population of free people of color (i.e., persons of African or mixed European and African ancestry who were born free or had been given their freedom). These families became rich by settling and building the city, but by the end of the nineteenth century many of their descendants were experiencing a period of economic decline. Others had moved out of the Quarter, or even out of New Orleans, becoming absentee landlords of the homes and business properties they left behind. Many buildings were bought and inhabited by families of Italian immigrants. Others were neglected, divided into small apartments, and rented to whoever was poor or eccentric enough to want to live amid the decay. This was the French Quarter of William Faulkner, the one portrayed by Tennessee Williams in *A Streetcar Named Desire*, and the one brilliantly satirized by John Kennedy Toole in *A Confederacy of Dunces*. It was a neighborhood that was home to descendants of once-proud families, but also to struggling writers, musicians and artists, to factory workers and manual laborers, to prostitutes of both sexes, to priests and nuns, to the children in the schools and orphanages they ran, to the black and immigrant working classes, and, of course, to many gays and lesbians, who seem instinctively drawn to areas full of beautiful old buildings in need of repair.

A preservation movement that overcame surprisingly strong opposition, followed by several waves of real estate speculation, left the Quarter of the early twenty-first century in considerably better repair than it was fifty or sixty years earlier, but the population considerably less diverse. Most of the nuns and all of the orphans are gone. So are the dock workers and the manual laborers. It has now been years since Ruthie the Duck Lady roller-skated the streets with her pet duck, or when it was common to see working-class black women sitting on their steps as they watched their children play in the street. Successful writers, musicians and artists still inhabit the Quarter, but the struggling ones have been displaced to areas like the Tremé, the Marigny, the New Marigny and the Bywater, where real estate prices are much lower and the crime rate is much higher. Many of the old homes, stores and warehouses in the Quarter have been converted to condominiums purchased by upscale singles and couples wanting a *pied-à-terre* to use during occasional weekends, Jazz Fest, and Mardi Gras. The result has been a gradual depopulation of the Quarter, which had about eleven thousand full-time residents in the 1940s, but which has only about four thousand now.[10] Both full- and part-time residents tend to be older and richer than the people they displaced, though gays and lesbians still figure largely among them.

Despite these changes, the Quarter still retains its reputation for vice and sin, and deservedly so, but the vice and sin fall into two fairly distinct categories.

There is Bourbon Street, of course, where vice is a bankable tourist attraction. Middle-class vacationers and conventioneers flock there to listen to jazz music coming out of nightclubs. They peek through doors to catch glimpses of women doing pole dances, and they drink brightly-colored cocktails in the courtyard of Pat O'Brien's. They watch the uninhibited men and women (usually fellow tourists) flashing their breasts and penises from iron-lace balconies, and sometimes, after a few drinks, they flash their own. Everything happens in a brightly-lit, police-patrolled environment, and when the vacations and conventions end, the tourists go back home and tell people how wild New Orleans is.

There are other parts of the Quarter where vice isn't so brightly-lit and tourist-friendly, but is perhaps more reminiscent of the red-light districts in other cities. Iberville Street is one such area.

Iberville Street is the upper boundary of the French Quarter, though hotels fronting on Canal Street, one block away, will often advertise themselves as French Quarter hotels. The Vieux Carré Commission, which is the municipal agency responsible for maintaining the architectural integrity of the Quarter, has jurisdiction only over the lower side of Iberville.[11] What this means is that the large stores and hotels fronting on Canal Street can go many stories high, literally overshadowing their older, more historic neighbors, and it also means that the upper side of Iberville consists largely of back entrances, service entrances and garage entrances for Canal Street buildings, giving Iberville a gritty, industrial character, and leaving the street feeling slightly dark and sinister. Even today, it is not the most desirable property in the French Quarter, and the difference in the sixties and seventies was even more pronounced. Much of Iberville was then devoted to flophouses and hustler bars that lacked the brightly-lit, wide-open, tourist-friendly ambiance of their Bourbon Street peers.

In 1970, a man named Phil Esteve inherited $15,000 from his mother. He was thirty-nine years old, and interested in investing the money, so he decided to start a business. His original plan was to open a gift shop in the Quarter that would cater to the tourist trade. He was having a drink at a bar called The Galley House, and talking with the owner, Alice Brady, when she said, "Well, if someone has a dollar, they'll buy a drink before they'll buy a gift" (Townsend 43). That's when Phil started thinking about opening a bar.

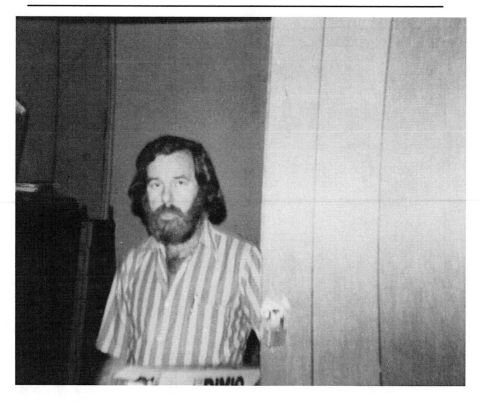

Phil Esteve, owner of the Up Stairs Lounge (photograph courtesy Johnny Townsend).

Soon after, he was having a drink at a gay bar on Iberville called The Cavern and discussing his plans with a bartender named Buddy Rasmussen. Buddy told Phil that if he were going to open a bar, the one thing he needed above all else was a bartender he could trust. Phil seems to have hired Buddy on the spot.[12]

The space that Phil found was an unlikely one; though it overlooked Chartres Street and faced the site where the 41-story Marriot Hotel would open in 1972,[13] and though the elegant Monteleone Hotel was only a block away, the space Phil was looking at had two things working against it from the start: it was on the second floor, which discouraged walk-in traffic, and the only entrance was an easily-overlooked door on Iberville Street.

A canopy over the door with the name of the bar on it would help attract attention, but when Buddy and Phil first saw the entrance stairwell, they knew that there was a lot of work to be done. This space was anything but inviting; uncarpeted stairs twisted their way around an ugly mass of utility meters and plumbing. Potential customers were not going to go any further if their first

Buddy Rasmussen, head bartender and general manager of the Up Stairs Lounge (photograph courtesy Johnny Townsend).

view through the door was an ugly one, so Phil and Buddy planned to carpet the stairs and to soften, if not conceal, the plumbing, by draping the walls and the pipes with yards and yards of fabric.[14]

The space upstairs was unexpectedly large. It spanned all three of the row houses fronting Chartres Street. The first room was about twenty feet wide across the Chartres Street front by about forty-four feet long.[15] There were seven windows, all of them stretching virtually floor-to-ceiling; four of these overlooked Iberville Street, and three overlooked Chartres. While the windows made the room sunny and bright, they actually presented a safety hazard; when the large lower sash was raised, it would be easy for somebody to fall out a window onto the street below. However, a previous tenant had installed horizontal bars across the windows to prevent that happening, and most of the sash cords were broken, making the windows difficult to open, anyway.

Through an arch nearly sixteen feet wide was a second room, which had another three windows overlooking Chartres Street, and the far wall had a solid, fire-rated door leading into a third room. This third room was dark, because its three windows had all been painted black on the inside. That, and the fact that this room was connected to the middle one only by a narrow, solid door, left it isolated from the rest of the space.

Phil and Buddy got to work, concentrating their initial efforts on the first two rooms. They felt as though the many large windows destroyed the feeling of private intimacy a bar should have. They walled over the two windows behind the bar counter, and all three of the windows in the middle room. The lower halves of the remaining windows were covered on the inside with louvered shutters.

The space, which had been vacant for a year, had formerly been a bar that catered to hustlers and their clients. Small tables and chairs covered the floor space, and each table had its own telephone. The idea was that a hustler or a john sitting at one table could phone someone sitting at another to see if the interest was mutual. Phil didn't want a hustler bar, so he removed all the telephones, but left the tables, so that people would have an option other than standing at the bar or sitting on a tall stool.[16] Paul Killgore, who still lives in New Orleans, used to like going to the Up Stairs for precisely this reason, and says today that the small tables and chairs made the place "conducive to friendly chit-chat."

Phil didn't have the money for major interior renovations, so several existing features determined the color scheme: pink-orange laminate covered the top of the bar counter, the floors had red indoor-outdoor carpet, and red flocked wallpaper covered the walls.[17] The extremely tall ceilings had previously been lowered slightly by a dropped ceiling of acoustic tiles. Phil and Buddy concealed these with fabric draped, in streamer fashion, between the archway and the bar in the first room.[18] They built a small stage in a corner of the first room, which was known as the bar area, and on top of this stage they put a white baby grand piano. In time, they built an elevated platform across the Chartres Street end of the middle room. This room was called either the lounge or the dance area, and the platform became a dance floor. Francis Dufrene, a former Up Stairs patron who survived the fire, still recalls the bar very fondly, saying, "I had some of the happiest times of my life there. You could sit at the tables and talk to people, and then you could get up to dance, and at the end of the evening, you didn't want it to end." The Up Stairs reportedly was the first gay bar in the city to receive a license that allowed for dancing. If the police paid a visit, Napoleon wouldn't be arrested a second time.[19]

Though the descriptions of red carpet, red drapes and flocked wallpaper strike people today as garish, the Up Stairs, in its day, had a reputation for "discreet elegance" (Fosberg 7). Perhaps the character Sally Bowles from *Cabaret* better catches the spirit with her phrase "divine decadence." Mardi Gras decorations lingered for months after the celebration, and Independence Day regalia went up weeks before July 4. And, of course, it wouldn't be a gay bar if there weren't beefcake pictures. Surviving photos show that the Up Stairs had two classic posters from the early 1970s tacked to the walls: a nude Burt Reynolds on a bearskin rug (blown up from the famous *Cosmopolitan* centerfold of 1972), and Mark Spitz wearing nothing but a tiny swimsuit and his seven Olympic gold medals.

Before the bar could even open, of course, Phil had to get the required permits and pass a fire inspection. Surviving documents show that the inspector paid several visits to the Up Stairs. One of the issues that needed resolution was the main entrance to the bar area from the stairwell. The code demanded an approved fire door with automatic closure to stop the spread of flames. The number and visibility of other fire exits were also issues. When the inspections process was resolved, the Up Stairs had two other exits approved for use during a fire. One was the window overlooking Iberville Street that was closest to the main entrance. This window was the only one that was not barred, and it opened to a fire escape connected to an exterior staircase leading to the third floor. The last approved exit was a doorway in the rear wall of the third room, which opened onto the roof of an adjacent building.

Though unresolved code issues meant that the Up Stairs was not in complete compliance with all fire regulations until March of 1971, it still was able to open in time for Halloween 1970 with the first of many costume parties.[20] It was a good way to open a new bar, but the business frankly struggled in its early days. Because the Up Stairs was removed from the gay bars in the center of the Quarter, it wasn't a place that lent itself to drop-in visits; a person had to have a specific intent to go there.[21] When business was slow, Buddy danced with the patrons or gave them shoulder massages. These efforts created good feeling—literally as well as figuratively—but they weren't enough to make the bar successful. Phil could possibly have created more business by following the example of other Iberville Street bars and opening it up to hustlers, but he was insistent that he was not going to run another hustler bar. To be sure, some of the patrons were known hustlers; they would come in to relax when they weren't working, or they would bring in an already-secured john for a drink on their way to or from a trick. But if Phil or Buddy suspected someone was actively soliciting a john on the premises, he was told to leave. Similarly, they didn't want the Up Stairs to be a place for a quick hook-up in the men's room; people known to be soliciting or participating in tea-room sex were also thrown out.[22] In fact, Phil and Buddy were so eager to maintain a clean atmosphere in the Up Stairs that they reportedly issued open invitations to the police vice squad to drop in at any time.[23]

After some months of struggling, Buddy suggested to Phil that they try something Buddy had seen in a gay bar in Houston: a weekly "Beer Bust." They set aside the hours of five to seven on Sunday evening for the event, which had a cover charge of $1.50. Fifty cents paid a deposit on a mug, which was redeemable at the end of the evening. The other dollar paid for all-you-can-drink beer from pitchers on the tables. This was a pretty cheap way to get a buzz. The Beer Bust wouldn't make any money for the bar—in fact, it would almost certainly lose money—but it would be a way to draw people in. Hopefully, some of these people would become regulars and would come to drink when the prices were at normal levels.[24]

At first, the Beer Busts were held in the third room. Its separation from the main bar and lounge areas made it easy to keep track of who had paid the cover charges, leaving the other two rooms available for people willing to pay full price. The patrons didn't like being put in that room, however. They complained that they felt cut off from the action. When Phil and Buddy moved the Beer Bust into the main bar and lounge spaces, its popularity exploded; instead of attracting only about a dozen people, it now attracted a hundred or more.[25] The crowds grew even more when Buddy hired a musician, David Stuart Gary, to play the white baby grand on Sundays. David, quickly nicknamed "Piano Dave," was a handsome young man who played piano at several bars and hotels throughout the Quarter during his career. He would leave his principal job at the Marriot Hotel and sit at the piano at the Up Stairs, looking around at his audience and saying "Ready kiddies?" (Newhouse "Smokie"). When he was at the keys, every Beer Bust turned into a sing-along, encouraging people to stay long after beer pitchers had been taken off the tables.

Just as holiday decorations and posters of hunky men tended to accumulate over time, so did rituals and traditions. One of these rituals was introduced by Richard Cross, known usually by the nickname Ricky, unless he was being called by his other nickname, Mother Cross.[26] He was only in his twenties, so it is unclear how he received such a maternal name, but during the sing-along portion of one or more of the Beer Busts, he requested a song that was first recorded by The Brotherhood of Man in 1970, and that was covered a year later by Sonny and Cher. Its title was "United We Stand."[27]

It became a ritual to sing this song at the end of every Beer Bust, often not just once, but again and again. Even today, several former patrons of the Up Stairs make a point of mentioning this song and its prominence in the Up Stairs culture.[28]

Other Up Stairs traditions included parties to celebrate Mardi Gras (of course) and Halloween (which was the bar's anniversary), but there was also an annual Easter Bonnet contest, and a regular celebration, which was suggestively named the Moonlight Cruise.[29] Another of Phil's popular innovations was the Tricycle Race, inspired by a running gag from the television show *Rowan and Martin's Laugh-in*; the show would regularly feature a video clip of a man riding a tricycle, hitting an obstacle, and falling down. For the Up Stairs tricycle race, Phil would tape out a course zig-zagging between the tables, and competitors would get on a child-size tricycle to see who could ride the

Buddy (center) in costume at a Mardi Gras party. Note the wallpaper (red-flocked), the Burt Reynolds poster over his head, and the Mark Spitz poster barely visible behind his shoulder (photograph courtesy Johnny Townsend).

course in the shortest amount of time. Partially because the tricycle was so small, and partially (one suspects) because many of the racers were drunk, it was common for them to fall off the tricycle during the course of the race. But that was part of the fun.[30]

The word "fun" is frequently associated with memories of what the Up Stairs Lounge was like, and a great deal of the credit for that seems to belong to the bartender and manager, Buddy Rasmussen. Now that business was picking up, he didn't have as much time to dance with the patrons and give them shoulder massages, but he still had several tricks for creating a warm atmosphere. Buddy wasn't afraid to look silly, for example. Jumpsuits enjoyed a vogue in the 1970s, despite the fact that they made it difficult for a man to raise his arms above shoulder level. Buddy had bought a white one and had tie-dyed it in shades of red and pink; he used to joke that he wore it to work so that he would match the wallpaper. Buddy kept a microphone behind the bar and, in the manner of Johnny Carson's perennial sidekick, Ed McMahon, he would announce the entrance of the regulars. "Here's Luther!" he'd say, or, "Here's Uncle Al!" (Townsend 278). When he didn't know their names, he would just call people "Honey" or "Sweetheart." Buddy had no hesitation about asking patrons to help him with his duties, requesting that one take a pitcher of beer over to the table by the piano, or that another ask the man standing by the door to close it so that he didn't let the air conditioning out.[31] Buddy seems to have had a gift for making the regular patrons feel special, and making the other patrons feel like they were one of the regulars. The implicit message to everyone was, "You're at home here. You're one of us." Under Buddy's management, the Up Stairs became something of a haven. Even today, Francis Dufrene says, "He and the other bartenders always made us feel safe."

Stewart Butler liked to go to the Up Stairs, and he often brought his dog, Jocko, who would sit on a barstool with the other regulars and lap up a special mixture of milk and vodka. Today, Butler says, "It was much more than a bar in those days. It was, in fact, a social club, even though there were no fees or membership." Butler believes that the difference in tone between the Up Stairs and most other bars—especially the other bars on Iberville—had a lot to do with the presence of the Metropolitan Community Church.

The Metropolitan Community Church, or the MCC, had its beginnings in Los Angeles in 1968. Its founder, the Reverend Troy Perry, had been raised in a Protestant Evangelical tradition. While still in his teens, and before he had acknowledged his own homosexuality, he married a woman and became a minister. His marriage and his ministry both came to an end as he began to recognize his sexuality, and he actually attempted suicide in the wake of a failed love affair with another man. Ironically, through all these traumatic experiences, Troy Perry came to believe that God loved him, and that it was possible for homosexuals to live ethical, meaningful, spiritual lives. His own spiritual journey is encapsulated in the title of his 1972 memoir, *The Lord Is My Shepherd and He Knows I'm Gay*. Today the MCC boasts thousands of members and has branch churches on every continent except Antarctica. Back in 1968, the very first service was for only twelve people, and it was held in Troy Perry's living room.[32]

In founding a church for people who were regarded as untouchables by most other churches, Perry had tapped into a very real need. It wasn't long before the MCC had branches in cities like Atlanta and New York, and in 1970, one opened in New Orleans.

It originally organized under the name Elysian Fields Metropolitan Community Church, located, as the name suggests, on Elysian Fields Avenue, with a man named David Soloman as its original pastor.[33] It struggled under Soloman's leadership for a year or two. When he left, his assistant, the Reverend William Larson, took over the ministry. Bill Larson was in his mid-forties. Like Troy Perry, he had been raised in a conservative Protestant tradition, and had been married to a woman at a young age. In Larson's case, it was his spiritual calling that seems to have brought the marriage to an end, because his wife did not want to be married to a Methodist minister. Once it was over, he became free to acknowledge and explore his homosexuality. He was drawn to the Metropolitan Community Church and became a deacon. When he stepped into the role of pastor, he functioned as a de facto minister.[34] His congregation was so small that he continued to support himself by working as a carpenter.[35]

One of Larson's first jobs was to find a new place for his tiny congregation to meet. He approached Phil Esteve, asking if the Up Stairs could be made available, and for a time, Larson held regular Sunday Services in the third room, which was conveniently separate from the bar and lounge areas.[36] Services often included a rendition of "We Shall Overcome," with an added verse, "*Gay and straight together...*"[37] When the service was over, the congregation would spill out into the public areas, and many of the members would linger for a drink, calling the post-services gathering "cocktail hour."[38]

If holding services in a bar seems unusual, the custom was not unprecedented. In frontier areas in the American West, for example, saloons were often among the first structures in a new settlement, so itinerant ministers would hold services there until a church could be built. Even in the late 1960s, when Troy Perry's earliest MCC membership outgrew his living room, he had trouble finding a church that would welcome his congregation, so he held services in a Los Angeles gay bar. Unlike the Up Stairs, this bar had no separate, private room, and during this first bar service, Perry writes, "just as I lifted a silver chalice to consecrate communion, from the monstrous jukebox in the barroom Tammy Wynette's voice blared forth at full volume, singing 'Stand By Your Man'" (Perry and Swicegood 43).

The MCC only held services at the Up Stairs for a few months. Some of the members didn't like the idea of going to services in a bar, and they wouldn't attend, so Bill Larson was forced to look for an alternative. Fortunately, he found one through Father Bill Richardson, an Episcopal priest at St. George's Church, which was uptown on St. Charles Avenue. Richardson, in his sixties, was a widower with grown children. In the early 1970s he had been made aware of the spiritual needs of homosexuals and lesbians through a summer course offered by his seminary in New York City. Shortly after that, Richardson's assistant, Stewart Wood, asked permission to accept an invitation to preach to a gay congregation at the Up Stairs Lounge. Richardson agreed, so later, when he was approached by Bill Larson, Richardson was not entirely unprepared. He allowed Larson and the MCC to hold services in a small chapel in the St. George's complex. This caused controversy amid the regular congregation; one woman who attended St. George's told Father Richardson that she would not reenter the chapel unless he first had it exorcised.[39]

Fortunately the MCC soon found a new home—one that would be permanent, and one that would provide living space for Bill Larson as well. It was a small, two-family house at 1373–75 Magazine Street, some blocks above the French Quarter, and a block from Coliseum Square. By the standards of uptown New Orleans, this was a somewhat raffish, seedy neighborhood. Though the area around Coliseum Square had once been very desirable, by the 1970s it had fallen on hard times and had a "mixed" character: a neighborhood where churches, convents and single-family houses shared space with abandoned or neglected homes inhabited by hippies, drug addicts and prostitutes. It also had a gay presence, including several other Up Stairs figures who lived nearby. Buddy Rasmussen and his lover,[40] Adam Fontenot, owned a double just a few blocks away on St. Andrew Street. They lived in one side and rented the other to Rusty Quinton, who worked as a welder during the week, and at the Up Stairs on Sunday afternoons, keeping the pitchers full during the Beer Bust.[41] Perhaps the mixed character of the neighborhood meant that a gay church wouldn't ruffle feathers. Using his carpenter's skills, Bill Larson tore down walls between the two halves of the house to create a large room in the front for services sometimes attended by forty or more people. The back of the house and the upstairs became his living quarters.[42]

But even though the MCC was no longer meeting at the Up Stairs, a bond between the two institutions had formed. Congregants continued the habit of going to the Up Stairs on Sunday afternoons after services, and the Up Stairs repaid this loyalty by holding periodic benefits for the MCC.

Some of these benefits involved the use that had finally been found for the third room in the Up Stairs complex, and the idea came from a rather unexpected quarter: the wife of a narcotics agent with the New Orleans Police Department, who thought that the third room would be a good place to put a small theater.

Bill McAnar, the agent, and his wife, Betty, were part of a surprisingly large number of Up Stairs patrons who were not gay males. Bill had discovered the bar through his official duties; associating homosexuality with drug use, he tried to hit all the gay bars in the Quarter as part of his "beat." He did not seem to have found any active use going on at the Up Stairs, because drug use, along with hustling and tea-room sex, was something Phil and Buddy actively discouraged. Unquestionably, some of the patrons came into the bar already high; there would be no way to monitor or control that. However, people who tried to use or deal drugs on the premises were shown to the door. Perhaps because of this, Bill McAnar found the Up Stairs a relaxing place to go when he was off-duty, and he started bringing his wife along.[43]

Other straight regulars included Jean Gosnell, who lived directly across Iberville Street, and who was friends with Luther Boggs and several other gay patrons. There was also Uncle Al, a retired sailor in his sixties, who had a farm on the outskirts of the city, and who used to bring home-grown vegetables to the Up Stairs to share with his friends. Inez Warren used to come with her two gay sons for a family night out. She would sit at the bar, pointing out attractive men to her sons, or sometimes approaching those men and encouraging them to take one of her sons home.[44] Among the most notable of the straight regulars was Suzanne Fosberg. Suzanne was a young woman who had come to the city to study art at Newcomb College, which was then the women's branch of Tulane University. She taught visual art classes for the New Orleans Recreational Department, and drifted into acting at the Gallery Circle Theater. It was through her teaching and her acting that she built friendships with a number of gay men, as many women in theater do. One particularly close friend, Tad Turner, started inviting Suzanne to go to the Up Stairs Lounge with him.[45] When she learned that the third room was to be converted to a theater, she thought it was a great idea, and she was right on board.

Phil and Buddy built a stage along the rear wall, in front of the fire door that opened onto the roof of a neighboring building. Betty, Suzanne, and a number of the regulars threw themselves into the work. Their productions soon became famous, though only within "a certain small circle" (Fosberg 7). The main fare consisted of light-hearted melodramas, and their titles often

A scene from the "nellydrama," *Egad, What a Cad!* A performer known as Michael West (center) plays Mrs. Greystone, and Rick Everett (right) plays the infamous Memphis Queen. The man at left is unidentified (photograph courtesy Johnny Townsend).

suggested that these works were not to be taken seriously. They produced one play called *Egad, What a Cad!* Another was *He Done Everybody Wrong, or, The Devil's Comeuppance.* Characters in plays like these had "humor" names such as Harry Deviate, Nellie Heaven, Miss Queenie, and The Infamous Memphis Queen.[46] In part because the Up Stairs regulars included far more men than women, and in part because it would make the plays funnier, most of the female roles were played by men. The result was that people stopped calling these plays melodramas and started calling them "nellydramas."[47] When women were in the plays, they were often cast in male roles, though this some-times caused difficulties. Suzanne Fosberg was once cast as a husband and her friend, Tad Turner, was to play the role of the wife. Because Tad was many years older than Suzanne, and about a foot taller, he was concerned that he might not be convincing in the role, so he glued sequins in his moustache to make himself appear more feminine.[48]

When a play was being performed, Phil and Buddy sent an advance invitation to members of the vice squad.[49] At show time the audience crowded into the tiny theater. Instead of the chairs being placed in rows, they were clustered about little tables made of oversized spools used to hold heavy cables.[50] Buddy made huge batches of popcorn and put a bowl on each table. Some got eaten, but when the villain appeared on stage the audience threw popcorn at him.[51] Some of the plays at the Up Stairs actually had serious literary value. Among these were *Salome* and *Lady Windermere's Fan* by Oscar Wilde, *Antigone* by Jean Anouilh, and *The Tempest* by William Shakespeare. The productions were probably more playful than respectful. Suzanne, for example, was eager to do *The Tempest* with a gay cast because she thought that a lot of swishy men would work the costumes to advantage.[52] Besides, Shakespeare's original cast would have been all male, too—as she undoubtedly pointed out.

The original purpose of the plays was simply to have fun, but, perhaps reflecting the influence of the MCC, some of the productions became charity benefits, with the proceeds donated to help disabled children. Suzanne Fosberg also directed some productions specifically meant as children's theater; instead of being performed at the lounge, these were taken to other venues and produced for children as young as five.[53] One of her most talented actors was Buddy Rasmussen's lover, Adam Fontenot.

Buddy and Adam lived the adage that opposites attract. Buddy was raised in an urban environment in Houston. Adam grew up in a small Louisiana town called Ville Platte, the child of Cajun sharecroppers who spoke French rather than English. Buddy was discouraged from studying at home. His formal education ended with high school, followed by a stint in the Air Force, where he worked in fire prevention. After his discharge and a series of dead-end jobs, he entered the Navy. In contrast, Adam was encouraged to study, eventually getting multiple university degrees, some at the Master's level. Buddy was tall, strong and dexterous. His many manual skills allowed him to do a great deal of the work on their St. Andrew Street home. Adam was small and delicate, and his gifts were intellectual. He had a talent for languages and was said to have been fluent in English, Cajun French, Spanish, Portuguese, German and Russian.

There were other differences between them. Buddy was both confident and gregarious, mixing easily and well with a wide variety of people. Adam was not just shy, but socially anxious. He was said to have affected a British accent, signaling self-consciousness—or even shame—about his Cajun sharecropper origins. He would sit quietly drinking at one end of the bar while Buddy made sure all the customers were having a great time. In his early thirties, Adam already had a serious problem with alcohol, and after a few cocktails, his British

A crowd assembled in the theater at the Up Stairs Lounge. Michael Scarborough poses for the camera at lower left. Seated in the center, Reggie Adams shields his eyes. Luther Boggs, wearing a blazer and horn-rimmed glasses, is seated at lower right. Michael survived the fire and had important information for investigators. Reggie died in the fire. Luther survived the fire, but died in the hospital (photograph courtesy Johnny Townsend).

accent would fall apart. Though his education was far superior to Buddy's, he was continually either unemployed or underemployed, working, for example, as a ticket clerk at a Greyhound bus station, or as a docent on a tour bus. Jobs like these didn't last long. Sometimes he left them because they were too far beneath his intelligence, making him feel bored and stifled. Sometimes he was fired because his drinking interfered with his job performance. By intellect and abilities he was most suited to an academic career, but his one attempt at teaching was unsuccessful, probably because he lacked the confidence to lead the classroom.[54]

Adam Fontenot (left) was the lover of Buddy Rasmussen. Opposites attract (photograph courtesy Johnny Townsend).

But, as Suzanne Fosberg soon discovered, Adam was very good on stage. Given a script to follow and skillful direction, he could command the attention of an audience in a way that he had never been able to command the attention of a classroom, and since he had a nearly photographic memory, she could cast him in large parts and still be confident that he would be "off book" before anyone else. He was a careful and sensitive actor, and when performing for children, the audience liked him better than anyone else.[55]

Anyone who has experience with live theater knows that, sooner or later, every actor forgets his lines. This happened to Adam once in the middle of a performance. Adam was not a man who dealt well with the unexpected, and his always-fragile sense of confidence was destroyed. Anxious and fearful, he panicked and went into a state of near-paralysis on stage. The other actors covered for him, and they got through the rest of the performance successfully, but Suzanne and the rest of the troop had to give him many reassurances and much encouragement before he got on stage again. To his credit, he did continue to act, and Suzanne continued to find his work very, very good.[56]

Despite all emphasis on performance—the work of Piano Dave, and the excitement over the nellydramas—drag queens and drag performances were late in coming to the Up Stairs Lounge, and some people report that Phil and Buddy discouraged drag queens from coming into the bar.[57] But the presence of a theater made drag shows nearly inevitable; the first of these was in December of 1972, and it featured a brand new performer by the name of Marcy Marcell.

Marcy Marcell's birth name is Marco Sperandeo. As the name suggests, Marco was born to a Sicilian family, and he grew up in the Tremé (pronounced Trah *May*), an old New Orleans neighborhood next to the French Quarter. In the later sixties and early seventies, Marco had a job as a mail runner at the municipal court building. On weekends, he would go out in the Quarter, sometimes going to the Up Stairs, and sometimes going to Wanda's, a bar with a mixed clientele (including hustlers) a block away from the Up Stairs in the 700 block of Iberville.[58] Larry Raybourne was a bartender at Wanda's, and remembers Marco as a cute young Italian boy who used to stand by the jukebox and dance by himself.[59] Marco's slender build, dark hair, and large dark eyes were all reminiscent of Liza Minnelli. Marco's longtime friend, Regina Adams, takes credit, not just for being the first one to put Marco in drag, but for making him the first person to impersonate Liza in the city of New Orleans.[60]

Marco, performing as Marcy, was a smash, and Marcy Marcell was soon a regular performer in the theater in the Up Stairs Lounge. Her shows took place on Sunday evenings at eight, which was an hour after the Beer Bust ended. The hour between the events encouraged the Beer Bust crowd to linger, but also allowed for some patrons to leave and others to arrive before the performance began.

If Phil wanted the Up Stairs to be a pleasant, home-like place, one that was far different from the standard-issue gay bar, and if, as Paul Killgore remembers, its out-of-the-way location meant that you had to have a definite reason to go there, Phil and Buddy had been very successful at creating a warm, welcoming environment, and at creating an impressive list of attractions to bring people in: costume parties, tricycle races, nellydramas, drag shows, church benefits and the weekly Beer Bust. There was always something going on at the Up Stairs Lounge.

It was said to have the most literate conversation in town,[61] and it was a place where people had a lot of innocent fun, but it was not, in essence, an innocent place. The sometimes-ominous undertone to life at the Up Stairs owed something to its Iberville Street location. Today, Larry Raybourne describes Wanda's and most of the bars on Iberville as being pretty rough places, and since he tended bar in some of them, he was in a position to know.[62] Though the fist fights, hustling, drugs and tea-room sex common in some of these bars were forbidden at the Up Stairs, some infractions surely escaped Phil and Buddy's vigilance. There was, for example, a hole in the partition between the two stalls in the men's room,[63] and the bartenders couldn't simultaneously serve drinks and police the "glory hole." Even Suzanne Fosberg, who was in a mutual love affair with the Up Stairs crowd (they had voted her Honorary Lady Faggot of the Year), acknowledged some parts of the Lounge's darker side. She once wrote that the Up Stairs had a certain sense of despair, "deftly concealed beneath the glitter of wit, the artifice of powder and dyed hair" (Fosberg 7).

It could hardly have been otherwise; by the time most of the regulars had found the Up Stairs, there was too much history behind them for true innocence. A lot of damage, both direct and collateral, resulted from that history. Many of the men—like Bill Larson, "Mitch" Mitchell, and Larry Raybourne— had been married to women earlier in their lives, either because they hadn't yet faced their sexuality, or because they were hoping that marriage would "cure" them, or because the concept of heterosexual marriage was so pervasive they couldn't imagine a life in which it didn't play a part.[64] Many of these men had become fathers as well. Such marriages could have their blessings, often in the form of lingering affection for a spouse, or ongoing love for the children, but the marriages were invariably painful, and the divorces, which often followed, caused even more pain.

There were other ways people had been damaged by a society which didn't grant gays and lesbians any legitimate place. Larry Raybourne had lived in Ohio before moving to New Orleans, and while there, he had written and found a publisher for a gay-themed novel. Because the novel contained some sexual content, it was considered pornographic, and because in dealing with his publisher he had sent the manuscript through the mail, Raybourne was accused of violating federal anti-obscenity laws (these same laws had been used against the pioneering feminist Margaret Sanger, when she used the mail to distribute birth control information).[65] The manuscript was confiscated from Larry's home during a raid, but the charges were dropped when it was discovered that the police lacked a valid search warrant. However, Larry's lover had been roughed up by the police, who "outed"[66] him to his parents, and he had been so humiliated by the negative publicity resulting from the case that he committed suicide by running the engine of his car in a closed garage. Larry could no longer tolerate staying in the house where his lover had died, and in a state of depression, he left Ohio behind. With no employment or income, and having lost his lover, his novel and his home, he moved to New Orleans for a fresh start, taking a job as a bartender at Wanda's.[67]

Other people had suffered in ways less obvious and less dramatic, but still very real, due to the need to live at least partially in the closet, and the shame and internalized homophobia this often entailed. Even today the gay or lesbian who is out to family, friends, employers, colleagues and neighbors is far from universal. Among the regulars at the Up Stairs lounge, such a person was a rarity. Most of them were comfortable being out with their gay friends (and a few straight ones), or at a bar on the weekend. Come Monday morning, their water-cooler references to their weekends were deliberately few and vague. When writing or telephoning their families in Arkansas or Texas or New Jersey, they talked about their "roommates" and gave evasive or false answers to questions about whether they were dating any nice women.

Buddy Rasmussen seems to have been one of the few who was truly out of the closet. During his hitch in the Navy, an M.P. once almost caught him having sex with another man. Though he wasn't arrested, Buddy was tired of hiding, so he confessed to being gay and was discharged. When Buddy returned home, he came out to his family, and in looking for work, he made a point of telling potential employers that he was gay. His attitude was that if his sexuality was going to be a problem, he'd rather know up front than be fired for it later. Not surprisingly, this didn't go over well in the late sixties, and he faced long periods of unemployment before moving to New Orleans and going to work as a bartender.[68]

In contrast, his lover, Adam Fontenot, labored under a constant sense of shame. He once went into a panic when Suzanne Fosberg, on an early visit to the Up Stairs, brought her husband along. Adam hadn't met Suzanne yet, but he recognized her husband as a former college roommate, and felt humiliated that this acquaintance from the straight world now knew that he was gay.[69] Though Adam brought Buddy home on visits to Ville Platte, he reportedly never came out to his family or explained the nature of their relationship.[70] Adam's internalized homophobia was almost certainly a factor in his drinking, and even affected his ability to hold a job. He once said that the reason he had not lasted long as a teacher was because he felt "it isn't right for a queer to be up here teaching these students" (Townsend 269).

But despite the failed marriages, some failing relationships, the pressures and bigotry from the outside world—or perhaps because of them—the Up Stairs was a refuge for many of its patrons. Suzanne Fosberg described it as "a place to go if you wanted to have fun, a place to go, a place to talk, a place to find friends if you were in need. There was a brotherhood there. People who understood, people with whom you could let your hair down. A place, perhaps, to find love" (Fosberg 7).

This love was often healing, and sometimes life-changing. Napoleon, for example, met his lover, Stanley Plaisance, in June of 1972. Because Napoleon had been working as a hustler when they met, and because he had a history of many failed relationships, the Up Stairs regulars started a betting pool to predict how long Napoleon and Stanley would last. Nobody wanted to bet on the relationship enduring more than three weeks. Napoleon soon stopped turning tricks and took a job in construction, and in March of 1973 he and Stanley moved out of state for a fresh start. They remained together for decades.[71]

Horace Broussard had also reportedly been a hustler when he met his lover, Duane George Mitchell, known as "Mitch." Like Napoleon, Horace gave up hustling, taking a job as a barber. Mitch was divorced and had children living in Alabama, and his wife was sufficiently comfortable with Horace so that the kids came for an extended visit every summer. Mitch and Horace became involved with the MCC, and would take the kids to Sunday services with them. Sometimes they dropped the kids off at the movies afterward and went to the Beer Bust for a while. On other occasions, they reportedly brought the kids to the Up Stairs, letting them have a soft drink or a glass of milk.[72]

There are many other couples who are known to have been regulars at the Up Stairs, and some actually met there. A partial list of these couples includes Joe Bailey and Clarence McCloskey; Stewart Butler and Alfred Doolittle; Joe Adams and Sid Espinache; Marti Bates and Wayne Cottingham; Paul Killgore and Frank Scorsone, Jr.; Fred Sharohway and Earl Thomas. Many of these couples stayed together for decades, or until death did them part.

Not everyone was partnered, of course; some didn't want to be. There were a lot of handsome young men in the city, after all. Some of them had the long hair, beards and bell-bottoms that were still fashionable in 1973, though the vogue of the hippie look was beginning to pass. Other men had a more tailored, "preppy" appearance, or were beginning to adopt the sleek, shiny fashions associated with the dawning Disco era. Nearby military bases meant that there were usually at least a few soldiers in New Orleans, and, of course, the port brought a lot of sailors to town.

On Friday night, June 22 of 1973, Larry Raybourne met a tall, slender man with blond hair who was wearing tight jeans and a cowboy hat. "I thought of him as a Midnight Cowboy," Larry says today, alluding to the 1969 film, "not because he was a hustler—he wasn't—but because he looked like a young, beautiful John Voight." This man was Leon Maples. He was from Florida and was just in town for a brief vacation. Larry went with Leon to his hotel room, and they spent the night together.

There were no plans to meet again, nor any other expectations. When Larry briefly went to the Up Stairs the next night, he was pleased to see Leon again, and was not at all disturbed that Leon was with somebody else. The two of them spoke easily and pleasantly for a few minutes, discussing what Leon might do before he returned to Florida. Before Larry left the Up Stairs that night, he gave Leon a kiss, saying fondly, but inexplicably, "Leon, I'm going to miss you" (Raybourne).

II

Nineteen Minutes of Hell

The Fire at the Up Stairs Lounge

— ·· — ·· — ·· — ·· — ·· —

After a major disaster, stories invariably circulate concerning premonitions that something bad was about to happen. For example, Major Archibald Butt, a military aid to President Taft, sailed on the *Titanic* and is on record as having confessed forebodings to several friends beforehand. He died when the *Titanic* sank. George Quincy Clifford, another victim of this shipwreck, had such a strong sense of his own impending death that he took out a large life insurance policy shortly before sailing.[1]

Several survivors of the *Titanic* also reported having had premonitions, and in the days before the voyage, nearly fifty passengers cancelled passage.[2] Among them were Mr. and Mrs. Edward Bill, who chose to sail on another ship because Mrs. Bill had a dream about the *Titanic* being wrecked. George W. Vanderbilt and his wife, Edith, also cancelled, after being cautioned by a family member against taking the maiden voyage, because "so many things can go wrong on a new ship" (Eaton). In some of the accounts, people voiced concerns before the *Titanic* sailed; in others, the reports were after-the-fact, and may have been the result of 20/20 hindsight, or perhaps an impulse to embroider.

There are naturally parallels for the September 11 disaster; a web search using the terms "premonitions 9/11" results in more than 15,000 hits for sources documenting claims of foresight about the terrorist attack and the destruction of the World Trade towers. Skeptics dismiss claims of premonition as everything from coincidence to active fictionalizing, and reject suggestions that any form of extra-sensory perception might have played a role in 9/11, the *Titanic*, or any other disaster. Such skeptics would be quick to point out, for example, that controlled scientific studies have failed to demonstrate any actual existence of ESP, and that people who claim to have it are no more likely to know what is on the face of a card drawn from a deck than people in a control group with no claim to psychic ability.[3]

But if forms of psychic powers exist, perhaps they are sparked by specific significant occasions; unless a person is a professional gambler, the ability to predict what is on the face of a card is not exactly consequential. On the other hand, the ability to identify and act upon premonitions of future events could save lives.

The night before the fire, as Larry Raybourne said goodbye to Leon Maples, he said, "Leon, I'm going to miss you" (Raybourne). Since they had known each other for only twenty-four hours, and since it was clear from the start that Leon was just a tourist passing through town, the remark seems both out of place and eerily prophetic.

About ten years earlier, while living in Ohio, Raybourne had a vision that, in retrospect, also seems to predict the fire at the Up Stairs Lounge. Raybourne and his lover had once visited New Orleans, and had so fallen in love with its aura of nineteenth-century decadence that they had decorated their living room with a Vieux Carré whorehouse theme, complete with red velvet draperies and red flocked wallpaper. (After his lover's death, Larry moved to New Orleans. One reason he liked the Up Stairs was because the décor reminded him of his former home.) One night Larry was sitting in this living room after taking a hit of LSD. "It was legal then," he said in a 2009 telephone interview, "and it was pure, because it had been produced by a lab. I remember sitting in that living room and I saw the red flocked wallpaper being enveloped in orange flames. But I wasn't frightened by it. I was fascinated by it."

On Sunday morning, June 24, Marco Sperandeo woke up with a feeling that something was wrong. He was scheduled to perform at the Up Stairs, doing his regular Sunday evening drag performance as Marcy Marcell. Unaccountably, Marco didn't want to do it. In fact, he didn't want to do anything, so he spent the entire day in his apartment.[4]

The New Orleans summer, by itself, is enough to make anyone want to stay inside. Air conditioning wasn't as universal in 1973 as it is now, and even for those who had it, going outdoors would have meant exposure to horrible heat. In late June, the temperatures typically hit the nineties by mid-morning, and can easily get to one hundred later in the day. With humidity levels that often match or exceed the temperature, the city gasps for breath and searches for shade. Wheezy window units struggle to keep interior temperatures to a bearable level, and people on the street carry umbrellas to protect themselves from the sun rather than the rain.

The French Quarter is one of the hottest sections of town. Uptown and in the suburbs, lawns, shade trees and broad streets help ameliorate the effects of the pounding sun. In the Quarter, all is brick, slate, concrete, stucco and iron. Even the famous courtyard gardens provide surprisingly little relief, because the tall surrounding walls block breezes and absorb the sun's rays, releasing heat long after nightfall. In the nineteenth and early twentieth centuries, people of any means would leave the city for the summer months, traveling to the north shore of Lake Pontchartrain or to the beaches of Grand Isle or Mississippi, where winds blowing across the water provided some relief.

For those who can't get away, the only respite in the summer months comes in the form of thunderstorms, which take place on a near-daily basis, often around four in the afternoon. Longtime residents claim you can almost tell time by the summer showers. "It's raining," they'll say. "It must be four o'clock." The relief is only temporary, at best. The rain rarely lasts more than an hour, and in June, the sun doesn't go down until nearly nine. That means three to four more hours of sun burning down on wet streets and gardens. Being outside before the rain is like being in a hot, dry sauna. Being outside after the rain is like being in a steam bath.

Buddy Rasmussen, the head bartender and general manager of the Up Stairs Lounge, would certainly have been aware of the heat as he left his house on St. Andrew that day. Although the bar didn't open until two and the weekly Beer Bust wouldn't start until five, he had to be at work by noon to make sure the bar was clean and ready for the day's business. Adam Fontenot, Buddy's lover, accompanied him to work that day, as he often did during the week, and nearly always did on Sundays.

Buddy and Adam had been together for about four years. They had purchased and renovated their uptown cottage on St. Andrew Street, and they had a large circle of friends, many of whom they'd met at the bar. In spite of this, there were signs that all was not well between them. Suzanne Fosberg, Regina Adams and Troy Perry all remember Buddy and Adam as being lovingly devoted,[5] but Johnny Townsend describes their relationship as deteriorating,[6] and Stewart Butler claims that when the fire occurred they were on the verge of breaking up.[7]

As is usually the case, there were probably multiple stressors involved, but one of them seems to have been Adam's drinking. Alcoholism, which has a strong genetic component, seems to have run in his family,[8] and it wasn't helped on days like this particular Sunday when he accompanied Buddy to work for an entire eight-hour shift. Adam sat on a stool and chatted with Buddy as Buddy got the lounge ready for business. Buddy tallied the prior day's receipts and made a quick trip to the bank to make a deposit. After that, he spent the remaining time before two o'clock making sure the bar was clean and orderly before opening. Right before two, he poured a drink for Adam and unlocked the gate at the bottom of the stairs.[9] The Up Stairs Lounge was open for business.

The Reverend Bill Larson was pastor of the New Orleans chapter of the Metropolitan Community Church (photograph courtesy Johnny Townsend).

While Buddy was getting ready to open the bar, Bill Larson prepared for Sunday services for the Metropolitan Community Church. The services would take place in the little house at 1373–75 Magazine Street which provided his own living space as well as a place for worship. Bill, a carpenter, had already performed a lot of renovations on this little turquoise-colored house, but he was limited by the donations from the small congregation, as well as by his own modest salary. Troy Perry and Regina Adams both remember him as being very quiet, but also very giving in a gentle, fatherly way.[10] Once Sunday services were over, Larson and the congregation planned to go to the Up Stairs for the regular Beer Bust. They often did so, for some weekly "fellowship" after the services, but there were several additional causes for celebration: a church member had just donated an air conditioner to the new MCC home, a popular—and cute—local musician was doing a benefit performance for the MCC, and on top of all that, it was Gay Pride Day.[11]

The New Orleans chapter of the MCC met, for a time, in the room at the Up Stairs Lounge that was otherwise used as a small theater. Later, after Bill Larson became pastor, this modest house at 1373-75 Magazine Street was both his home and the MCC headquarters (author's photograph).

The last weekend in June is the traditional time for commemorating the Stonewall Riots. Four years earlier, on June 28, 1969, policemen descended upon a Greenwich Village bar called the Stonewall for what was then a fairly routine raid, arresting gay men for no particular reason, except that they were gay. On this particular night the bar patrons fought back with such ferocity that soon the police had locked themselves in the Stonewall for protection, and drag queens outside used parking meters as battering rams. Gays and lesbians staged riots the next four nights, signaling to the New York police, and to the nation as a whole, that their days of being frightened, passive victims were over. The last weekend in June is now known as Gay Pride weekend, with parades and festivities taking place in many major and not-so-major cities around the nation.

The annual Pride commemorations were still a new phenomenon in 1973, but events took place that year in cities like New York, Los Angeles and Atlanta. New Orleans now pays tribute to its gay population conspicuously (though the local Southern Decadence festival tends to be the focus), but in 1973, Pride weekend seems to have passed largely unrecognized by anyone outside of the local MCC. Some of the individual gay bars undoubtedly had their own parties, but the celebrations were probably fairly low key. It is perhaps understandable that the mainstream newspapers made no mention of Pride weekend—they would have been less inclined to do so back then—but the alternative weeklies like the *Vieux Carré Courier* were also silent, and there was no specifically gay press. This silence on the subject of gay pride reflects, perhaps, the *laissez faire*, apolitical nature of New Orleans gays then. Many of those who were closeted or semi-closeted would be reluctant to engage in any activity that might draw attention to themselves; many others saw no point in overtly political activity. Why bother about riots in New York four years earlier? In New Orleans in June, a Beer Bust, some live music, and a performance by Marcy Marcell were all reasons enough to have a good time.

The lure of a Sunday service followed by a long, fun afternoon at the Up Stairs meant that most of the regular church members were present. Among them were Mitch and Horace, along with Mitch's two young sons, Duane and Steve. The kids often accompanied their father and step-father to MCC services when they were visiting from Alabama, and would sometimes accompany Mitch and Horace to an after-church Beer Bust, where they drank milk or soft drinks.[12] Courtney Craighead, a longtime church member and MCC deacon, was there, too, as well as Perry Waters, a dentist who lived and practiced in the suburbs. Perry was unattached, and much of his social life involved the MCC and Vieux Carré gay scene. He liked for his patients to also be his friends, and for his friends to also be his patients, and he also had a reputation for being lenient when it came to payment terms, so a number of people involved with the Up Stairs and the MCC saw Perry for their dental work.[13]

Rick Everett was also present. At twenty-five, he was more than twenty years younger than the Reverend Bill Larson. Rick had a lover named Lenny, who was also involved with the MCC, but Rick seems to have had something of a crush on Larson nevertheless; he and Lenny, in fact, even argued about the attachment. Lenny does not seem to have been around that day, but Rick met a visitor, Ronnie Rosenthal, who lived in Atlanta and was active with the MCC chapter there. When services ended and the congregation dispersed, Bill Larson and Rick Everett took Ronnie Rosenthal out for a meal at a restaurant called The Fatted Calf. As the three of them sat around the table, Rick felt uneasy. He said that he had a feeling that something bad was about to happen to Bill, who replied, "I know it" (Townsend 171). They shared this moment in silence, and then dismissed it. When the meal was over, they paid their check and left the restaurant to go see their friends at the Up Stairs Lounge.[14]

Meanwhile, Marco Sperandeo, in his apartment uptown, could not shake the feeling that something was not right. He should have been getting his costumes ready to go downtown. He should have been preparing to transform into Marcy Marcell. Instead, he was watching television, and trying very hard to convince himself that there was no reason for his feeling of discomfort. Marco looked at the television listings in *The Times–Picayune*. A Bette Davis movie was coming on soon: *Watch on the Rhine*. It started at eight o'clock, which was when Marcy's performance was supposed to begin. But maybe, if he got all the costumes together first, he could watch just the first few minutes. Maybe it wouldn't hurt to be a little late.[15]

The apprehension that Marco, Rick and Bill experienced was not in evidence at the Up Stairs Lounge. The normal afternoon rain did not materialize, but the Beer Bust started promptly at five. With the weather too hot to do anything outdoors, it was a good day to go to a place that had air conditioning and bottomless pitchers of cold beer. The bar got crowded early and stayed that way. About twenty members of the MCC were there, along with a whole lot of others. It's impossible to know precisely how many were in the bar at any point, but Buddy Rasmussen later estimated that there was a core crowd of about ninety,[16] with people drifting in and out during the afternoon.[17]

A baby grand piano occupied a small, elevated area in the room with the bar counter. For several months, a man named David Gary had been playing there, taking requests and getting paid in tips. Young and handsome, "Piano Dave" was just about two weeks shy of his twenty-third birthday. David had been supporting himself by playing at various bars in and around the Quarter, including one of the lounges at the Marriott Hotel right across the street.[18] He had quickly become a regular at the Up Stairs, and played during the Beer Bust on June 24, but when the Bust officially ended, he ceded the stage to another pianist named Bud Matyi, who was going to play that evening for a benefit to the MCC.

At twenty-seven, Bud was just a few years older than David; in a surviving photograph, he looks like a shaggy, happy teenager. Despite his youth, he had already been married and divorced twice, and he had three children. One problem in both his marriages was his sexuality; he attempted to conform to societal and religious norms, but he could not make himself give up men. Additionally, as an aspiring musician, he made a meager living at best. Reportedly, he and his second wife sometimes fed themselves by scavenging for food in trash cans. After his second divorce, he moved to New Orleans, where he soon made a name for himself in local clubs, and his music career finally took off. He also met his lover, a local television personality named Rod Wagener. They moved in together, declared December 27 their wedding day, and wore matching rings. Bud also wore a holy medal with the image of two doves on it; a priest had once told them that the medal was a symbol of marriage. These outward signs were somewhat unusual at a time when most gays and lesbians tried to avoid signaling their sexual identities and relationships to the world. Even if they lived together and attended social functions together, wearing rings was less common than it is now, and gay and lesbian couples often did not come out in any explicit way. Straight acquaintances might speculate privately about the nature of a relationship between two men or two women, but the issue was not discussed in their company, and specific questions or comments would have been considered rude.

Bud and Rod had moved somewhat beyond that stage. Though a television personality like Rod would never, in 1973, come out to his viewership on the air, Rod and Bud had a large circle of straight friends who were in the know. Today they might be considered a local "power couple." They were connected to the music, arts and television scenes, and they maintained three residences: a condominium in an upscale development near Lake Pontchartrain, a trailer in the then-rural area of Slidell, and an apartment in Montreal. By the standards of the 1970s, they were as out, as open and as successful as two gay men could be.[19]

A couple of months before the fire, Bud and Rod were home alone, when Bud suddenly said, "You're going to miss me so much you're gonna ache for me" (Townsend 312). He couldn't explain to Rod why he had said it, except that he had been moved to say it.

Like a lot of gay men, even today, Bud and Rod took pride in appearing straight, and they had an aversion to gays who were too obviously queer. The effeminate, the transgendered and the "flamers" would not be counted among their friends. When Bud told Rod that he had been asked to play at the Up Stairs for a benefit for the local MCC, Rod did not, at first, understand the concept of a gay ministry, and he didn't want Bud playing for a church "for drag queens" (Townsend 236). They fought over the issue, but Bud stood his ground. Rod eventually agreed to drive Bud to the performance, but he didn't want to attend himself, or even go inside. He dropped Bud off at the ground floor entrance on Iberville Street and watched him walk up the stairs.[20]

Horace Getchell, who went by the name of Skip, also got dropped off. He had been out drinking with a friend named Jimmy Willamette that afternoon, and they visited several gay bars in the Quarter. By early evening, Jimmy had had enough; he had a meeting later, and he wanted to go home to clear his head beforehand. Skip, however, wanted to keep partying. As Jimmy let Skip off at the curb, he thought for a moment that he saw a black cloud-like aura hovering over Skip's head. He dismissed it as nothing.[21]

Francis Dufrene wasn't having premonitions about something bad being about to happen. In fact, he hadn't even gotten to the bar yet, and he was already enjoying himself very much. He was at a little hole-in-the-wall hamburger joint on Royal Street when a cute young man introduced himself. "And can you believe it?" Francis asked in an interview in 2013. "He was with his mother! And his brother, too!" The cute young man was Eddie Warren, who was, as usual, accompanied by his brother, Jimmie, and their mother, Inez. Francis enjoyed meeting the whole family, but was especially taken with Eddie, and by the time the four of them left the hamburger joint to go to the Up Stairs, it was clear that Francis and Eddie were on a date.[22]

Steven Duplantis was twenty years old and a member of the Air Force stationed at Randolph Air Force Base in San Antonio. "The military was really after gays in those days," Duplantis says now, "and it wasn't safe for me to go out in San Antonio." M.P.s would frequently visit gay bars in the San Antonio area, and any service members found in one would be arrested and made subject to dishonorable discharge. In part because New Orleans was safer, and in part because he was friends with Stewart Butler, Steven Duplantis would frequently drive through the night to get New Orleans, and at the end of the weekend, he would drive through the night to get back and report for duty on Monday morning.[23]

Out in the suburb of Lakeview, a man who will be called Steven Whittaker[24] had been enjoying himself at a party all afternoon. That party was winding down, and a man by the name of Jim Hambrick suggested they all go to the Up Stairs Lounge. Most of the guests weren't interested, and Steven had never even been to the Up Stairs before. He had taken a bus out to the suburbs for the party, so when Jim left, Steven decided to go with him.[25]

They arrived to find a whole crowd of people talking, flirting or singing. During the Beer Bust, Piano Dave was taking requests, as usual. Also, as usual, he was asked to play the same song over and over again. It was the song that had become the unofficial Up Stairs anthem, "United We Stand."

Phil Esteve, the bar's owner, was not at the Up Stairs; instead, he and his lover had decided to see *Damn Yankees* at the Beverly Dinner Playhouse.[26] But Uncle Al, the elderly, retired sailor was there. Jean Gosnell, the straight woman who lived just across the street, had come to the bar with her friend Luther Boggs. Mitch and Horace arrived after dropping Mitch's kids off to see a movie on Canal Street. Even Reggie Adams was there with his lover, Regina.[27]

Reggie, a young African American man, had come to the city to study at Loyola University in preparation for entering the priesthood. After meeting Regina, he had decided to give up his dream of becoming a priest so that he and Regina could build a life together. They often attended the Beer Bust, and they had special plans that night to go out to dinner with Buddy and Adam when the Bust ended.[28]

People sang continuously along with Piano Dave, and when Bud Matyi took over at seven o'clock, the singing continued. In the central room, couples swayed on the dance floor. Michael Scarborough and his lover, Glenn Green, enjoyed a companionable evening, talking to the many friends who came by to visit their table. Rusty Quinton, whom Regina Adams remembers as a happy, skinny red-head,[29] lived next to Adam and Buddy. He also worked in the bar on Sunday afternoons, and stayed constantly busy refilling beer pitchers and looking after the patrons.[30]

All the beer meant that there were a lot of full bladders, and a lot of trips to the men's room. The men's room had two stalls, and somebody had drilled holes in the partition between them for cruising or for quick, anonymous encounters. Buddy and Phil discouraged such tea room sex at the Up Stairs, and would throw out people caught engaging in it. But Phil wasn't there that day, and Buddy was very busy at the bar. In their absence, a young, dark-haired man had moved in. He had commandeered one stall, and as men entered the other, he peered through the hole and made comments. Steven Duplantis remembers seeing him in there, and also remembers seeing him in there on other occasions. In fact, this man was something of a regular customer, and not one whom the other patrons welcomed. Today, Steven Duplantis recalls, "When he came in that night, you could hear everybody groan, like 'He's here again.'" It isn't known what the dark-haired man was saying to people through the partition in the bathroom, though it was obviously sexual in nature. It is known that he'd been in there quite a while, and that he was bothering people. Including Michael Scarborough.[31]

Michael went to the men's room several times during the Beer Bust, seeing and listening to the comments of this dark-haired man each time. On Michael's last visit, which took place between 6:30 and 7:00, the man was still there, and Michael was sick of having to deal with him. When Michael left the restroom, he reported the conduct to Buddy. Buddy and a bartender named Hugh Cooley went into the restroom and told the man to get out of there and to leave people alone. This man left the restroom, but went to the table that Michael was sharing with his lover, Glenn, and harassed him further.[32]

Michael had had enough. He got up and punched the dark-haired man in the jaw, knocking him down. From his position on the floor, this man looked up at Michael, growling something in response. Buddy and Hugh saw the disturbance, so they grabbed the troublemaker and escorted him to the door.[33]

Within a few minutes, there was a second disturbance, over, of all things, cheap beer mugs.

During the Beer Bust, any patron could purchase a pitcher of cold beer for one dollar, and this pitcher could then be refilled again and again at no extra charge. But to drink the beer, the patron had to put down a fifty-cent deposit on a beer mug, which was redeemable at the end of the evening. One of the patrons that afternoon was a young man who appeared to be between eighteen and twenty with long blond or light brown hair (the legal drinking age in Louisiana was then eighteen). This youth had punched and kicked some of the patrons, pretending to be playful. Several times, he approached Rusty Quinton, saying that he wasn't drunk, but that he had taken pills and was stoned. Rusty had also seen him approaching customers and asking them for beer. He would fill his beer mug to the brim, drink it down, and then intentionally spill a little on the carpet so that he could have an excuse to ask someone else for a free refill. It was clear his behavior was irritating people, but Rusty was too busy to do anything about it.[34] At seven o'clock, as the Beer Bust wound down, the long-haired kid started walking through the room, picking up unguarded beer mugs and taking them to the bar to be redeemed for fifty cents each. As soon as Buddy saw what he was doing, he ordered the kid to leave. Mumbling that he would be back,[35] this young man grabbed two beer mugs on his way out, and when he reached the street level he smashed them at the bottom of the stairs.[36]

Right after this young man was thrown out, another man named James Smith decided to leave the bar. He met the young man on the sidewalk, they spoke a few words to each other and then walked away together. Buddy's assistant, Hugh Cooley, went downstairs to sweep up the broken glass.[37]

The Beer Bust was over. Some patrons lingered over that last pitcher of beer. Others switched to different drinks and paid the regular prices. As new patrons drifted in for the evening's performances, some of the others decided to leave, and in the next hour, the crowd dwindled from approximately ninety to about sixty-five. Stewart Butler had been at the Beer Bust with his lover, Alfred Doolittle. Stewart was having fun, but Alfred wanted to move on. They were encouraged to do so by their friend, Steven Duplantis, who had witnessed the earlier scuffles, and who was worried that there might be more trouble. Between 7:30 and 7:45, Stewart and Alfred decided to go down the street to see what was happening at Wanda's. They said their goodbyes and left.[38]

Right about this time, Buddy also prepared to leave. He had been at work since noon, and he and Adam were supposed to go to dinner with Reggie and Regina. He started closing his cash register and giving instructions to Hugh, who would take over at eight.[39]

William White and Gary Williams, two teenagers from the small, rural town of Pineville, were exploring the French Quarter on a rare visit to New Orleans. They poked their heads into the stairwell, but saw two men having an argument at the top of the stairs. "I don't like no kinds of fights," White later said, "so we left" (Lind, Thomas, and Philbin A6).

Inside the bar, Reggie and Regina took a quick look at their wallets. They didn't have much cash, so if they were going out to dinner with Adam and Buddy, one of them would have to run to their apartment on Conti Street to get a checkbook. Reggie wanted to go, but Regina insisted that she go instead. Today Regina recalls telling him, "I've already finished my drink. You stay here and enjoy yours." Regina also had another reason for wanting to leave: she had borrowed a hat from Jean Gosnell, who was at the bar that evening, and Regina wanted to return it.[40] If Regina was the one who went home, she could take care of both matters at once. Giving Reggie a quick kiss goodbye, Regina said that she would be back in ten minutes.[41]

Eddie Gillis wanted to go out and enjoy himself, but he was short of cash. Although straight, he had some gay friends, one of whom owed him a few dollars. Eddie knew that he would find that friend at the Up Stairs Lounge, so he went there to see if he could collect on the debt. He arrived and went inside at about a quarter to eight.[42]

Across the street, at 601 Iberville, Charles and Katherine Kirsch were in their fourth-floor apartment watching *The FBI* on television. They were out of cigarettes, so Katherine offered to go to the Walgreens drug store at the corner of Iberville and Royal. At about 7:53 she reached the sidewalk and started to cross the street when she heard a woman's voice saying something about a fire. She looked in the doorway to the Up Stairs and saw a small fire at the bottom of the staircase. Running into the Midship bar next door, she got a bartender's attention, telling him that there was a fire and that somebody had to call for help right away.[43] He went outside with her and looked in the doorway. Though the fire was still small, confined to the bottom two steps, it was beginning to climb the staircase. He raced back into the Midship and grabbed the phone. The fire department recorded the call and dispatched units by 7:56.[44]

In the Up Stairs Lounge, a buzzer sounded. The button controlling this buzzer was at the street entrance; it was there so that, before the doors were opened for business in the afternoon, people bringing supplies could signal Buddy or Phil that they had a delivery. During business hours, if one of the bartenders phoned for a cab to take a patron home, the cabbie would ring the buzzer to let them know he had arrived. But nobody had phoned for a cab, and the buzzing was relentless. Buddy was busy behind the bar and Hugh was in a storeroom getting supplies. Requesting help from a patron, as he often did, Buddy asked Luther Boggs to go to the top of the stairs and tell whoever was playing with the buzzer to quit.[45]

When Luther opened the door at the top of the stairs, a huge shaft of flames exploded into the room.

The flames pushed Luther backwards, and immediately caught on his clothes. A spring was supposed to close this fire-rated door. At the very moment it was most needed, it malfunctioned and remained open.[46] Because the fire came from downstairs near the street entrance, and because the door to the lounge didn't close properly, the stairwell acted as a massive chimney flue, funneling heat, flames and combustible gases into the lounge.[47] Soon, everything ignited: the carpeting, the wallpaper, the wood paneling on the walls, the velvet drapes at the windows and the large archway, and the posters and holiday decorations hung around the room. Everything was in flames, and the source of the flames was the most obvious way out.

A lighted red sign clearly marked a fire exit overlooking Iberville Street.[48] This exit consisted of a window opening to a fire escape with stairs leading to the third floor. Eddie Gillis had been moving toward the door when Luther opened it and the flames burst through. Eddie dodged and ran toward this side window, his clothes already on fire. He picked up a chair and broke the glass, got onto the fire escape and realized there was no way down to the street. In a panic, he ran up the fire escape toward the third floor. The street was already full of people watching. They screamed to Eddie, encouraging him to jump. He hesitated, then leapt over the fire escape rail. A man named Gerald Tyler from the Midship poured a pitcher of ice water over him to extinguish the flames.[49]

Jean Gosnell and Luther Boggs followed Eddie. Jean went first, and Luther, himself on fire and in a panic, tried to hurry her by pushing her through the window; he accidentally shoved her into the casing, breaking two of her teeth. By the time they got onto the landing, they were both on fire and tried to slap out the flames on each other with their hands. But Luther was almost totally ablaze, and there really wasn't anything Jean could do to help him. Like Eddie, Luther jumped over the railing into the street, and Gerald Tyler poured a pitcher of water over him, too. Jean, afraid and unable to jump, despite the urging of the crowd on the street, climbed the fire escape to the third floor and remained there as she awaited rescue.[50]

Most people could not make it to the fire escape because it was at the same end of the room as the stairwell from which flames bellowed. Two lovers, Eugene Thomas and Fred Sharohway, took the courageous step of ignoring the fire escape and running directly into the flaming stairwell, down the stairs and into the street. Amazingly, both survived, though they were severely burned.[51]

For those unwilling to run into the flames, there was another fire escape, but it wasn't immediately visible. It was in the rear wall of the room that was used as a theater. Buddy Rasmussen knew about this exit, of course, and despite the flames and the chaos all around him, he kept his head. He shouted to everybody to follow him, and as he walked through the bar, he touched each person he passed. "Come with me," he said, calmly. "Come with me" (Sclosser and Gebbia 30). Those who listened to him soon formed a line. Some followed his example, touching others as they passed, saying, "Come with me." Amazingly, many people did not follow; they remained frozen, sitting or standing where they were.[52] It didn't help that many of them had been drinking for hours. Buddy led his group across the central room, opened the narrow, fire-rated door into the theater, and brought them onto the stage where another fire door allowed them to get onto the roof of a neighboring building.

Duane Mitchell, known as Mitch, was one of the people who had followed Buddy, but as the group filed onto the roof, he realized that he didn't see his lover, Horace, among them. He turned back, reentering the flaming lounge to look for him. They died together.[53]

Rick Everett worried about not seeing Ronnie Rosenthal, the young visitor from Atlanta. Like Mitch, he ran back to the door connecting the theater to the lounge, but the flames were too hot for him to go further; he rejoined Buddy's group, and later found Ronnie safe on the street.[54]

After assembling on the roof of the next building, Buddy's group entered a window of an apartment in the building beyond that, ultimately making it down to the street outside of the Midship at 606 Iberville. Buddy saw that everyone was headed to safety, then went back into the theater. He found yet another man contemplating a run into the burning lounge to look for someone. Buddy told him to leave, then he stood at the door himself, calling to

Duane George Mitchell (left), known as Mitch, and his lover, Louis Horace Broussard, known as Horace. Both were active with the MCC. Mitch escaped the fire, then reentered the burning bar to try to save Horace. Their bodies were found together (photograph courtesy Johnny Townsend).

whomever who could hear him. There was no response. Conscious of containing the flame, he closed the fire-rated door between the theater and the lounge, making sure to fix the latch.[55]

Steven Whittaker had been in the men's room when he heard people shouting about a fire. He was a bit drunk and not thinking clearly. At first he thought it was a prank—as though someone had lit some napkins with a lighter—and he planned to stay where he was until the shouting stopped. When he realized it might be a real fire, though, he decided he didn't want to die in a men's room. He opened the door and saw a main room full of dense black smoke. He made his way to a nearby window, which was the one giving access to the Iberville Street fire escape. When a shaft of flame burned his upper arm, he dropped to his hands and knees and attempted to open the window. At that moment, Eddie Gillis used a chair to break the glass. After Eddie Gillis, Jean Gosnell and Luther Boggs rushed through this opening, Steven crawled out to the fire escape and, hanging down by his arms, dropped himself to the street.[56]

Investigators later estimated that there were about sixty-five people in the bar at the time of the fire.[57] With Buddy's group of about twenty, two coming down the stairwell, and four using the fire escape on Iberville Street, that meant more than forty people were left to find some other way out, or to die trying. After a brief, paralyzed panic, most tried to escape through the large windows overlooking Chartres Street. They ran to the windows, ripping down flaming drapes, tearing aside the louvered interior shutters, raising sashes when they could and breaking glass panes and wooden frames when they couldn't. As the windows opened and broke, more oxygen entered the room, feeding the fire and making immediate escape ever more necessary. But few got out. Ironically, the single factor that caused the most deaths was a safety feature.

These windows were forty-two inches wide and more than nine feet tall. When the lower sashes were raised, the openings were almost the size of doorways, with the window sills near floor level. A previous tenant had anchored horizontal bars across all the window openings, except the one at the fire escape overlooking Iberville Street. These bars were designed to keep people from falling out of the windows onto the street, and now they did their jobs only too well. The lowest of these bars were fourteen inches above the windowsill, and the other bars were spaced ten inches apart.[58] Slowly, with agonizing effort, people squeezed between these bars. Incredibly, about twelve men made it out this way.[59] Those who did tended to be young, slender and agile. Rusty Quinton was one of them.[60] Once outside of the window, he managed to grab onto a drain pipe and slide down. Rusty ran up the street to a bar called Gertrude's, urged someone to phone the fire department, then returned to the Up Stairs and encouraged people at the windows to try to jump. Some couldn't make themselves do it, though the fire was at their backs and the street only twelve feet below. These fearful people blocked the way for others trying to get through.[61]

Francis Dufrene was able to get out of a window. A man was actually standing in front of Francis, but let Francis go first, despite the fact that the flames were upon them. Francis sustained third degree burns over much of his body, but still counts himself as fortunate. "These days," he says, "being gay is all about muscles. Back then, if you were thin, you were in. And I was thin, thank God. I squeezed between the bars and dropped down to the sidewalk, and a few weeks later I woke up in the hospital."

Michael Scarborough got through a window as well, but not before the flames were pouring through, severely burning his hands, arms and face.[62]

Regina returned from her apartment with the checkbook and Jean Gosnell's hat. She expected to rejoin Reggie, Adam and Buddy and go out for a pleasant dinner. Instead, she heard sirens and saw flames shooting out of the windows of the bar. She remembers standing in the middle of Iberville Street, scream-ing.[63]

Stewart Butler and Alfred Doolittle had just gotten to Wanda's, one block away, when they heard that there was a fire at the Up Stairs. Stewart ran back to see the building in flames.[64]

Uptown, Marco Sperandeo had decided that he couldn't keep putting off his departure. He had packed his costumes and props for the show and had phoned for a cab to take him downtown. The television was still on as he waited for the cab, and he was catching just a few more minutes of his Bette Davis movie when the broadcast was interrupted by a news bulletin: there was a fire in a French Quarter bar....[65]

Meanwhile, a swelling crowd of people watched the blaze: tourists from the Marriott Hotel across the street; patrons from the Midship and the Hideaway and Jimani. The onlookers now included people like Rusty Quinton and Michael Scarborough, who had managed to get through the windows, as well as Buddy Rasmussen and the twenty people he had led to safety. These sur-vivors watched in horror as their friends pressed against the windows, blocked by the wooden framing, or the iron bars or their own blind panic, their bodies engulfed by billowing smoke and angry red fire.

Bill Larson, the pastor of the MCC, had not followed Buddy's group. Mem-bers of his congregation watched from the street as he tore an air conditioning unit from beneath one of the large, heavy windows. Once it was gone, he tried to crawl out between the windowsill and the lowest bar, but the sash slid down and he couldn't move. He managed to pull himself out of the window and to push the sash down to the sill. Using his hands, he smashed the glass and broke through several of the wooden mullions. He tried to squeeze through again, his head and one arm making it through, but he got stuck, the lowest bar and parts of the window frame forming a trap. As the flames reached his body, he screamed, *"Oh, God, no!"* (Laplace and Anderson 3). In the next window, three more people were being burned alive.[66] As much as Larson struggled, he could neither move forward to get through the window, nor backward to try and find another way of escape. As billowing smoke and flames engulfed him, an air conditioning unit fell from a third floor window, hitting Bill on the head. By the times the flames subsided, he was dead.[67]

All this happened within moments. With the call received at 7:56, the first fire truck had arrived by 7:58, and three more were there by eight o'clock. By then, nearly everyone who would survive had already escaped the Up Stairs.[68] With the entrance blocked, and with flames shooting out of the building by as much as twenty feet,[69] the firefighters could only connect their hoses to hydrants and shoot powerful streams of water into the windows.

Buddy got a clear view of his lover, Adam, through one of these windows.[70] Like others, Adam had gone helpless at the sight of the fire, never leaving his position at the end of the bar. Before Buddy reached the street, Adam's whole body was ablaze. Adam remained in one spot, screaming in agony, until the powerful stream of a fire hose hit him and knocked him to the floor.[71]

Soon there were no more signs of life. The fire was declared fully extinguished at 8:12 p.m., just sixteen minutes after the first unit had been dispatched.[72] Only nineteen minutes had elapsed since Katherine Kirsch first noticed a small flame at the bottom of the stairs.

The work of the fire department was far from over, and the police arrived to control the crowds and begin their investigation. The streets were now even more crowded than they had been during the fire. Print and television journalists arrived. Three Catholic priests, attracted by the sirens and the swarms of people, gave comfort to the living and said prayers of conditional absolution for the dead.[73] Buddy Rasmussen also tried to give comfort to those who had escaped.[74] Heavy scents of burned wood, fabric, carpet and flesh poisoned the hot summer air. Bystanders gazed in morbid fascination at the tableau of dead bodies in the windows, though with their faces scorched and their clothes, hair and skin all smoke-stained to the same sooty gray color, these bodies scarcely looked human anymore. A photographer for one of the local newspapers arrived at the scene knowing only that there had been a fire. Seeing the figures at the window, he thought the fire had been in a mannequin factory, and that what he was looking at was damaged inventory.[75] He said as much to a colleague, who replied, "Those aren't mannequins" (Townsend 193).

Despite all he had been through, Buddy went from survivor to survivor on the street. At one point, he caught sight of the dark-haired man whom he and Hugh had thrown out of the bar for bothering patrons in the men's room and making a nuisance of himself with Michael Scarborough. Grabbing this man by the arm, Buddy asked where he had been. The dark-haired man claimed to have been at Wanda's. Buddy dragged him through the crowd, looking for a policeman, because he wanted the man arrested for questioning.[76] The police officer Buddy found seemed to be more interested in crowd control than with who had caused the fire. Buddy asked that the dark-haired man be arrested, but the officer ordered Buddy to let go of the man and move on. When Buddy did so, the man disappeared into the crowd. Buddy later found a plainclothes officer and told him about the troublemaker from the restroom. He also mentioned the young man who had been redeeming other people's beer mugs, and who had smashed some of them at the bottom of the stairs when told to leave. With prior training in fire prevention, Buddy had a feeling that the fire was arson, and also had a feeling that at least one of these men was involved.

Though he didn't know either man by name, he recognized them as sometime-patrons of the bar. He was able not just to describe them physically, but to name some of the people he knew to be their friends.[77]

Medical personnel collected the injured survivors on the streets and rushed them to Charity Hospital. For many years, Charity was famous throughout the nation for the quality of its emergency medical treatment. A new burn unit had been scheduled to open in just two weeks. When the director of Charity, Dr. Isidore Brickman, heard of the disaster, he gave orders for the unit to be opened right away.[78] Police reports indicate that fifteen people were taken to Charity for treatment. A few, like Rusty Quinton, had only minor injuries, and were soon released. Most required hospitalization. Three later died.[79]

After reaching Iberville Street with only a burned arm, Steven Whittaker wandered onto Chartres where he saw the dead faces in the windows glowing orange like jack-o-lanterns from the heat. Jim Hambrick, the man who brought him to the Up Stairs, was lying on the street, bloody and unconscious, his toupee askew, matted with blood, and still attached. He had escaped from the barred windows only to hit his head as he fell to the street. He was put on a stretcher and taken to Charity Hospital.[80]

It was a gruesome night at Charity, the halls full of people screaming in pain, the hideous odor of charred flesh in the air. Clancy DuBos, a journalist from *The Times–Picayune*, described two priests giving solace to survivors, a nurse's aide mopping blood from the floor, and a man moaning while doctors cut burnt skin from his chest. One of the less-injured, a young man of about nineteen, asked for assistance in using a pay phone so he could tell his room-mate what had happened. This young man had tears running down his face. He couldn't make the call himself because his fingers were burned so badly that he could neither remove change from his pocket nor dial the phone.[81]

Rusty Quinton told his story to several journalists that night, describing his escape from the fire, and also describing what it was like to watch people being burned alive. "I knew almost everyone in that bar," Rusty said. "They were my friends" (Laplace and Anderson 3).[82] By coincidence, a *Picayune* photographer had taken a picture of Rusty at the scene, his face twisted in agonized horror as he gazed at the windows. This photograph accompanied the DuBos story on the front page of the June 25 edition. The caption reads, in part, "My friends are up there."

Regina Adams has only scattered memories of the night. After she returned from her apartment to find the bar ablaze, her next memory is of being in the emergency room at Charity, hoping to find Reggie. "I was running up and down the halls, looking for him," she said in 2009, "asking people if they knew

Lindy Quinton, known as Rusty, was an Up Stairs regular who was a part-time bartender on Sundays. He escaped from the fire by squeezing between the bars at the windows. This photograph was taken as he watched the fire from the street. The caption beneath the photo on the front page of *The Times–Picayune* read, in part, "My friends are up there" (photograph by Ronald LeBoeuf, from *The Times–Picayune*, Times Picayune/Landov).

anything about him. And then I don't remember anything for about another two weeks."

Vince Fornias, a twenty-year-old student worker at the LSU Medical Center, was sometimes required to make trips back and forth between the morgues at LSU and Charity. He was on one of those errands on June 24. The city morgue could not handle the number of dead, and Fornias arrived at the Charity morgue just after some bodies had been sent there; later, other bodies were sent to the LSU morgue. In a 2009 interview, Fornias recalled, "What I remember first of all is the smell. There was a burning stench that I could smell even before I entered the room. But when I went through the doors, the sensation of the stench was overpowered by the look of abject horror frozen in the eyes...."

Fornias continued, "It was my second summer working in the morgues, and I thought the first had prepared me for all that I was ever going to see. I had seen what I thought was every form of violent death in that morgue room. I had even seen other burn victims. But I never saw in any other faces what I saw in those eyes that day."

Steven Whittaker doesn't recall how he got to Charity Hospital. He wanted to check on his friend, Jim Hambrick. He had sobered up a bit by then and was worried about the consequences of being identified as a man who had been in a fire in a gay bar, so when he was asked to sign the register, he signed

This photograph shows the foot of one of the fire victims hanging partially out of the window of the Up Stairs Lounge. Many of the victims were fully visible, including their faces (Times Picayune/Landov).

in as Steve White. When a list of survivors appeared in the paper that was the name that appeared.[83]

Long after the fire was over, survivors and curious onlookers lingered, looking up through the windows and trying to see what the police and the fire investigators were doing. A neighboring bartender set up a station on the street to sell drinks to the crowd.[84] The electricity in the building was out, so the investigators were forced to work with klieg lights mounted atop fire trucks and aimed through the windows.[85] Due to the amount of damage in the building and the number of corpses that had to be tagged, catalogued and taken away, the process dragged on for hours. Firemen paused frequently to give themselves short breaks from the sickening odors.[86] Meanwhile, the klieg lights illuminated the bodies of Bill Larson and other victims who remained in the windows where they had died.[87]

A block away, at the bar called Wanda's, a surreal scene unfolded. Larry Raybourne had planned to be at the Up Stairs that night, but he was delayed and arrived to see the firefighters battling the flames. When it was over, Raybourne and a number of others went to Wanda's to try and make sense of it all. "A lot of the survivors were there," Raybourne said in 2009. "They were soiled, stunned and crying."

One man who had escaped was telling the story to those who had not been there, crying out, "The fucking fire just came through the goddamned door!" As he continued his story, his fear and relief expressed by bursts of profanity, he was interrupted by a woman who obviously did not understand what had happened. "Young man," she said, "I wish you would watch your language" (Raybourne).

A jukebox at Wanda's contained a recent hit record about the heat of passion. Recorded by Elvis Presley, its title is "Burning Love."

"It played over and over again that night," Raybourne said in 2009, "and it was about somebody who was on fire and burning. But nobody screamed, 'Take that damn record off the jukebox!' It was kind of ironic. But it was kind of appropriate."

III

Thieves, Queers
and Fairy Carpetbaggers
How New Orleans Responded

—·—·—·—·—·—·—·—

It was a grisly time in New Orleans.

In November of 1972, a fire had broken out in the Rault Center, a 17-story office building in the central business district. It started on the fifteenth floor, spreading rapidly and working its way upward. Although between three and four hundred people were able to make it down to the safety of the street,[1] many on the top three floors were trapped. Eight men having lunch in a private club in the penthouse were able to get to the roof. Incredibly, they were rescued by a private helicopter pilot who had been out on a job and who had responded to distress calls. He lifted these men off the roof a few at a time, bringing the last two to safety minutes before the roof caved in.[2]

Others were not so lucky. Five women in a beauty parlor on the fifteenth floor had their escape cut off before they even realized there was a fire. They stood in a window, waving and screaming for help, until the fire spread into the room they occupied. Faced with a choice between certain death by fire, or an uncertain fate if they jumped, they leapt from the window, falling to the roof of the Travelers Insurance Companies building eight floors below. Only two of the five women survived.[3]

In all, there were six deaths: the three women who died in their falls, a man on the fourteenth floor who died of smoke inhalation, and two men who had escaped the fire at first but reentered the building to try to rescue others.[4] The Rault Center stood empty for many years, a mute, ruinous monument to a tragic event. Only recently has any renovation work begun.

The spectacular tragedy elicited an outpouring of sympathy and grief. Mayor

Moon Landrieu was out of town at a convention when the fire occurred. When he heard the news, he held a press conference in Indiana, and ended his trip a day early to come home.[5] The day after the fire, he published a statement in all the papers, saying that the dead were "mourned not only by those who knew them, but by New Orleanians in all walks of life." On behalf of the city, he offered "heartfelt prayers for those who were injured, and thanks to all those who risked their lives to save others" ("Mayor Offers Sympathy" 11). The next day Governor Edwin Edwards drove to the city from Baton Rouge. While touring the Rault Center he, too, issued a statement of sympathy to the survivors and the families of all the victims.[6]

In the early 1970s, the New Orleans area was about 47 percent Catholic, a number which is not quite a majority, but certainly a substantial plurality.[7] Thus, while the pope is sometimes known as the Bishop of Rome, it wouldn't be too much of a stretch to call the city's archbishop the Pope of New Orleans. Philip Hannan took his duties as Archbishop very seriously, writing a weekly column for the archdiocesan newspaper, *The Clarion Herald*, and issuing public statements upon significant events. The day after the Rault Center blaze, the local papers carried a press release in which he, like the mayor and the governor, offered condolences and sympathy to the survivors as well as to the families and friends of all the victims. He also requested "that prayers be recited in all our churches, begging God's mercy on the deceased and His grace and support of their families as well as of those hospitalized by the fire" ("Condolences" 3).

Less than six weeks later, tragedy struck again. On the morning of Sunday, January 7, a young black militant by the name of Mark Essex infiltrated the downtown Howard Johnson's at the corner of Loyola Avenue and Gravier Street. Essex first began to experience pronounced racial prejudice while in the Navy, which ultimately led him to associate with the Black Panthers in New York when that group was on the decline. Essex eventually found his way to New Orleans, his racial views fermenting and hardening due to several scrapes with the police, as well as to the obvious social and racial inequality he saw around him. Eventually something caused him to snap, and he went on a renegade mission to kill as many people—especially as many white police officers—as he could.[8] After entering the Howard Johnson's, he climbed the stairs to the eighteenth floor, where he shot and killed two young newlyweds visiting from Roanoke, Virginia. He set fire to their room and several others to create a disturbance, shooting at guests and hotel personnel as they tried to escape, and at policemen and firefighters as they tried to put out the flames and rescue guests.

Police blocked all the streets in the vicinity of the hotel, bringing traffic to a halt. Marco Sperandeo, due to perform as Marcy Marcell, was not able to make it to the Up Stairs Lounge, so he stayed home and watched the nonstop news coverage.[9]

The police eventually pursued Essex to the roof, where he took cover behind a concrete structure housing mechanical equipment. With nearly one hundred police on the scene and a Marine helicopter sweeping the area and surveying the roof, Essex was held in a standoff that lasted long into the night.[10] He finally emerged from cover at around ten o'clock, at which point he was killed by policemen, who shot him dozens, perhaps hundreds, of times.

The event was not over, however; based on witness reports, police believed that at least one and possibly two other men were working with Essex, and they thought those other snipers were also hiding in or near the concrete bunker on the roof, and so the standoff continued through the night and well into Monday.[11]

With key streets blocked and the violence continuing, many schools in New Orleans announced closures Monday morning. Other schools met, but classes were effectively suspended, as teachers brought portable televisions into classrooms so students could follow the story.

Meanwhile, the police remained on the roof of the hotel, periodically charging the bunker and firing upon it, retreating when other officers were wounded by what they believed to be returned fire from the other terrorists, but what was actually friendly fire or police bullets that ricocheted off the bunker.[12] When it was all over, there were eight dead, including the deputy police superintendent, two patrolmen, the young married couple, the manager and assistant manager of the Howard Johnson's,[13] and Mark Essex himself, who turned out to be working alone. Investigators eventually discovered that Essex had been behind another shooting incident on New Year's Eve that killed one police officer and wounded another, bringing the total number dead to nine.[14]

Once again, the community rallied behind the victims. Charity Hospital was literally overrun with people eager to donate blood for the wounded and the hospital called upon the 4010 Army Hospital Reserve Unit for assistance. Other hospitals and blood banks opened their doors to the willing donors as well.[15] Mayor Moon Landrieu was actively on the scene, issuing public statements of sympathy for the victims and their families, and declaring a city-wide period of mourning to last until January 14, when the last of the funerals for the victims would take place.[16] In honor of Deputy Superintendent Louis Sirgo and the other police killed in the incident, Mayor Landrieu started a tragedy fund that would be distributed to the wives and families of all police and fire personnel killed in the line of duty, effective from January 1, 1973, and continuing in perpetuity.[17]

Archbishop Hannan's most notable public act was to be celebrant at the funeral mass of two of the three slain policemen: Deputy Superintendent Louis Sirgo and Patrolman Paul Persigo. This was covered in depth by the papers, and a photograph on the front page of the January 11 edition of *The Times–Picayune* shows him embracing Sirgo's widow after the funeral service. In the *Clarion Herald,* Executive Editor Father Elmo L. Romagosa wrote a lengthy piece that, in its tone, crossed the line from admiration to hero worship, documenting in its entirety the archbishop's participation in the crisis: how he "spent almost nine hours ... at Charity Hospital as a shepherd consoling his flock"; how he "went in person to the homes of Mrs. Louis Sirgo and Mrs. Paul Persigo to comfort them in the loss of their husbands" (Romagosa 1). Archbishop Hannan even offered himself to the mayor and the police superintendent as an intermediary or an exchange for hostages being held by the terrorists, a brave offer which both the mayor and the police superintendent respectfully vetoed,[18] and which proved ultimately unnecessary, since Essex never took any hostages.

Given that race relations in the city are historically charged, and given that Essex was a black man who was reportedly out to kill white people,[19] it is surprising that the incident did not ignite a controversy between the black and white populations of the city. Perhaps some of the credit for this can be given to the archbishop, who used his regular weekly column in the *Clarion* to offer a prayer asking God to give His mercy and healing power to the city. Stating that "every member of this community [is] united in common tragedy," the prayer goes on to ask God, "may we stand as a single family of every race, every culture, every religion; may we stand as brothers united under the fatherhood of God.... Give us Your strength to overcome the evil of this tragedy as you overcame death by the Resurrection of Your Son" (Hannan 1).

Less than six months later, a fire started in the stairwell of the Up Stairs Lounge. Killing twenty-nine people in minutes, and sending fifteen to the hospital where three more would later die, the fire at the Up Stairs Lounge still stands as the single deadliest fire in the history of New Orleans.

Ronnie Rosenthal had been lucky enough to survive. A young visitor from Atlanta who was active in the Metropolitan Community Church there, Ronnie had sought and attended services at the New Orleans chapter of the MCC. After services, he accompanied Rick Everett and the MCC pastor, Bill Larson, to The Fatted Calf for a meal before the Beer Bust. Ronnie had followed Buddy Rasmussen to safety through the theater's fire exit, and had watched the horrific spectacle from the street. When it was over, Ronnie got to the phone and called the MCC in Atlanta. He reached the pastor, the Reverend John Gill, and said the fire had killed Bill Larson and many members of the New Orleans

MCC. When John Gill got off the phone with Ronnie, he called the MCC's founder, Troy Perry, who lived in Los Angeles.[20]

Troy Perry had been out celebrating Gay Pride weekend and didn't get home until after midnight Pacific time. Troy found a note on his door telling him about a fire, and he walked through the door to hear his phone ringing. It was John Gill, calling from Atlanta after 3 a.m.

John gave him a brief account of what had happened. Troy immediately suspected arson, because the Up Stairs Lounge was the third location associated with the MCC that burned in 1973: the first was the Mother Church in Los Angeles, and the second was the MCC's meeting place in Nashville. True, the Up Stairs was not an MCC meeting place any longer, but it had been, and many of the MCC members were present when the fire started. He wondered if the latest fire was part of a pattern of targeted violence.[21]

Troy and John decided that they needed to get to New Orleans as soon as possible. They also decided that they needed others to help. One of the men they called was Paul Breton, another MCC minister who lived in Washington, D.C. Paul supported himself by working with D.C.'s Department of Social Services and had experience helping victims of illness and violence find health care, social and financial assistance, and, in worst case scenarios, burial assistance.[22]

Troy and John also called in two other men: Morty Manford, the director of the Los Angeles Gay Community Services Center, and Morris Kight, a New York resident and the president of the Gay Activists Alliance,[23] a group which had been formed in the aftermath of the Stonewall Riots four years earlier.[24] Both men had experience dealing with the press, city officials and police. Troy, John, Manford and Kight all flew into New Orleans on Monday. Paul Breton joined them Tuesday.

As the business day started in New Orleans, most residents treated it just like any other day. To the extent that the fire affected routines at all, it largely elicited snide jokes or moralistic statements about the evils of homosexuality. What some of these workplace pundits didn't know was that, sitting at the next desk, or standing behind them at the water cooler, were people keeping carefully silent, not daring to reveal that they had been at the bar, or had close friends who died there. Others were simply gay or lesbian, hoping to hear some sympathetic remarks about the dead. Today, both Marcy Marcell and Stewart Butler recall how painful it was to go to work the morning after. Butler says, "What was particularly difficult was this horrible thing happened, and I was so close to it. And I couldn't say anything about it, because *I wasn't out at work!*" This was the logical—and excruciating—extension of the need so many gays and lesbians felt to live life at least partially in the closet.

Troy Perry and John Gill met at the New Orleans airport after flying in from opposite coasts. Morty Manford and Morris Kight would join them later that day.

Troy and John drove to Bill Larson's house on Magazine Street, which was also the New Orleans headquarters for the MCC. People filled the little turquoise cottage, the phone rang incessantly and the door kept opening. Some of the people there had survived the fire. Others searched for news. Still others were offering or seeking comfort. Troy and John heard several firsthand accounts of the fire from those lucky enough to walk away. The two visitors had intended to stay at Bill Larson's house, but they soon realized that it contained too many distractions and too much raw emotion. Troy phoned a friend employed by the Marriot chain, who arranged for rooms. A generous member of the MCC covered the costs.[25]

The Marriot sat directly across Chartres Street from the Up Stairs Lounge, and from their tenth-floor room, Troy and John could look down on the site of the fire, smoke still issuing from the windows. When Paul Breton arrived the next day he could see cooked blood on a windowsill, and was told that it was Bill Larson's.[26]

Troy and John rested in their room for only a few minutes. Morty Manford arrived shortly after, and Morris Kight was expected that night. Morty said he felt like the people of New Orleans were acting "like a bunch of jackasses." He continued, "At the airport when we arrived, I mentioned to a man that we were here because of the tragedy. He laughed and said, 'What tragedy? I don't know of any tragedy. Only some faggots got burned!'" (Perry and Swicegood 87).

The three men went to visit the site of the fire, planning to leave yellow chrysanthemums at the door. Over the next few days, hundreds of flowers were left at the entrance to the lounge.[27] Vandals started stealing them, so a man known only as Smokie appointed himself guardian. Smokie had been released from prison a few months earlier. After his release, he had gone to New Orleans and somehow found his way to the Up Stairs Lounge. Despite the fact that he was straight and an ex-con, he had been befriended by some of the Up Stairs regulars, including Horace "Skip" Getchell, who had purchased some new clothes for Smokie to help him get a fresh start on life. Smokie had been working on a boat offshore when the fire happened. Smokie heard about it upon his return to the city, but had not yet been paid and had no money to purchase flowers of his own. "'But I can watch [these],' he said, pointing to the iron grill entrance." He added, "It sounds kind of silly, but while I was sitting here I could see the boys walking around again up there, their drinks in hand, beer, vodka, grapefruit juice ... whatever. And I keep

The day after the fire, a curious onlooker peered through the open doorway to inspect the stairwell where the fire began. Soon this doorway would become an improvised memorial altar, banked with flowers and flickering candles, and guarded by someone named (of all things) Smokie (Times Picayune/Landov).

thinking 'I've got to get back up there and with them again'" (Newhouse "Smokie").

Smokie's friend, Skip Getchell, was among the dead, although the body would not be identified for some days.

After leaving their own flowers at the scene, Troy Perry, John Gill and Morty Manford returned to the Marriot. They had a press conference scheduled for five o'clock on the roof of the hotel. Troy and Morty both castigated the press at large for its callous and insensitive treatment of the fire, especially since they claimed to know that many members of the press were gay. They criticized police and city officials for the content of some of their statements, and announced plans for a memorial service to take place at eight o'clock that evening.

Perhaps chafing under the criticism of their work, one of the journalists at this first news conference described Perry and the other activists (off the record) as "fairy carpetbaggers" (Perry and Swicegood 88), i.e., gay men who had come to the city to exploit the fire for their own ends, just as men from the North reportedly came South after the Civil War, all their possessions contained in a single carpetbag, allegedly in order to exploit and impoverish the former Confederacy.

Perry later described his behavior at this press conference, including his explicit criticism of the media, as "harsh, but not unfair" (Perry and Swicegood 89). That may not be completely accurate. Some of the articles written even on the night of the fire were quite compassionate. For example, Clancy DuBos of *The Times–Picayune* wrote an extremely poignant story detailing the suffering of injured survivors who had been taken to the emergency room at Charity Hospital. At the *States Item*, Angus Lind, Lanny Thomas and Walt Philbin all wrote about the fire scene, creating sympathy for the victims by describing their suffering and deaths in horrific detail. There are references to the fire being like an inferno, a holocaust, and even Hitler's incinerators.[28] Where callous or insensitive remarks appear, or where misinformation is transmitted, this is often because the newspaper articles are reporting remarks made by witnesses or city officials, rather than editorializing themselves.

After the news conference, the out-of-town delegation hurried uptown to attend a hastily organized memorial service for the victims. Expecting a crowd too large for the MCC headquarters, which held only around fifty people at most, they had arranged to use a church facility loaned to them by Father Bill Richardson.[29]

Father Bill Richardson was the pastor at St. George's Episcopal Church on St. Charles Avenue. He had befriended Bill Larson, and had formerly made a small chapel at the St. George's complex available for MCC services before Bill Larson found his house on Magazine Street. As noted in the first chapter,

Bill Richardson's generosity to the MCC was not universally appreciated by his congregation, one member telling him that she would not re-enter that chapel until it was exorcised.[30]

Despite past opposition, he made his church available for the June 25 memorial, which started at 8 p.m. almost exactly twenty-four hours after the blaze began. Though organizers expected a large crowd, a contemporary newspaper account puts the number in attendance at about fifty.[31] The service had been so hurriedly organized that there was little time for word to get out to people who would have gone, but didn't know it was taking place.[32] Other people were too stunned to go to a service, and since most of the dead were still unidentified, people weren't quite sure who the memorial was for.

Troy Perry led the service, with two other ministers assisting. One was Bill Richardson; the other was David Soloman, the founding minister of the New Orleans chapter of the MCC. Troy opened by saying, "Somebody said that [the fire killed] just a bunch of faggots ... but we knew them as people, as brothers and sisters, and we will never forget them." Noting that the victims were at peace, Troy said "The individuals who [set the fire], we have to pray for them, because they have to live with this. This will be on their consciences for the rest of their lives" (Nolan and Segura 3). Toward the end of the memorial, Troy announced that he and Morris Kight were calling for a national day of mourning within the Gay Liberation Movement. He also announced plans for a relief fund to aid the survivors and the families of those who had died.[33]

The day after the service, Bill Richardson received a telephone call from the Episcopal bishop of Louisiana, Iverson B. Noland. Bishop Noland was reportedly so conservative that he didn't even like having divorced people in the church. When he read newspaper accounts of the service, he phoned Bill Richardson to let him know exactly how unhappy—and angry—he was.

Bill Richardson asked, "Do you think Jesus would have kept these people out of his church?" (Sears 104–5).

Bishop Noland had no interest in discussing what Jesus might have done. In a later phone conversation, he informed Bill Richardson that he had received more than one hundred calls protesting the memorial, many of the callers demanding Richardson's resignation. Richardson himself started receiving hate messages by phone and through the mail. His vestry board met, and only one member out of twelve supported his decision to host the memorial. They were outraged, asking questions like "What kind of Christian are you to allow a thing like this to go on in our church?"(Sears 105).

Depressed and dispirited, and thinking it best to resign, he took a walk. He encountered a woman on the street, who simply said, "Thank you." A few minutes later, he met a second woman who said, "I'm from Trinity Episcopal, and I think it was wonderful that you did this" (Townsend 38).

Soon, Bill Richardson took a step which his vestry board could (and probably did) regard as open defiance: he wrote an open letter to the congregation. In it, he pointed out that "St. George's is not a private club but a House of God." He described the dead Bill Larson as "a fine, humble, devoted Christian, and Minister," who "was trying to exercise his pastoral ministry that evening at the bar." He went on to write:

> While there has been considerable criticism from some of our own members, and from a few outsiders, most of which has been relayed not to me but to several ladies of the parish (who are not the authority), there is a mounting number of people in the community, both clergy and lay persons, who are voicing their entire agreement that the memorial service was a very Christian thing for St. George's to permit, and the question again comes up, "Would Jesus have barred these grief-stricken people from His church? Or would he have welcomed them?"
>
> Therefore: If any considerable number of St. George's members still feel that our church is to minister only to the select few, and not to the whole community, then I shall seriously consider resigning as your Rector in the near future, so the Bishop and the Vestry can look for someone else [Richardson].

The letter did its job. Bill Richardson did not resign.

Bishop Noland was not alone in disparaging the dead and looking askance at the tragedy because of the sexual identity of its victims. Most of the clergy in town seem to have harbored similar attitudes, though these attitudes were often revealed through silence rather than hostile words.

Take, for example, Archbishop Hannan, who had made himself such a public presence during the Rault Center and Howard Johnson's incidents. The Up Stairs Lounge had a much higher death toll than either of the other events; in fact, its final toll would be *double* that of the Rault Center and Howard Johnson's, *combined*. How did the archbishop respond to an event of this magnitude?

Publicly, there was no response at all. In contrast to his behavior during the earlier events, he did not go to Charity Hospital to console the families of the dead or dying. He did not help break the news of a son's death to a mother. He did not write a prayer. He didn't even issue a press release. Given his habit for making public statements upon disastrous occasions, these were rather stark omissions, which the mainstream news outlets either didn't notice, or chose not to report.

Admittedly, the Catholic Church continues to regard homosexual activity as "an intrinsic moral evil" and homosexuality itself to be, in the words of Cardinal Joseph Ratzinger (now the former Pope Benedict XVI), an "objective disorder" (Ratzinger). Still, Hannan might have taken a moment to ask people to pray for the families of the victims and for the souls of the dead. He could have gone so far as to request that people donate blood for the benefit of the hospitalized victims. Given that even the earliest news reports mentioned the possibility of arson, the archbishop might have issued a statement against violence, and offered a prayer that the culprit soon be found. Any and all of these statements seem consistent with the Christ who associated with lepers, tax collectors and prostitutes, who enjoined us to love our neighbors as ourselves, and who urged people to visit and comfort the suffering. None of these statements would have been either an explicit or an implicit endorsement of homosexuality.

In the journalistic community, only Bill Rushton, writing for a small, alternative weekly called the *Vieux Carré Courier*, seemed interested in holding the archbishop accountable for his silence. He phoned the Archdiocesan Human Relations Committee to ask for a statement, only to be told that they had seen no reason to issue one, nor did they have plans to do so in the future. Pressing forward, Rushton called the chancery office and asked to speak to the archbishop himself. The priest who answered the phone responded to Rushton's inquiries with long, embarrassed pauses, followed by evasive answers, but still made it very clear that the archbishop would not be coming to the phone.[34]

Despite the archbishop's lack of a public statement, he apparently made some private ones, instructing his clergy not to give Catholic funeral services to any of the victims, nor to allow them burial in Catholic cemeteries. Paul Killgore recalls, "There was many a Catholic family in tears because a son or a brother had died and they couldn't give him a Catholic funeral or a Catholic burial." Paul Breton, one of the MCC ministers who came to New Orleans with Troy Perry, describes the funeral of one of the Catholic victims, although he unfortunately does not record names. A priest conducted this funeral, but it was a generic service instead of a specifically Catholic one, and during the funeral itself the priest made derogatory comments about the dead man.[35] Troy Perry's memoir, *Don't Be Afraid Anymore*, also mentions the archbishop's prohibition of Catholic burial for any of the Up Stairs victims.[36] Many years after the fire, during his exhibit entitled "Remember the Upstairs Lounge," the artist Skylar Fein was approached by several viewers who told him that they remembered hearing about the archbishop's prohibition of Catholic burial to any of the victims, and today he tells the story of one woman crying, "Even then, I knew he was *wrong!*" Archbishop Hannan retired many years ago and died in September of 2011. Although in his late nineties when he passed away, he had remained active in community affairs, making public appearances and issuing occasional statements. He was contacted in 2009 in connection with this book and was given the opportunity to comment on his behavior following the fire, in particular the reports that he denied church burial to the Up Stairs victims. He chose not to do so.[37]

Many civic and political leaders were also indifferent to the victims, some using the fire to advance their own agendas. The state's assistant fire marshal, Timothy A. Driscoll, mentioned the loss of life but tried to blame it on the Vieux Carré Commission, the municipal body entrusted with preserving the architectural integrity of the French Quarter. According to Driscoll, the VCC was actively obstructing the work of the fire marshal's office. "Life is more important than old bricks," he charged ("VCC Blamed A3). VCC director Wayne Collier fired back, hinting at corruption in the fire marshal's office, and arguing that Driscoll was "trying to pass the buck for a fire that occurred out of the Vieux Carre Commission's jurisdiction" ("Passing the Buck" A8). Indeed, while Iberville Street is one of the official boundaries of the French Quarter, the boundary itself and the VCC's jurisdiction runs along the center of the street. The building housing the Up Stairs Lounge falls outside of VCC jurisdiction by about 20 feet.

Wayne Collier blamed the fire marshal for not doing his job by providing regular inspections of French Quarter gathering places, and by not looking for inadequately marked exits or false ceilings like the one at the Up Stairs that provided air for a growing fire.[38] The Up Stairs had, in fact, passed its most recent fire inspection, though that had occurred two years earlier.[39] In the meantime, three major fire-related tragedies—the Rault Center, the Howard Johnson's and the Up Stairs Lounge—had given the fire marshal's office a distinct black eye.

Lost in all this intramural bickering was any discussion of the fire victims themselves, and it wasn't coming from any leaders further up the ladder. The office of Governor Edwin Edwards was as non-responsive as the archdiocese. Edwards once famously quipped that the only way he would lose an election would be if he was "caught in bed with a dead girl or a live boy" ("Remembering Edwin Edwards"). After the fire at the Up Stairs, his only public comment indicated that he would call for changes in the fire code. There was neither an expression of sympathy for the dead, nor an explicit acknowledgment that anyone had died.[40] Troy Perry and the other activists who had come to New Orleans sent a telegram to Edwards' office, asking he make a public statement and declare that Sunday, July 1, be a statewide day of mourning. The governor's office did not respond. When Morty Manford made a follow-up phone call, the governor's secretary first claimed that no telegram had been received, then claimed to have just found it, then said that the governor was busy and could not come to the phone, then said that he was away from the office and would continue to be away throughout the entire week. Morty Manford and the other activists noted multiple times during the week when Edwards made statements from his office, despite being "away."[41]

Just as Archbishop Hannan and Governor Edwards refused to address the issue, no word was forthcoming from Mayor Moon Landrieu. In a move that was unusual then, when Moon Landrieu was running for mayor he actually visited the local gay bar, Café Lafitte, in Exile. According to local historian Robert Batson, this was such an unexpected event that word spread immediately.[42] Now the gay community needed him, and he was silent.

As had been the case with the Rault Center fire, Landrieu was out of town when the fire at the Up Stairs Lounge took place. Unlike the Rault Center fire, he did not hold a press conference from a remote location, he did not issue a press release calling for city-wide mourning, and he did not abort his trip to come home and oversee the tragedy. Again, nearly alone among New Orleans journalists, Bill Rushton of the *Courier* was willing to press the issue. He documented multiple calls to the mayor's office, during which he was repeatedly told that Landrieu was out of town, that he had made no statement on the Up Stairs to date, but that "he might say something at his press conference July 11" (Rushton "Forgetting" 1). That meant Landrieu's earliest comments would come seventeen days after the fire.[43] When Mayor Landrieu was finally questioned at that news conference about his lack of response to the fire, he tried to sidestep the issue by saying that he hadn't spoken because changes to the fire code were under state rather than municipal jurisdiction. Asked about the "homosexual angle" and the failure of the major power brokers to acknowledge the fire's victims and their families, Landrieu said, rather tepidly, that he was "just as much concerned about that life as any other life," and that he was "not aware of any lack of concern in the community" (Rushton "Fire Three" 7).

Perhaps he had not been reading the paper. The chief of detectives of the New Orleans Police Department, Major Henry Morris, discussing the problems of identifying the victims, said that it was difficult to know if the identification found with the bodies even belonged to them. Elaborating on that comment, he said, "Some thieves hung out there and you know this was a queer bar" (Lind, Thomas and Philbin A1). A second, unnamed member of the police department explained Major Morris' statement, telling the press that it was "not uncommon for homosexuals to carry false identification" (Lind, Thomas, and Philbin A1). These remarks not only linked homosexuality with thievery by association, but also implied a practice of widespread deception by gays, yet they seem to have had little basis in fact. Larry Raybourne, who frequented New Orleans gay bars during the sixties and seventies, and who even worked in some (which meant that he was periodically required to check identification), calls Major Morris' remark "preposterous." He says, "The only people I've ever known to carry fake IDs were kids trying to pass as legal age, not gay men pretending to be somebody else."[44] Stewart Butler, who has been going to gay bars since the mid-sixties, says that he never heard of people carrying false identification, though he concedes that, at a time when men were frequently arrested just for being present in a gay bar, there would have been a motive to do so.[45] In his book *The Gay Metropolis*, Charles Kaiser gives extensive attention to the police patterns entrapping and arresting gay men in New York, and to the ways gays sought to avoid arrest and criminal records. Contacted by email about this question, Charles Kaiser responded, "No one I ever interviewed in New York ever mentioned a fake ID tradition. It's possible there were different habits in New Orleans, but I am skeptical about that."[46] No one interviewed for this book who was frequenting gay bars in New Orleans in the 1960s or early 1970s either carried false identification or knew anyone who did, including those people who, by request, appear in this book anonymously or under an assumed name. Only one account seems to corroborate Morris' charge, and it is not directly tied to the Up Stairs fire; in the book *Stonewall*, David Carter discusses how some people in the Stonewall on the night of the famous police raid had no identification at all, so other people passed them things like library cards and credit cards, which would have confused the police when they tried to book multiple people with the same name.[47] But this deals with an improvised, situational strategy, not a habitual practice of carrying forged or stolen documents. If police in New Orleans did, in fact, sometimes encounter men who carried false identification in gay bars, it seems to have occurred in isolated instances, not as part of a widespread behavioral pattern.

The statements having to do with thieves, queers and false identification were among those that Troy Perry protested during the press conference he held the first day he was in town,[48] and the *Vieux Carré Courier* criticized local gay reporters working at mainstream papers, saying that they should have known better than to let such sensationalistic and prejudicial remarks go to press unchallenged.[49] Morris Kight, who was not yet on the scene when the remarks were made, but who would arrive in New Orleans Monday night, spoke via telephone to reporters from *The Times–Picayune* on Monday, and lambasted Morris for the comment as well. He is quoted as saying:

> I'm terribly sorry the detective has made such a prejudicial statement at a time when gay people all over the nation are mourning over their gay brothers and sisters. And at a time when everyone needs a little more understanding. We are indeed human beings in this society. We're trying to eliminate that kind of preju-

dice. [There is] absolutely no justification to believe gay persons are in the habit of carrying false identification [Nolan and Segura 3].

The city administration's Human Relations Committee sent Major Morris a note reprimanding him for his comment. In response, the police department issued a statement saying that the remark had been a misattribution, and that Major Morris hadn't made the comment at all.[50] The statement also included an oblique apology for the member of the force who said it was common for gay men to carry false ID, saying "he meant that the 'transient' lifestyles of many of the bar's patrons might make identification difficult" ("How the Media Saw It" 6). Apparently this was a reference to the French Quarter tourists and Iberville Street flophouse residents who might have been in the bar when the fire happened, and whose lack of a permanent local residence might make them hard to trace. Ironically, among the earliest victims to be identified was a tourist named Guy Anderson. The plastic fob of his hotel key was made of a hard plastic similar to that used in manufacturing ashtrays. It survived the fire and therefore provided a clue to Guy Anderson's identity.[51]

Still, the dubious and prejudicial assertion that all gays, or at least large numbers of them, were in the habit of carrying false identification was picked up by several news outlets, which passed it on to their readers and viewers without question. The remark surfaces, for example, in a national broadcast by Bruce Hall of CBS News. This news broadcast has been posted on YouTube and includes a clip of New Orleans newsman Bill Elders of WWL-TV, who reported from the site of the Up Stairs Lounge shortly after the fire had been extinguished. Elders speaks to two survivors who would only consent to be interviewed if he did not use their names or show their faces.[52] One of them, a man with a slender build and light hair, seems to be Rusty Quinton, and is even wearing a mesh tank top identical to one Rusty is seen wearing in newspaper photographs taken at the scene.

Their fear of appearing on the television news probably reflects more caution than paranoia. In the early twenty-first century, when gays and lesbians are far more open and openly accepted than they were forty years ago, a 2009 study still suggests that a majority of LGBT employees remain closeted on the job.[53] It is hard to overstate how much stronger the pressure to stay in the closet was in the early 1970s.

In fact, it is arguable that the values of the closet were adopted by the society as a whole, and that differences of any kind—not just sexual or affectional— were seen as threatening and best suppressed. Today, books, movies and television series such as *Harry Potter*, *True Blood*, *Twilight* and *Charmed* present the possibility of being different as attractive, desirable, and even erotic. The messages in the popular culture of the sixties and early seventies were quite different.

Consider, for example, the television series *Bewitched,* which ran from 1964 to 1972, and which has been in syndication ever since. The series featured Elizabeth Montgomery playing Samantha Stevens, a witch married to a mortal named Darrin (played first by Dick York, who, because of health reasons, was later replaced by Dick Sargent). The plot of nearly every episode was driven by Samantha and Darrin's desire to keep secret the fact that she was ... different, and the entire series had a gay sensibility that Montgomery (who was straight) and Sargent (who was gay) both later commented upon.[54]

There was always something unusual about Samantha, even if the mortals around her couldn't quite identify it. Darrin had imposed a household prohibition against Samantha practicing witchcraft, but it was ultimately unenforceable, as her difference continually found ways to express itself. Still, she did her best to fit into the middle–American world around her, and her success as a woman and a wife was determined by her ability to keep this world in the dark about who she really was. No matter how enviable Samantha's magic powers might be, or how witty and sophisticated her relatives were, the series encouraged us to identify with Darrin, who resented Samantha's family and disdained their good opinion. Instead, he courted the approval of their neurotic neighbor, Gladys Kravitz, and his greatest wish was for his family to be—in perception if not in reality—as banal as his soulless boss, Larry Tate.[55]

This was a common theme in television shows of the period. Whether the unusual characteristic was magic power (*Bewitched* and *I Dream of Jeannie*), a special talent (*The Flying Nun* and *The Girl with Something Extra*), an undesirable marital status (*Occasional Wife*) or alien origins (*My Favorite Martian*), these shows featured a character who differed from the norm, and whose difference was obsessively concealed, even if doing so meant a life of lies, fakery and subterfuge.

In the immediate aftermath of the fire, if gay men like Rusty Quinton and Stewart Butler were behaving with caution—or even paranoia—in trying to make sure their sexuality remained concealed, they were playing by the rules, and the people of New Orleans were giving them more than adequate reason to continue doing so. Citizens were not overrunning Charity hospital, volunteering to give blood. Instead, the Up Stairs fire became an occasion to vent a lot of anger and homophobia. One gay man, for example, went to a government office the very next day to conduct some personal business. The clerk waiting on him perceived he was gay, and with a look of hatred on her face, she said, "You should have died in that fire!"(Townsend 210). Many jokes began circulating, including this one.

> Q: What major tragedy happened in New Orleans on June 24?
> A: That only thirty faggots died—not more! [Townsend 40].

Another joke managed to blend set-up and punch line into one: "Did you hear the one about the flaming queens?" (Townsend 40). Still another made reference to a popular children's cereal, and suggested that the fire had turned a bunch of fairies into Crispy Critters.[56] The most infamous joke was spread by a New Orleans radio personality, an early "shock jock,"[57] who suggested that the best way to dispose of thirty gay men was to "bury them in fruit jars" (Rushton "Forgetting" 6).

This last joke, disgusting as it is, touched very real issues: The first memorial had been sparsely attended, partially because it had been organized so quickly, but partially because the identities of most of the dead were still unknown. How would their lives be honored? How would their passing be recognized?

Although the names of the injured were printed in Monday's edition of *The Times–Picayune*, none of the dead had been identified by the time it went to press, so at the time of the Monday night memorial, the identities of most of the dead were mere speculation. By the time Tuesday morning's paper came out, there were only two positive identifications, though the paper listed names of twelve more who had been tentatively identified. By Wednesday, there were ten positive identifications, by Thursday that number climbed to eleven, and by Friday the number climbed to twenty-one, with three additional tentative IDs.[58] Meanwhile, a man injured by the fire had died in the hospital, bringing the total number dead to thirty, with six having neither a confirmed nor a tentative ID. Two weeks later, when the thirty-first and thirty-second victims died in the hospital, there were still six dead men who had not been identified.[59] Three of them never would be.

So many friends and survivors were at a crossroads. So many people didn't know whom or how to mourn.

The night after the fire, Larry Raybourne was in a French Quarter bar having a drink when one of the customers said, "I hope the queens in the fire had the dresses burned right off of them!" Another man took offense and charged the speaker. Larry and several patrons had to struggle to separate them (Raybourne).

A day or so later, Larry went to the Up Stairs. The sidewalk outside the door was covered with flowers. As Larry stood gazing at them, somebody passing in a car screamed a single word at him: "Faggot!" By Larry's visit, the names of many of the dead or suspected dead had been printed, including the name of Leon Maples, Larry's beautiful Midnight Cowboy. Although Larry doesn't remember who, somebody was able to open the door and take him into what had been the Up Stairs Lounge to look at the devastation. As they wandered through the burned interior, walls, floor and furniture all charred black, the friend picked up something that looked like a big charcoal briquette.

It was a wallet. There was a picture of Glenn Green inside. "Glenn Green and I ... we were sort of 'frenemies,'" Larry says today, though that term came to use long after the fire. "I moved to New Orleans with another man, who abandoned me for Glenn. There were no hard feelings. I knew we weren't going to last. I was not a man of means in those days. That man later left Glenn to move on to somebody else."

By the time of the fire, Glenn Green had found a lover in Michael Scarborough. Michael lived, though he was seriously injured as he tried to escape. Glenn died in the fire.

Three nights after the fire, the drag queen Miss Fury was having a drink in another French Quarter gay bar. A distressed-looking woman came into the bar carrying a photograph. She approached several patrons, telling them that the picture was of her son. She said, "[He] hasn't called in four days. His pickup truck is parked on Chartres.... Do you know if my son is alive?" (Townsend 210).

Regina Adams does not remember the week after the fire. She has no connected memories of anything after leaving Reggie there a few minutes earlier so that she could run to their apartment to get their checkbook and a hat she had wanted to return to Jean Gosnell. She recalls seeing flames shooting out of the windows of the Up Stairs, and she remembers standing in the middle of the street, screaming. She knows that every morning after the fire she would wake up and lay out Reggie's clothes so he would have something to wear. She was in such a state of stunned denial that she refused to believe he was dead. It didn't help that Reggie was among the last of the victims to be identified; he had the bad luck to share a surname with Joseph Henry Adams. Both men were burned far beyond recognition, and police and autopsy records suggest that at some points in the identification process the identities of the two men became confused.[60] Regina last saw Reggie alive in the bar just minutes before the fire started, and because he hadn't been seen since, there could be little doubt about what had happened. Until there was a positive identification, however, there was no closure.

Regina's mother moved in to take care of her, and every day she watched Regina wake up and lay out Reggie's clothes. When Regina finally came to herself, and was able to accept that Reggie had died, her mother said, "Yep. For a couple of weeks there, you were gone" (Adams).

Some people felt that the first memorial service at St. George's hadn't been enough, and that a second one was needed. Troy Perry, Morris Kight and Morty Manford had encouraged gay communities across the nation to have memorials in honor of the Up Stairs victims on July 1, one week after the fire. Surely the city of New Orleans should have one, too.

The MCC delegation got to work. First they needed a location. They approached Father Bill Richardson of St. George's, but he understandably declined. He had prior plans to be out of town, anyway, but having attracted so much criticism for hosting the first memorial, he was not eager to host a second.

John Gill remembers Paul Breton spearheading the effort to find a location, opening a phone book and calling every church listed.[61] They hoped to find a church in the French Quarter so that the memorial would be close to the scene of the fire, but they knew that they might have trouble finding one.

They made call after call and got nowhere. Some of the clergy simply said no. Troy Perry learned that Bishop Noland had informed the Episcopal clergy that they were not, under any circumstances, to host or participate in the memorial, and when he phoned the bishop directly, he received a hostile response. He went to a Baptist church in the French Quarter, and the people he spoke to laughed in his face. A board member of one Lutheran congregation refused the use of his church, but suggested that the MCC call an associated church outside of the French Quarter, saying that it had a black congregation and that "they are more tolerant of aliens there" (Breton journal). Troy Perry called the office of Archbishop Hannan to see if a Catholic church could be made available. As when Bill Rushton had phoned for a statement from the archbishop, the person Troy Perry spoke to responded to questions with long pauses and evasive answers, refusing to put the archbishop on the phone. Eventually, somebody told Troy Perry that Catholic churches were for the use of Catholics only.[62]

The search for a church occupied several days, but that was not all that the MCC delegation and the activists from out of town were doing. Each day they took turns going to the hospital to check on the people who had survived the fire. Troy Perry reports that Larry Stratton never lost his sense of humor, despite severe injuries that would eventually take his life. "Next time I go out drinking," he told Perry, "I'm wearing an asbestos jock" (Perry and Swicegood 93). Paul Breton witnessed the touching devotion that two other patients showed each other. Luther Boggs and Jean Gosnell had been enjoying a drink together when the fire broke out. Now they were in the same hospital in different rooms. Whenever Breton visited Jean, she immediately asked how Luther was, and whenever he visited Luther, Luther asked about Jean.[63]

Luther was reported to be one of the straight men who liked the friendly atmosphere at the Up Stairs. He was also between jobs when the fire occurred, so he asked both Paul Breton and Troy Perry to help him prepare to interview for another job, but Luther died on July 10, without ever leaving the hospital.[64]

Aside from comforting the living, Paul Breton spent a lot of time trying to assist in burying the dead. Used to working with social services agencies in the D.C. area, he was appalled at how little assistance people in New Orleans were given. In D.C., the indigent were guaranteed the services of a funeral home, a priest, minister or rabbi, a church and a burial plot. In New Orleans, the city would supply only a wooden box and space in a potter's field. Breton approached several funeral directors about either reduced rates or *pro bono* services. Speaking of them today, Breton simply says, "Some were very kind. Others were not."

In the evenings, Perry, Gill and Breton would go out to meet gay people wherever they could find them in numbers. Sometimes they attended gatherings in private homes, but nearly every night they went to the gay bars. Breton recalls being greeted and hugged by hundreds of people that week, some of them weeping on the MCC ministers' shoulders. Breton says today, "There was so much pain at the harsh treatment gays had received from their local clergy—particularly with the archbishop's denial of Catholic burial—that people were grateful to see any positive ministerial presence." In 2010, John Gill recalled a different contingent:

> I remember being in a bar one night. We were emotionally exhausted. There was disco music, and strobe lights were flashing. In some ways, people didn't seem to want to acknowledge what had happened. It was like they wanted to pretend things were the same way they had always been.
>
> While we were in that bar, Troy noticed the emergency exits. They were those kind of doors that lock from the outside, but have panic bars on the inside [so they can be pushed open in an emergency]. Troy noticed that the doors had heavy chains and padlocks on them to prevent them from being opened from the inside. He got hold of somebody—I'm not sure if it was the owner or the manager—but whoever he was, *Troy let him have it!* [Gill].

That week, Perry, Gill, Breton, Kight and Manford did what they could to raise consciousness in New Orleans about gay issues calling inside and outside of the gay community. They issued a steady stream of press releases requesting aid to the survivors and assistance in burying the dead. They also granted numerous interviews to local television stations. Perry recalls, "We often found ourselves being interviewed ... with hosts and hostesses who became increasingly familiar with, and less afraid of, words like gay, lesbian and (gulp!)—homosexual" (Perry and Swicegood 92).

Other people, too, began to speak up. The newspaper editorials referencing the fire tended to avoid its more controversial aspects and limited their comments to the fairly safe topic of the need for improved fire codes, but in the June 28 issue of the *States Item*, in an article entitled "Have Labels Overshadowed 29 Deaths," staff reporter Lanny Thomas wrote, "Is there as much public sympathy and concern for the victims as there was for those of the Rault Center and Howard Johnson's? If there is, where are all the statements of sympathy from the clergy and public officials?" (A16). Both the *States Item* and *The Times–Picayune* ran multiple letters from readers who defended the Up Stairs Lounge against Major Morris' charge that it had been a hangout for thieves and queers. At least two of these were written by straight men who made a point of saying that the Up Stairs had such a welcoming and nonthreatening atmosphere that they felt comfortable taking their wives there.[65] One of these men mentioned the theatrical productions done as charity benefits, asking, "Does this sound like the work of thieves? They wanted to give, not receive" (Rutland A10). A letter signed by Mrs. Barbara Bouden also took on the remark about thieves and queers, but did so in a way that examined its broader implications. She observed that Morris' language "denotes not only an ingrained bias, but implies a condemnatory stance on the part of the police department." She continued, "I venture to say that, had a French Quarter restaurant filled with prominent Orleanians gone up in smoke with a comparative death toll, investigations would be pulling the town apart" (Bouden 12).

But not all of the criticism was being levied against the city's clergy, politicians and police department. Some of it was directed toward the gay community. On June 30, the *States Item* ran a letter written by a Richard M. Hargrove, who opened with a salvo against Major Morris' infamous remark about thieves and queers, and stated that Morris' perception seemed to be shared by local leaders. Hargrove, a gay man himself, then wrote, "What is even more appalling is that seemingly no individual in the extremely large gay population of New Orleans has seen fit to give anything but guarded and anonymous over-the-shoulder interviews and comments on the tragedy." Hargrove went on to say that he was a frequent patron of the Up Stairs, and that "if there were ever any thieves or perverts with false identification there, I must have missed them" (Hargrove A6).

Perry, the MCC ministers and the activists quite possibly had succeeded in creating an atmosphere in which people like Bouden and Hargrove felt free to criticize city leadership and sign their names to pro-gay letters. It is also possible that the townspeople who wrote to the papers would have done so even if Perry and the others had not arrived on the scene. Still, it is undeniable that the efforts of Perry and the others were extending and amplifying a city-wide conversation on gay issues that Mayor Landrieu, Governor Edwards, Bishop Noland, Archbishop Hannan, and a lot of gay people didn't particularly want to have.

During this week, the label "fairy carpetbaggers" began to stick to Perry and the men he had brought to town. Asked about it today, Troy Perry laughs and says, "The gay folks who were calling me that didn't understand that I was from the South." It is a response that seems to miss the point. The term "carpetbagger," as previously noted, has historically referred to northerners who moved south after the war, reportedly in order to exploit the people—both black and white—for their own political or economic gain.[66] The term "fairy carpetbagger" seems to have much less to do with Perry's place of birth than with a perception that he and the others with him were exploiting the Up Stairs fire for their own political purposes. Before Morris Kight even got to the city, he was asked if he would be using the fire "to further organize support for the gay cause." Kight responded, "Not at all. That would be terribly offensive" (Nolan and Segura 3). Nevertheless, some people felt that was precisely what was happening.

Surprisingly, even some members of the New Orleans chapter of the MCC felt this way. Courtney Craighead seems to have been one of them. Like a lot of gays and lesbians in New Orleans, Courtney was not a native. He had come to New Orleans from his home state of Arkansas, finding a place where he could live in easy, anonymous comfort and where he could express and explore his sexuality far from prying, familial eyes. He also discovered the MCC, a church which allowed him to reconcile his spiritual and sexual natures. A charter member of the New Orleans chapter, and a deacon at the time of the fire in 1973, Courtney remained active in the MCC until his death in 2005.[67]

The Reverend Dexter Brecht, pastor of the New Orleans MCC from 1994 until 2007, knew Courtney well. He says that despite Courtney's longtime loyalty to the MCC, he was resentful of Troy Perry's presence in New Orleans following the fire, particularly regarding the ways in which Perry kept gay issues in that week's news coverage. Courtney was one of the people who survived by following Buddy to the fire escape in the theater. Although neither the *Daily Record* nor *The Times–Picayune* specifically identified the Up Stairs as a gay bar in Monday morning's editions, the Sunday evening television news coverage and the Monday edition of the *States Item* both did. *The States Item* even identified Courtney both as a survivor of the fire and as a deacon of the MCC. By Tuesday morning, all three papers described the Up Stairs as a gay bar and the MCC as a church for homosexuals, and Courtney's name appears in more than one of these articles. Because the AP wire services picked multiple stories and circulated them nationwide, Courtney—like others connected to the fire—was "outed" to his family by the press. One member of the MCC who had survived the fire lost his job when his name appeared in the news coverage.[68] Eric Newhouse, a reporter from the AP wire services, went to MCC headquarters to get a story. Bill Rushton provided a record of Newhouse questioning Courtney Craighead in a manner that seems less like an interview than an interrogation. Ruston records Newhouse asking Courtney what kind of man Bill Larson had been. Courtney began his reply by saying, "[The Reverend Larson] believed in freedom and love because he wanted the right of the individual to make his own choice." Probing for the *"real"* story, Newhouse asked "What was he doing at the *bar?*" (Rushton "After the Fire" 1).

Episodes like these were not endearing the press to some of the MCC members, or to the gay community at large. Courtney and many other gays and lesbians wanted the story to die down as quickly as possible.[69]

This attitude surfaces in a letter to the editor that was published in *The Times–Picayune*. This letter, which ran under the title "Hurt by Label," once again asks why Major Morris felt it necessary to make his remarks about thieves and queers. Though the letter does not mention the out-of-town activists, the author was clearly uncomfortable with the high profile given to the "homosexual angle" in the coverage, asking, "Why did the news media find it necessary to refer to the bar time and time again as a homosexual bar? I am sure that not all the people who were killed were gay, but even if they were it is grossly unfair to put labels on them" (10). Unlike every other letter concerning the Up Stairs in *The Times–Picayune*, the *States Item* or the *Daily Record*, this one was published without the author's name, and was accompanied only by the initials M.F.

Soon a group of gay business leaders—mostly the owners of gay bars—demanded a meeting with Troy Perry. The reports of possible arson at the Up Stairs had made gay men afraid to go out. This wasn't helped by rumors that a terrorist group planned a series of similar attacks on other gay bars. Because of the crime threat, police patrolled the bars heavily, reportedly harassing the patrons in the course of doing so. Continuing news coverage scared men who didn't want to be "outed" by print journalists or television cameras. Business suffered and bar owners blamed Perry for keeping the spotlight on the gay community. They, too, felt like life would be better if the story passed as quickly and as quietly as possible, without the "fairy carpetbaggers" continually granting interviews and issuing press releases.[70]

Perry was not one to be cowed by opposition. In fact, in speaking about the experience today, John Gill says, "The more negativity we found, the more we got fired up!"

Perry answered the business leaders:

> In case you hadn't heard, people have died here! Gay people are hurt, and official New Orleans isn't lifting a finger to help. Are you going to keep letting this be just "another queer happening?" Are you just going to go to sleep and forget? No, no! The time has come my friends, for you to reexamine your priorities. What are you able and willing to do? [Perry and Swicegood 91].

The question does not seem to have been rhetorical in intent, but it might as well have been. Perry does not say that the meeting ended with any substantive agreement, and there does not seem to be any record of coordinated aid given to the MCC, the victims, or the victims' families by the gay business community.

Plans for the memorial went forward, and suddenly there were several offers for possible locations. Clay Shaw, a prominent local businessman who had ties to the Vieux Carré Commission, said that if no other alternative could be found, the VCC was willing to close off a block of Iberville so that the memorial could take place in the street outside of the Up Stairs Lounge. Troy Perry had held a similar outdoor service when his church in Los Angeles had burned, and he found this to be an acceptable fallback position, but he was still reluctant. "Nobody died when my church in L.A. burned," he says today, "but people died in this fire, and a lot of them were associated with the MCC, so I felt strongly that we needed to have a church service." Still, Perry was warmed by the offer, and now says he was particularly warmed because he later learned who Clay Shaw was.

In 1969 New Orleans district attorney Jim Garrison tried Clay Shaw for an alleged role in the assassination of John F. Kennedy. Garrison accused Shaw, a gay man, of taking part in a far-reaching conspiracy that involved the cooperation of the Mafia, the C.I.A., Cuban exiles, and New Orleans homosexuals, among others.[71] Though the jury acquitted Shaw in less than an hour, he was still stung by the case, much of which focused on his sex life and effectively put him on trial for his homosexuality. Troy Perry now says that because of this painful prior experience, "Shaw might have had a very good reason for denying us permission to do this. If Shaw had a reason to be frightened, it didn't stop him from doing the right thing."

Shaw's offer got serious consideration, despite the preference for a church. Morty Manford seems to have been both grateful and angry, saying later, "We were prepared to go out into the streets because we were turned down right and left by the Sunday Christians who aren't even Christians on Sunday" ("200 Attend" A3). Paul Breton quotes Manford in his journal, following Manford's words with the note "This sentiment was shared by everyone."

Then, after Shaw's offer, a Unitarian minister named Evelyn Barrett approached the MCC and invited them to use her church. Perry, Gill and Breton were touched by the invitation, especially since they had experienced so much hostility from other churches, but the Unitarian church was too small for the expected crowd, and it was also far outside the French Quarter.

Finally, the MCC found St. Mark's Methodist Church, a rather austere stucco building at the corner of North Rampart and Governor Nicholls. This church was quite a bit more liberal than the average Protestant church in New

Orleans in the early 1970s. A woman named Mrs. Harold, Troy Perry's contact on the St. Mark's board, knew there would be controversy, but dismissed it with good humor, saying, "Here in the South, when you have a church with a black pastor and five white women on the board—! Oh, my dear, we've been called everything" (Perry and Swicegood 98). Her friendship with Troy Perry was cemented when they discovered that Mrs. Harold was an old friend of his mother.[72]

The service was scheduled for 2 p.m. on Sunday, July 1, exactly one week after the fire. Since Troy Perry was scheduled to preach at a memorial for the Up Stairs victims—in Los Angeles—at eight o'clock that same evening, he would have to race for the airport after the service ended.

The MCC, which Troy Perry had started in his living room five years earlier, now had chapters in forty-six cities across America and in Great Britain. All forty-six of those chapters would be having memorial services at 8 p.m. on July 1. Gay bars and night clubs in cities such as New York, Atlanta, Chicago, Los Angeles and San Francisco had also agreed to close their doors and "go dark" for sixty minutes starting at 8 p.m., and many straight bars and night-clubs belonging to the Tavern Guild chapters in L.A. and San Francisco agreed to do so as well. Gay organizations such as the Mattachine Society, the Gay Activists Alliance, the Oscar Wilde Book Shop and New York's Gay Synagogue all helped coordinate efforts and all pledged participation. Though neither Mayor Landrieu nor Governor Edwards was willing to declare a day of mourning at home, there would be one, and it would take place on a national, and even an international, scale.[73]

After Troy Perry spoke to the Reverend Edward Kennedy, the pastor at St. Mark's, he and the other MCC ministers printed three thousand handbills announcing the memorial. They made a conscious decision not to include the words "gay" or "homosexual" on the handbill, in part because some of the victims had been straight. They also wanted to avoid further controversy that could be caused by labeling victims, since labeling had been so injurious in the aftermath of the fire. The organizing committee even decided that television cameras would not be allowed, so that people wouldn't avoid the service for fear of being outed by the coverage.[74]

In Louisiana's oppressive summer heat, with temperatures approaching one hundred, and with work interrupted by brief but near-daily thunderstorms, all the out-of-town activists and a group of local volunteers distributed the handbills. Paul Breton's journal includes the note "The horribly hot, humid weather down there is hard for a damn Yankee ... to bear. But that is not really a complaint." Many of the handbills went to the owners and managers of small businesses, and Troy Perry was happy to see them later displayed in shop and restaurant windows. Others went to individuals on the street who were sometimes hesitant—or even afraid—to take them. Some were fearful because of rumors that other gay bars or gay gatherings would be firebombed—and what better target than a church full of people memorializing the Up Stairs victims?[75] Others undoubtedly just didn't want to be convicted of guilt by association.

When he talks about the experience today, Paul Breton recalls meeting someone like this. Walking the streets handing out flyers, he encountered a slender young black man. Breton gave a flyer to the man, who returned it, wordlessly.

Breton asked, "Is there a problem?"

The man said, "I'm afraid if I go to the memorial, people will call me a queer lover."

Breton said, "I live in Washington, D.C., which is about seventy-two percent black. I've been called a nigger lover for going to the funerals of black people."

The young man stared at Breton for a full minute before finally taking the flyer.

As people began arriving at St. Mark's for the memorial service, Troy Perry received word that one of the people attending was Finis Crutchfield, the Methodist bishop of Louisiana. Troy recalls his heart sinking at the news; after the bad experiences he'd had with Archbishop Hannan and Bishop Noland, he expected nothing but trouble. Much to his surprise, he learned that Bishop Crutchfield was in attendance as a show of support to the fire victims, to the people organizing the memorial, and to his own minister, Edward Kennedy. Of course, by showing his support, Bishop Crutchfield also opened himself to criticism, and Troy recalls, "In a spiritual sense, I immediately fell in love with him" (Perry and Swicegood 98).

Aside from attending himself, Bishop Crutchfield had encouraged other ministers and members of the Methodist spiritual community to attend, so several young seminary students were present.[76] So were Stewart Butler and his lover, Alfred Doolittle, who had left the Up Stairs only minutes before the fire broke out. Paul Killgore and his lover, Frank Scorsone, Jr., also went. Though they used to sometimes go to the Up Stairs, they were unfamiliar with the MCC until they read about it in the fire coverage. Part of what drew them to the memorial was their curiosity about this gay church. In particular, Paul Killgore wanted to see Troy Perry. Today he says, "I hate to say this about myself, but maybe I was celebrity-stalking. Maybe that was it, but I hope I'm not that shallow." Charlene Schneider, who would later open the lesbian bar Charlene's, was in the congregation that day, along with Marco Sperandeo, who performed at the Up Stairs as Marcy Marcell. Both the *States Item* and *The Times–Picayune* sent journalists to cover the event. In all, between two and three hundred people attended the service. A few seats remained open, but people also stood in the rear.[77] Some were survivors of the fire, some had lost lovers, friends or relatives, and some were merely there to acknowledge a loss of life so vast in its dimensions. After a week of shock, mourning, pain, homophobic jokes, hostile clergy, intrusive media coverage and indifferent public officials, there was, at last, a moment when people could sit peacefully together and share a common grief.

Troy Perry led the service with the assistance of multiple concelebrants: Edward Kennedy, who had made the church available; John Gill and Paul Breton, who had accompanied Troy Perry to town; and Lucien Baril, a recently-ordained MCC minister who lived in New Orleans, who had assisted Bill Larson, and who had become the local MCC pastor upon Bill's death. Morty Manford, though not a rabbi, also took part in the ceremony, representing the Jewish faith. From the altar, Paul Breton spied the young black man to whom he had given a flyer on the street; he had decided to attend after all.[78]

Though it followed the funeral service in the Anglican *Book of Common Prayer*, the ceremony was ecumenical in its spirit and intent.[79] After an organ prelude, Paul Breton opened with a prayer, asking, in part, "O Lord, grant us in this memorial worship the inspiration and courage to take on the task of human fellowship that never again will brothers and sisters die with branding and the social stigma of name-calling, but rather they will all live in peace, in freedom, in hope and in love" (Breton journal).

John Gill led the congregation in a hymn and then read selected scripture, and then Morty Manford addressed the mourners. After a brief opening, he said:

> Many of our brothers and sisters who died at the Upstairs Bar were Gay. They know what it was like to live in a condemning society where churches call us sinners, psychiatrists call us sick, legislators called us criminals, where capitalists denounced us as subversives and communists denounced us as decadent. The irony of it all is that we are loving, feeling, productive human beings. This we know—that we are no more, we are no less. In the face of such knowledge, we stand together proudly [Breton journal].

Discussing the relief and memorial efforts that were taking place nationwide, Manford noted in particular that people throughout the country were donating blood and stipulating that it was for the benefit of the Up Stairs fire victims in New Orleans. He urged the mourners to go to Charity Hospital's blood bank to do the same. He closed by saying:

> The spirit of community, of concern, of caring and love of sisters and brothers in far away cities is with us—this must make our burden lighter. In the words of

[Isaiah 9:2]: "the people that dwelled in darkness have seen a great light. They who lived in the land of the shadow of death—upon them hath the light shined" [Breton journal].

The Reverend Lucien Baril then read telegrams of support that had arrived from all over the country. Many came from MCC chapters, but not all. One, in fact, was from the American Baptist convention. Some people thought this telegram must have been a mistake, though Troy Perry "preferred to believe that some Baptist leaders knew to whom they were sending their condolences" (Perry and Swicegood 99).

Troy Perry spoke near the end of the service. "We are thankful for men like Reverend Kennedy and Bishop Crutchfield who have the guts to support us today." He went on to say that there would continue to be a problem "as long as one brother or sister in the world is oppressed.... Such names as faggot, queer, fruit and fairy are [the] language of the bully and the bigot—insensitive labels that will never put us down" (Perry and Swicegood 100). He had printed the lyrics to the unofficial Up Stairs anthem, and they had been distributed to all present at St. Mark's. With some people crying, the congregation sang "United We Stand."

A collection was taken for the benefit of both living and dead victims. Then Paul Breton called for a moment of silent prayer, after which Lucien Baril provided the benediction. As John Gill led the congregation in the closing hymn, somebody passed a note to Troy Perry: despite the specific request for no television coverage, news cameras were outside waiting to film the people as they left the service. When Troy Perry made the announcement, a palpable feeling of alarm pervaded the church. Many of the congregation were gay or lesbian, and many still in the closet. Others who were straight probably feared being branded by association. Troy Perry announced, "We didn't expect this, but we still made contingency plans for the situation. Anyone who desires can leave without being observed. Reverend Kennedy can show you out through the alley by way of the back door" (Perry and Swicegood 100–101).

An anxious moment followed as the mourners looked to each other, trying to decide what to do. The tension broke as a woman, who has never been identified, stood up and shouted, "I'm not ashamed of who I am or who my friends are. I came in the front door, and I'm going out that way" (Butler; Killgore; Marcell; Pizanie).

She had made a collective decision. In stark contrast to just one week earlier, when survivors of the fire consented to a television interview only if they were filmed from behind, the entire congregation rose out of their pews and walked out the front doors to face the cameras.[80]

IV

"Nothing there"

The Investigation of the NOFD and the Coroner's Office

— — — — — — — — — —

There were actually three investigations into the fire at the Up Stairs Lounge: one conducted by the New Orleans Police Department (NOPD), one conducted by the Fire Prevention Division of the New Orleans Fire Department (NOFD), and one conducted by the Arson Investigation Unit of the Louisiana State Fire Marshal (SFM). For good measure, the Orleans Parish[1] coroner's office essentially conducted a fourth, parallel investigation.

The report of the fire department is really more interested in the prevention and safety lessons to be learned from the fire than in whether or not it was arson. Leaving the question of *who* almost entirely out of the picture, it concentrates, instead, on *what*, *why* and *how*. What caused the fire to spread the way it did? Why did so many people die? How could another fire be prevented?

The first part of this report is a handwritten statement which was required to be turned in within twenty-four hours of the incident.[2] It includes a description of the scene, indicating that the fire seemed to originate in the stairwell. It also indicates that inspectors found an empty lighter fluid can which was in the possession of the police. The report notes that there was no sign of broken glass at the scene, suggesting that firemen were responding to rumors of a Molotov cocktail. No statements from survivors were taken at the scene because "all in the bar were dead, and those treated at Charity were in the intensive care unit, transferred to another hospital, or released when arrived there" (NOFD Investigation Report 3).

Following the description of the scene is a list of fatalities. Compiled long before the identities of many of the victims were known, the list merely notes

84

the locations where bodies were found, along with the gender. So, for example, body number one is "in corner of bar on Iberville side—male" (NOFD Fatality List 1). Numbers two and three are "in Entrance to Restroom male" (1). Two more were in the restroom, one under the basin and one alongside the toilet. Number six was in front of the piano, seven through nine were under or near the piano, and ten through twelve were on the stage in front of the middle Chartres Street window. The largest group by far was in the front corner, where windows overlooking both Iberville and Chartres streets falsely promised the best hope for escape; seventeen bodies were found piled in this corner. At the time this preliminary report was filed, only five tentative identifications had been made, including the only female victim, Inez Warren.[3] Her two sons would later be identified among the dead as well.

The next item in the report is a list of the survivors who were taken to Charity Hospital, along with their names and conditions. Most were in intensive care in serious condition. Two were listed as critical. Four had already been transferred to other hospitals because Charity could not handle everyone. The last five names on the list are those of people, like Rusty Quinton, who were fortunate enough to be treated and released the night of the fire.

Finally, there is a hand-drawn diagram of the interior of the Up Stairs showing the locations of the dead. Only the first two rooms (the bar and the lounge areas) are drawn in the diagram, apparently because the theater neither contained bodies nor sustained fire damage.

In addition to this brief handwritten report is a much longer document labeled "Supplemental Information." Though it is typed, it bears neither a signature nor a date, but internal evidence indicates it was compiled six or more months after the fire took place. For example, this supplemental report refers to the fact that, in the fall of 1973, a man named Raymond Wallender, in jail in California for another charge, falsely confessed to setting the fire so that he would be extradited to Louisiana.[4] The report also refers to an article about the fire published by Elwood Willey in the January 1974 edition of a professional publication known as the *NFPA Journal*.[5]

Mentioning the empty can of lighter fluid, the report states that "it is believed that a small amount of flammable liquid was used to start the fire at the foot of the stairs" (NOFD Supplemental Information 1). After that brief reference to possible arson, the report arrives at its main focus, which is answering these two questions: Was the Up Stairs Lounge in compliance with fire regulations, and how could the deaths have been prevented? The report describes the presence of emergency illumination, for example, but says, "It is not known if these lights were functioning properly at the time of the fire" (1). The last fire inspection at the Up Stairs had taken place in March of 1971.

Figure 1. Floor plan of Upstairs Lounge.

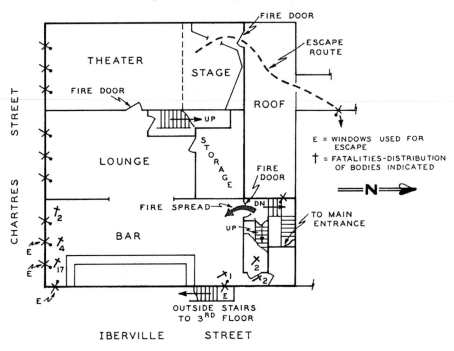

This diagram accompanied an article about the fire which appeared in the January 1974 issue of the *NFPA Journal*. It shows the general layout, the path by which the fire entered and spread, the locations of the fire exits, the locations of the windows, and the locations where fatalities occurred. One body was inadvertently omitted from the original, hand-drawn diagram made by the New Orleans Fire Department (reprinted with permission from *NFPA Journal* (Vol. 68, #1) © 1974, National Fire Protection Association, Quincy, MA. All rights reserved). *NFPA Journal* is a registered trademark of the National Fire Protection Association, Quincy, MA 02169.

Phil Esteve, the owner of the bar, was questioned about carpeting and interior finishes after the fire, and he told investigators these finishes had remained unchanged since the last inspection. The flammability of such finishes was a question of some concern, but "these materials were consumed in the fire and no samples were available" (2). The report assumes that interior conditions were largely the same as at the time of the last inspection—which the Up Stairs had passed—though possible exceptions are allowed for the working conditions of lights, the wire and hasp on the rear exit door, and a possible accumulation of combustible rubbish.

At 1880 square feet, and with an allowance of 15 square feet per person, the Up Stairs had a total permissible capacity of 125 persons (though it had only been officially approved for 110). Specifying that only about sixty people were present at the time of the fire,[6] the report notes that the number and travel distances of the fire exits were all adequate for safe egress.[7]

The supplemental report is heavily critical of finish materials.[8] Many other criticisms were leveled against the fire exit in the theater: the door was not readily visible, concealed behind stage properties; this door opened into the room instead of pushing outward; it did not have the requisite panic hardware, and the lock was substandard, only a wire and hasp; once people using this exit got to the roof of the neighboring building, there was no clear indication of what to do next. However, "none of the exit deficiencies appear to be contributors to the loss of life" (4). Indeed, as the report notes, this sub-standard exit saved more than twenty lives, and could have saved more if people had not panicked, because the theater and the roof outside "could have been a safe place of refuge for all occupants in this fire" (5).

As the New Orleans Fire Department tried to determine whether unsafe conditions led to loss of life, the Orleans Parish coroner's office had a formidable job to do. The autopsy reports for all of the victims are now archived in the Louisiana Collection of the New Orleans Public Library, and reading them is a grim experience. In most cases, the examining doctors did not spend a lot of time determining a cause of death for the twenty-nine victims; the causes were obvious.[9]

Shortly after the blaze, Fire Superintendent William McCrossen was quoted as saying that he didn't think the victims had burned to death. Instead, he said that he thought they died from carbon monoxide. "I call it the cobra ... superheated gas that will knock you unconscious in just a couple of whiffs. The tiger ... fire ... will finish you off. I doubt that any felt the flames" (Swindall "Tourist" 7).

Witnesses had watched several people scream as they had, in fact, felt the flames. Those victims died in or near windows, where the broken glass let in oxygen, perhaps counteracting the effects of the carbon monoxide. Hopefully, though, McCrossen was right about asphyxiation having killed—or at least rendered unconscious—the majority of the victims. Seven autopsy reports indicate asphyxia due to carbon monoxide as either a primary or a secondary cause of death. Some of these note that carbon monoxide inhalation produces a pink color in the skin. Those for whom this cause of death was noted were not burned as severely as most other victims, leaving the pink coloring obvious. The cause of death for the others was listed as severe burns over much of the body.

With causes of death easy to determine, the real job the coroners faced was identifying the twenty-nine bodies found inside the burned lounge. This job, taking place long before the days of DNA testing, had its challenges. In theory, clothing, jewelry and the contents of wallets—such as driver's licenses—can provide clues to the identity of a body, but these had not fared well. When the police department caused a controversy by claiming that it was common for homosexuals to carry false identification,[10] they were actually misidentifying the problem the coroner would face: much of the identification found after the fire was in fragments, melted beyond use or "not near enough to any body to confirm identification" (Lind, Thomas, and Philbin "29 Dead" A6). Most bodies had no identification cards of any kind. The cards, the wallets that contained them, and the pockets containing the wallets had all been destroyed in the fire. The autopsy report on body #18 is typical, noting that "brown shoes are still in place, together with fragments of pants." Nothing else that #18 wore survived the fire.

The chief of pathology at Charity Hospital, Dr. Monroe Samuels, was also an assistant to the Orleans Parish coroner. He described the condition of the victims in one word: "Bad" (Swindall "Blaze Victims" 3). On many bodies, facial features had burned beyond recognition. Trying to use fingerprints was frequently impossible because the finger pads, or even the fingers themselves, were entirely gone. A Charity Hospital physician said, "There is simply nothing there" (Katz "Labeling" A6b).

Thus, even more than usual, the examining physicians paid particular attention to any remaining marks or items that could provide a clue. Although the autopsy report of William Douglas Maxwell notes that he had "second third and fourth degree type burns involving 85 percent of body surface," two tattoos, amazingly, remained intact; one was of an animal, the second "an emblem and the capital letters 'MOM.' The identity of Reginald Adams, later confirmed by dental records, was partially established by a high school ring, which actually belonged to Regina. "A lot of people lose their high school rings, and don't know where they are any more," Regina says today, "but I know where mine is. It was buried with Reggie, because it was melted onto his finger." George Steven Matyi, known as Bud, was the cute young pianist who was playing at the Up Stairs for the first time that night, and he, too, died in the fire. The autopsy report indicates he had "third and fourth degree burns over 95 percent of body surface," and that "there is loss of the fingers of the hands and there is extensive charring of the face rendering it unrecognizable." However, the medal his lover had given him, which contained the image of two doves, and which was said to represent marriage, survived the fire and provided a clue to his identity.[11]

Major Morris urged all those who suspected a friend or loved one had been in the fire to call the police so that the department could contact the dentists of the alleged victims and request records.[12] Dental records were crucial. The autopsy report for one body, listing cause of death as "extensive 4th degree body burns [over] 90 percent of the body surface," notes that the victim wore a complete set of dentures, adding that this would be a valuable aid to identification since "the fingers are charred completely." In some cases, the real teeth were removed from unidentified bodies so they could be used for possible identification in the future.

One of the victims had actually been a dentist. Perry Waters, a single man with no lover or steady boyfriend, had a wide circle of gay friends and had been active in the MCC. When he did not arrive for work the day after the fire, his secretary contacted the police and added his name to the possible dead. She provided a tentative identification of him based upon a watch and a ring taken from his body. That identification was later confirmed by dental records. Because Perry Waters had encouraged his friends to see him for their dental work, his patient files became a valuable aid to the parish coroners, helping to establish the identities of Glenn Green, Adam Fontenot and Horace "Skip" Getchell.[13]

In the end, three men remained unidentified. A fourth, Ferris LeBlanc, was identified, but never claimed.[14] The MCC wanted to claim these bodies and give them proper funerals, but the city would not release them.[15] The issue was a legal one; when a person dies, that person's body becomes the property of the legally recognized next of kin, and the next of kin makes decisions regarding funerals, cremation or burial.

Today, gays and lesbians are often legally forbidden to make funeral decisions for beloved deceased partners, because in the absence of marriage, they are not legally recognized as being next of kin. In 2009, the Rhode Island legislature passed a bill to address this inequity by giving domestic partners— including same-sex partners—the right to make funeral arrangements. Governor Donald L. Carcieri vetoed the bill, citing it as evidence of "the incremental erosion of the principals surrounding traditional marriage" (Gregg).

The MCC fought to be able to bury the unidentified victims of the Up Stairs fire, but since no one could determine the legal next of kin, there was no one with the legal authority to release them to the MCC. Ferris LeBlanc's family neither claimed him nor released their rights. Thus, Ferris LeBlanc and the three unidentified men met the same fate as other indigent, unclaimed or unidentified dead in the city's possession: they were buried in a potter's field.[16]

Bill Larson, the MCC pastor, nearly met a similar fate. His mother had never fully accepted her son's sexuality. The AP wire service spread newspaper reports of the fire nationally, and these stories clearly identified Bill Larson as the homosexual minister of a homosexual church who had died in a homosexual bar. Shamed by the news coverage, Mrs. Larson did not want him sent home for burial, but she ultimately released him to the MCC for cremation and allowed the MCC to keep his ashes. These remained in an urn at the New Orleans MCC headquarters for years, until a church member donated mausoleum space.[17]

As the coroners labored, the death toll continued to grow. On June 28, Jim Hambrick died of burns over 50 percent of his body. Luther Boggs died on July 10, with similar burns, but he had also developed bronchopneumonia and cerebral edema. The last to die, Larry Stratton, survived until July 12; he had burns over 80 percent of his body, and like Luther Boggs, he developed bronchopneumonia. These three men brought the final death toll to thirty-two.

Though most of the final autopsy reports are only one or two pages long, occasionally supplemental items are included in an individual's file. This is the case with David Gary, the twenty-two year-old man who had been nicknamed Piano Dave because he had been playing at the Up Stairs for several months before the fire. David's file contains some agonized letters written to the Orleans Parish Coroner by his parents, as well as a more business-like letter written by their attorney. David's parents had maintained an insurance policy on him, and they were trying to get a settlement, but the insurance company would not pay until a final death certificate had been issued. In July and August of 1973, when these letters were written, the death certificate was still provisional, with the cause listed as "Under Investigation." If the police and fire marshal determined arson, the death would become a fire fatality due to homicide. If no determination of arson was made, the death would be classified as an accidental fire fatality. With the investigation still underway, and with the death certificate remaining provisional, David's parents wrestled with their grief at the same time as insurance executives made them jump through bureaucratic hoops.

These very questions, though, were still unsettled: Was the fire accidental or arson? Were the deaths accidental or homicide? These are the questions that the police investigation was supposed to answer, though few people are satisfied that it did.

V

Passive Voice
The Police Investigation

On June 25, the night after the fire, a local television news anchor named Alec Gifford issued a bulletin: a terrorist group calling itself *Black Mama, White Mama* had phoned the station, taking credit for starting the fire at the Up Stairs Lounge. The caller said its members had been victims of homosexual attacks and they had burned the Up Stairs as a means of retribution. This group, Gifford earnestly warned his audience, said that the Up Stairs Lounge would be the first of many such fires.[1]

In retrospect, the claims were patently ridiculous. The putative terrorist group took its name from a B movie of 1973. *Black Mama, White Mama* starred the blonde Margaret Markov and the African American Pam Grier, who made a name for herself in the "blaxploitation" film *Foxy Brown* that same year. In *Black Mama, White Mama,* Markov and Grier play two inmates confined in the same women's prison where they are predictably menaced by a lesbian prison matron. Ultimately they escape while handcuffed together, pausing long enough to strangle the evil matron with the chain linking their cuffs.

While this brief synopsis suggests an anti-gay theme, the subtext of the film relies heavily upon the erotic possibilities of lesbianism. Early in the *Black Mama, White Mama*, Markov and Grier frolic innocently—and nakedly—in a group shower. Later they are punished by being locked together—naked—in a tin sweatbox the size of a phone booth. They make their handcuffed escape wearing implausibly short and low-cut prison shifts. As they run through rough countryside, their breasts and buttocks jiggling beneath the thin, clingy dresses, they periodically stop to slap each other, but their handcuffs restrain their battle.[2] In the trailer (available on YouTube), a deep male voice chants, "Women in Chains! Women in Chains!" *Black Mama, White Mama* is a film

91

replete with fantasies involving bondage, S&M, and, above all, female homo-eroticism. While the film punishes "bad" lesbians, it excites a straight male audience by making it eager to see Markov and Grier get it on.

This is probably not a movie to which an anti-gay terror group would be eager to attach its name. Much more likely, homophobic pranksters thought it would be funny to phone the media outlets and see what would happen. The alleged terrorist organization was never heard from again, and no other news organizations in New Orleans ran the story.

But even if Gifford had not seen the movie (one hopes that he had better taste), there was still some feeling that he should have known better than to go public with his "scoop." This broadcast was unquestionably responsible for rumors of further firebombs that helped create the aura of fear in the French Quarter gay scene. The police department itself debunked the story[3] and the *Vieux Carré Courier* publicly criticized Gifford's gullibility and poor judgment, stating, "Any prison authority ... could have told Gifford that gay people are usually the *victims* of [rape and violence] rather than the perpetrators" ("How the Media Saw It" 5). The *Courier* went on to suggest that if Gifford wanted to examine conspiracy theories, he might want to pay attention to the fact that the fire took place on Gay Pride Day.[4] Might the fire, the article implies, be punishment for no offense other than being gay? The *Courier* states, "Strong social disapproval of homosexuality—defined by psychiatrists as 'homopho-bia'—usually sanctions such anti-homosexual attacks" ("How the Media Saw It" 5).

In short, the *Courier* is asking if the fire was a hate crime, though the term is not used, because it does not seem to have been coined until the 1980s.[5] In fact, there were many people in the city whose thoughts of the fire were pro-pelled by two core assumptions: that the fire was a case of arson, and that the arsonist was motivated by homophobia.[6]

Troy Perry, the founder of the Metropolitan Community Church, was one person employing these assumptions, and with justification. The MCC's Mother Church building in Los Angeles was completely destroyed by a fire in January of 1973.[7] The fire department started by treating it as arson, but later changed its position and said the cause was probably bad wiring, though Perry continues to doubt this conclusion.[8] In March of 1973, the MCC meeting place in Nashville also burned. Again, investigators termed the fire "of suspi-cious origin" (Perry and Swicegood 76). No arrests have ever been made in either of these cases.[9]

The Up Stairs Lounge was the third fire within six months. Though the bar was no longer a site of MCC worship, it was still actively associated with the MCC, and now such a fire involved injury and loss of life, including the life of the MCC pastor, Bill Larson. Did these MCC fires represent a coherent pattern? Were they equivalent to the church bombing in Mississippi a decade earlier? Or did they merely represent a remarkable example of coincidence? Was the fire at the Up Stairs Lounge even a case of arson? Among investigators, opinions varied early and widely. The speed and deadliness of the fire made many people, including police chief Major Henry Morris, suspect that the fire had been intentionally set.[10] The city's fire chief, William McCrossen, was initially guarded in his public statements, saying, "It may come in the definition of an explosion. It was 'bang' and it was all over" (Lind, Thomas, and Philbin "29 Dead" A1). An explosion, of course, could result from something malign, like arson, or something accidental, like a gas leak. The morning after the fire, McCrossen was quoted in the *States-Item* as saying that people reported smelling gasoline before the fire, but McCrossen emphasized that the reports were unconfirmed.[11] As weeks passed, McCrossen became more and more convinced that the fire was, indeed, arson, eventually saying as much on a local television talk show.[12]

Assistant State Fire Marshal Timothy Driscoll had his doubts from the beginning. He didn't think, for example, that someone could have spent the afternoon wandering through the bar pouring gasoline on the floor without being noticed, and said that flammable interior materials or finishes could have accounted for the rapid spread. Asked about the possibility of a firebomb, such as a Molotov cocktail, he said, "A firebomb would affect only one area. This thing went *whoosh!*" ("Charred Rubble" A1).

As these men debated whether the fire was arson, others wondered who the arsonist might be. The newspapers documented reports that two men had been thrown out of the bar earlier, and that one of them was being questioned.[13] They also noted reports that someone had seen four men running away from the lounge just before the fire started.[14] An employee of the Marriott across the street claimed that he heard a guest saying he wanted to burn down the Jimani bar.[15] This was in the same building as the Up Stairs, and directly beneath the room where twenty-nine people died.[16] Might an arsonist have accidentally burned the wrong bar?

The police began their investigation immediately after the fire on June 24. Copies of their General Case Report, filed on August 30 of 1973, are archived in three separate locations. One is in the Williams Research Center of the Historic New Orleans Collection. A second can be found at the Louisiana Collection of the New Orleans Public Library. A third is on microfiche at the Louisiana State Archives as part of the extensive file left by investigators for the state's fire marshal. The NOPD case report makes for a fascinating read, though one that might disappoint a fan of mystery and detective fiction. Crime novels often feature a first-person narrator with a jaded, cynical tone and a propensity for richly figurative metaphor. In an actual case report, all is in third person, all is in passive voice, all is crafted to create an impression of detached objectivity. Adjectives are rare, and seem to be chosen for the fewest possible connotations, and slang terms almost never surface. In fact, in the entire 67-page case report, the word gay only occurs once, and then it is both capitalized and in quotation marks. It is thus deliberately framed as an unaccustomed replacement for the allegedly more objective (and infinitely more clinical) term "homosexual," which occurs with a curious frequency. The studied use of objective language and passive voice results in effects that are sometimes startling, sometimes chilling, and sometimes unintentionally funny.

The first page of the General Case Report merely notes the date and time of the occurrence, and that the case was assigned to Detectives Charles Schlosser and Sam Gebbia of the Homicide Division. They were assigned to the case at 8:35 p.m. on June 24, only about twenty minutes after the fire had been put out. Page one goes on to record that the fire was in a lounge, that death, injury and property destruction all resulted, that the fire marshal had been notified, and that the fire department gave emergency aid. Pages two through five consist of a list of the thirty-two victims. Each entry consists of a name, a race and gender, an age (if known) and an address (if known). The names are not in alphabetical order, nor are they in the order that identifications were released to the public. The report bears witness to the difficult and confusing job that the Coroner's office faced in establishing identity; Joseph Henry Adams, Jr., was initially listed as a negro male residing at 1017 Conti. He had been confused with Reginald Adams, Jr., who lived at the Conti Street address. The two men bore the same surname, and both used the title Jr., but only Reggie was black.[17] Entries thirty, thirty-one and thirty-two are—and remain— unknown white male.

A list of the injured people treated at Charity follows. Though Schlosser and Gebbia note that fifteen people were brought to Charity the night of the fire, they only list twelve names. The disparity can be accounted for by the fact that three of the fifteen—Jim Hambrick, Luther Boggs and Larry Stratton—had died by the date the report was filed, and thus their names are among the deceased.

The narrative portion of the report begins on page seven. Written presumably by Schlosser and Gebbia, the use of passive voice and the emphasis on detached observation are so complete that Schlosser and Gebbia even refer to themselves in the third person. Hence:

> Detectives Schlosser and Gebbia were notified by Sgt. Eugene Geary that there were six persons known to be dead at the scene of the fire and one person in

Charity Hospital, in serious condition, who could possibly have information relative to the fire. Detectives Schlosser and Gebbia were instructed to go directly
to Charity Hospital and attempt to interview this person, name and other information unknown at that time, before going to the scene [Schlosser and Gebbia 7].

This short paragraph reveals that, at the time Schlosser and Gebbia were
assigned to the case (8:35 p.m. on June 24), nobody had any idea how many
people had died in the lounge; instead of six dead at the scene of the fire, there
were twenty-nine.

At Charity, they found the victims of the fire, but were not able to speak to
most because of the severity of their injuries. They did get to speak to "one
Lindy Quinton" (i.e., Rusty), who told them about the Beer Bust, about how
he had been singing at the piano at the time the fire broke out, and about how
he escaped. They were interrupted when the doctor came to treat Rusty's
injuries. Because the doctor was working, and, "because of [Quinton's] emotional state, it was impractical to continue the interview" (Schlosser and Gebbia 8). They interviewed Adolph Medina and Philip Byrd, two more men who
had escaped through the windows, and who gave Schlosser and Gebbia basically the same information as Rusty Quinton. The other survivors at Charity
were too seriously injured for interviews, so Schlosser and Gebbia went to the
fire scene, arriving there at 9:27.[18]

Several subsequent pages involve a description of the building, including
what businesses occupied the street level. Once they enter the Up Stairs itself,
the report notes "detectives Schlosser and Gebbia observed the charred body
of what appeared to be a human male in a crouched position leaning against
the lake side[19] of the bar. Near this body was a window which leads to the fire
escape" (11). This almost certainly refers to Adam Fontenot, who had been
too frightened to either follow Buddy's group or follow the four people who
used the Iberville Street fire escape. Instead, Adam remained at the end of the
bar until an errant stream from a fire hose knocked him down.[20]

The report goes on to describe the room and makes multiple notes about
the positions of bodies, some lying singly, most clustered together. Schlosser
and Gebbia describe a man on the sill of the middle window overlooking
Chartres Street and speculate that he died trying to escape.[21] This, of course,
is Bill Larson, who was seen trapped and dying in the window by many witnesses standing on the street. Later, Schlosser and Gebbia mention seeing several bodies on the piano platform and two bodies behind it: one female, one
male, with the male lying on top of the female.[22] The lone female was Inez
Warren. The bodies of her two sons lay in the same room.

Concluding that the first room and the middle room were completely
destroyed by fire, Schlosser and Gebbia entered the theater to find it almost

As people gathered in the street below the Up Stairs Lounge, they could see the body of the Reverend Bill Larson in the lower center window. He remained visible for hours (photograph by Ronald LeBoeuf, from the States-Item, Times Picayune/Landov).

completely without damage, again indicating that the theater could have saved everyone if people had only followed Buddy's lead.[23]

At 9:40 p.m. the parish coroner, Dr. Carl Rabin, arrived and pronounced all the victims dead at the scene. Patrolman Tidwell began to photograph the bodies, and at 9:50 the fire department finally received clearance to remove them. Because of uncertainty about the structural integrity of the staircase, bodies had to be carried to the Iberville Street fire escape and lowered with a fire department "snorkel," a crane not unlike the "cherry pickers" used by people who work on telephone and power lines.[24]

Today some gay people speaking or writing about the Up Stairs Lounge criticize city emergency personnel for insensitivity—or outright homophobia—as evidenced by the slow pace with which they removed the victims from the windows, some of whom remained on display there until midnight.[25] The Reverend Dexter Brecht of the MCC equated the delay with the police chief's dismissive description of the bar being filled with queers and thieves, suggesting that firemen moved slowly because they just didn't care about the victims.[26] In a 2009 interview, Stewart Butler placed the blame upon members of the fire department, saying, "Fire Chief McCrossen was totally unsympathetic. The firemen probably felt like they had to wash their hands when it was over. Not because of the cadavers, but because of the *gay* cadavers."[27] It is worth noting, however, that the fire department was not allowed to begin the removal process until 9:50 p.m. more than ninety minutes after the fire was declared extinguished. Removal involved a lengthy, painstaking process. Each body was carefully examined and photographed, and any personal property that was likely to belong to the victim was collected and labeled.[28] Ravaged by fire, many of the bodies were extremely fragile, and had essentially been seared together, making intact removal difficult.[29] In the front corner of the lounge, seventeen people had died clustered together. There would have been no way to get to the victims in these windows without removing a number of other victims first. The gruesome sights and sickening smells meant that firefighters had to take frequent breaks.[30]

During this slow and grisly process, Major Henry Morris and Detective Steve Marshall uncovered what seemed to be a significant clue: they found an empty, seven-ounce can of Ronsonol lighter fluid at the bottom of the staircase.[31]

As Schlosser and Gebbia labored inside, two other detectives interviewed survivors. Most recalled the fight between Michael Scarborough and the man who had been bothering patrons in the restroom. They also remembered Buddy and Hugh making this man leave the bar. Descriptions are fairly consistent: a white male in his twenties, somewhere between 5'4" and 5'7" tall, medium-length dark brown or black hair, white or light-colored shirt and bell-bottom pants.[32] No one seemed to know his name, though one witness, Mark Allen Guidry, said he thought the man lived in the 2700 block of Esplanade and was called either Gerry or Johnny.[33] This was not much for police to go on, and it didn't help that the physical description was general enough to apply to any of a dozen—or a hundred—men in the French Quarter that night. Louisiana's French and Spanish heritage means that dark-haired men under six feet tall are plentiful.

A few witnesses also said they had seen someone thrown out for redeeming other people's beer mugs. Again, the man was not named, but people described him as nineteen or twenty, slender, with long, dark blond or light brown hair.

All these survivors said the fire burst through the door, and told how they escaped. With most of the accounts consistent in most details, the major variations were in the timeline; estimates of how much time lapsed between the ejections of two men and the start of the fire range from five minutes to an hour. Part of this wide range can be attributed to the survivors not paying all that much attention. It is hardly uncommon for a troublemaker to be thrown out of a bar, and such an event rarely has significant consequences. Part of the discrepancy can also be attributed to either the alcohol witnesses had consumed before the fire or the adrenaline-fueled horror they experienced later, either one of which might result in an imprecise sense of time.

A man named Floyd Villareal, who had not been at the Up Stairs, also filed a statement; he was on the street when the fire broke out and said he saw a man running out of the entrance of the Up Stairs. Though Villareal was too far away for a close look, someone else on the street described this man to Villareal as approximately nineteen and wearing a blue t-shirt advertising the Pontchartrain Beach amusement park. Villareal told police that he knew a man named David who worked at Pontchartrain Beach and lived with a man named Pepper.[34]

The most important statement taken that night was Buddy Rasmussen's. Buddy covered his entire day, from taking Adam to work with him that morning,[35] to opening the bar at two o'clock, to staffing the Beer Bust, to ejecting the two customers. He talked about the fire, and about leading people out of the bar. He also talked about apprehending one of the ejected customers on the street, and being made to let him go by a uniformed officer. Buddy was not able to name either man, but said that he recognized both men as occasional patrons of the bar. He provided physical descriptions consistent with others the police had been given, and partially corroborated Floyd Villareal's statement when he said that the man who smashed the beer mugs lived with someone named Pepper.[36]

Two more reports were taken on site; one was from a man named Harold

Bartholomew who had been driving in slow-moving traffic on Iberville Street when the fire broke out. He claimed to have seen two men outside of the entrance. One said to the other, "I'm telling you, you better get out of here" (Schlosser and Gebbia 32). He had also noticed two other men lurking suspiciously on the other side of the entrance. Though he did not see a fire in the entrance then, within moments, the fire exploded out of the second floor windows. Bartholomew had his young children with him, and the fire frightened them, so he drove until he could park and calm them down. By the time he returned to the Up Stairs, the men he had seen were gone.[37]

The final statement taken at the scene came from Gregory Gieselman, manager of the Levee Skipper Lounge at the Marriott Hotel. He told them that a man named Brady, a regular guest at the Marriott, bore a grudge against the Jimani, the lounge on the ground floor of the same building as the Up Stairs. When the fire broke out, one of the employees had said, in reference to Brady, "He finally burned it" (Schosser and Gebbia 34). Gieselman was not able to provide a full name, but was able to provide a room number, for Brady had charged his service to his room. Gieselman also affirmed that Brady had made curious remarks about the fire.[38]

By the time Schlosser and Gebbia had taken all of these statements, it was 3:25 a.m. on June 25. Despite the Gieselman and Bartholomew stories, the two most obvious suspects were the two men ejected from the Up Stairs for misbehavior; police had no name at all for one, and nothing but "David" for the other. When they arrived at the office of the Criminal Investigation Division at 3:40 a.m. they must have been surprised to find that one of these suspects had already been apprehended and brought in for questioning.[39]

After Schlosser and Gebbia left Charity Hospital much earlier that evening, two other detectives, George Florane and George Heath, remained, questioning people who were able to talk. According to the report Schlosser and Gebbia later filed:

> As a result of what [Florane and Heath] learned at Charity, they determined that a possible suspect for arson in this matter was one David Dubose, white male, age 18, who had been evicted from the lounge a short while before the fire started and who was heard saying that he would return by several of the patrons of the lounge at the time he was evicted. It was determined by these officers that Dubose frequented homosexual bars and usually lived with homosexuals. It was further learned from patrons of the lounge, that Dubose was living with a homosexual by the name of Francis Barker, alias "Pepper" [35].

Their tips led Florane and Heath to the Golden Slipper Lounge, about two blocks from the Up Stairs in the 100 block of St. Charles Avenue. Florane and Heath arrived at the Golden Slipper at 10:30 p.m. When they asked the bartender if Pepper was there, he pointed to a man talking on the phone in the back. As the detectives approached Francis Barker, they could hear part of his conversation. Apparently anxious, Barker said something which Detective Florane understood to mean that the man Barker was speaking to would have to provide an alibi for somebody else. Francis Barker held a card in his hand as he spoke. When he got off the phone, the detectives identified themselves and took the card away. It bore the name, address and telephone number of a James Smith.[40] They asked Barker if he knew where David Dubose was. He told them that David, too, was at the Golden Slipper, sitting at the bar. The police found him, "a white male subject approximately 18 years old" (Schlosser and Gebbia 36). They brought David Dubose and Francis Barker in for questioning.

Francis Barker's statement was brief; according to Schlosser and Gebbia's case report:

> Barker stated that at about 9:30 p.m. or sometime near that time David Dubose came into the Golden Slipper Lounge. He stated that there had been several people (homosexuals) in the lounge a short time before asking where David Dubose was and that the police were looking for him to question him as a possible suspect in the fire at the Upstairs Lounge. Barker added that he asked Dubose if he had set the fire and that Dubose informed him that he didn't. Dubose told him that he had been thrown out of the lounge at about 7:00 p.m. and that he left the lounge with a subject named James Smith who lives at 1508 Erato Street. According to Barker, Dubose told him that he stayed with Smith in his apartment until about 9:15 p.m. at which time the subject, Smith, drove him to the Golden Slipper Lounge. Barker, in reference to the conversation overheard by Detective Florane, stated that he had called James Smith and asked him if he would be willing to come forward and stated that Dubose was in fact with him during that time period [36].

Florane and Heath turned their attention to David Dubose. According to the case report, he said he had been thrown out of the Up Stairs for causing a disturbance in the bathroom, which is inconsistent with earlier reports of him taking and redeeming other people's beer mugs. He initially confessed complicity in the fire, saying that he had brought a can of gasoline back to the lounge after being thrown out, but stated that James Smith had actually set the fire. Later he denied having had any part in the fire at all, and provided a different account of his actions that evening: he said that after being thrown out of the Up Stairs, he had met James Smith on the sidewalk and they went to Smith's apartment.[41] The police report records Dubose saying that "they ate supper and that Smith then performed an act of oral copulation on him. Dubose stated that Smith gave him ten dollars and drove him to the Golden Slipper Lounge" (37).

There are two curious things about this second account of his actions. The first is that David Dubose had not been thrown out of the Up Stairs for causing a disturbance in the bathroom; that is a much closer description to the reason the other man had been thrown out. Had he been confused by aggressive or leading questions? Was he drunk, and not remembering clearly? Does this merely represent a minor factual error in a final report compiled two months after the fire? There is no way to tell.

The second is the language of the report. Clearly, David Dubose did not say, "James Smith then performed an act of oral copulation on me." He would have said something very different. The passage shows the police substituting official language in place of slang or vernacular in the summary of a witness statement. While the shift from slang to official language here involves no real "translation" issue (and may even produce a chuckle), in other places, the word choice raises questions about possible prejudices and preconceptions.

Detectives Florane and Heath left David Dubose at police headquarters while they drove uptown to talk to James Smith, a man of about thirty. Smith let them into his apartment and told them his version of what had happened. He said he met David on the sidewalk outside of the Up Stairs Lounge and brought him back to his apartment. James Smith said that they had, indeed, had supper together, and that he drove David back to the Golden Slipper, dropping him off around 9:30. The report notes:

> Smith denied that he performed an act [of] oral copulation on David Dubose while they were in his apartment, but upon being questioned ... he became very nervous and stated that he wanted his attorney before he answered any questions concerning that line of questioning, indicating that he had apparently performed the act [37].

It seems odd that Smith would react calmly to a line of questioning concerning a fire that had killed so many people, only to get nervous and demand a lawyer when asked a question about an act of "oral copulation." Perhaps he had a clear conscience in relation to the fire, but was worried about the consequences of the sex act. Louisiana, like many other states, had "crime against nature" laws, or, as they were often termed, anti-sodomy laws. Until 2003, when the United States Supreme Court overturned them in *Lawrence v. Texas*,[42] such laws typically criminalized consensual but non-procreative sexual acts between adults, such as "oral copulation."

Some states criminalized *all* sexual acts defined as sodomy or crimes against nature, no matter who engaged in them. Other states criminalized only acts performed by two people of the same sex. The Louisiana law applied to everyone, and penalties could be as steep as a $2,000 fine and five years in prison.[43] About the time of the fire, Charles Ward, a New Orleans criminal judge, stated on the bench that he thought the Louisiana statute was unconstitutional. This briefly led a number of gays and lesbians to believe that their sex lives had been decriminalized—or soon would be—but Ward clarified his statement, saying that, in his opinion, "the crime against nature statutes were not applicable to heterosexual relationships" (Treadway "It's Not Illegal" 14). Straight people, in Judge Ward's opinion, should be constitutionally entitled to oral copulation.

James Smith was clearly aware of the legal realities; not only was he being asked about oral copulation, but he had given David ten dollars, an act which, if seen as *quid pro quo* (which it probably was), would violate prostitution laws as well. Fortunately for James Smith, the police had larger issues on their minds and did not pursue the morals charges. Detectives Florane and Heath were satisfied that David Dubose had an alibi. One can only imagine their surprise when they returned to headquarters and discovered that, in their absence, David Dubose had made—and retracted—a second confession to starting the fire.

False confessions are fairly common, and can be caused by a variety of factors, including intoxication, coercion, or duress. People being questioned by police may find the process so grueling that they will admit anything just so it will come to an end.[44] There is no way to tell whether Florane and Heath engaged in behavior that might have been coercive or have put David Dubose under duress, but it seems very clear that he could have been both drunk and stoned at the times he confessed to setting the fire. He had, after all, been drinking at the Beer Bust where he told Rusty Quinton that he had been taking drugs. He drank some wine during his visit to Smith's apartment. He might have taken more drugs during the evening, and, of course, when Florane and Heath found him, he was in the Golden Slipper Lounge.

Because he had now confessed and retracted his confession twice, the police gave David Dubose a polygraph test, which indicated that he was telling the truth when saying that he had not brought gasoline to the lounge, and when he said he had not started the fire. The section of the case report covering David Dubose ends with the words "No other evidence, other than the fact that Dubose was thrown out of the Upstairs Lounge, has been uncovered to implicate him in the fire at the present stage of investigation" (38).

The police questioned one other suspect in the hours immediately following the fire. This was Alfred Edward Brady, the guest at the Marriott who was heard by employees making hostile remarks about the Jimani bar and who seemed to want to see it burned down. After a brief interrogation, the police determined that he was too drunk to be usefully questioned, and that whatever remarks he had made about the Jimani were similarly the result of a "high state of intoxication" (39).

By 7:30 a.m. on Monday, June 25, Schlosser and Gebbia were back at the

Up Stairs. They had been on the case for eleven hours without a break. They met William Roth and Edward Hyde, two deputy state fire marshals. Together these four men combed the scene, taking carpet and drapery samples for flammability tests, and looking for bits of personal property that might help identify victims. They found a burned yellow watch, a set of keys, several metal cigarette lighters and cigarette cases, and two wallets, one of which belonged to Leon Maples,[45] who had been Lawrence Raybourne's handsome young Midnight Cowboy.

While at the scene, the police and fire marshal investigators performed a quick inspection of the electrical system. It seemed to be in good condition, but they did not rule out the possibility of an electrical fire. They also discussed the empty seven-ounce can of Ronsonol lighter fluid that had been sent to the lab for testing. Finally, at 12:45, more than sixteen hours after first being put on the case, Schlosser and Gebbia cleared the scene,[46] meaning that the on-site investigation was finished, and that civilians were now allowed to go inside.

Later that day, the two men conducted an informal fire test. They got scrap lumber and took it to a vacant lot. They had intended to douse it with the contents of a seven-ounce can of Ronsonol, but they couldn't find that size, so they used two 4 ½ ounce cans instead. After pouring the Ronsonol on the wood, they threw a lit match on it. Although the Ronsonol ignited readily, it burned away quickly and left the wood unscathed. Their description ends with the words "Of course, the results of this test are inconclusive" (45).

It doesn't take much of a scientist to find at least three flaws with their methodology. The first is the nature of the wood. According to records on file at the Williams Research Center of the Historic New Orleans Collection, the buildings that housed the Up Stairs Lounge are known to have existed in 1848, and may have been constructed as early as 1821. Assuming the staircase was original, the wooden treads were between 125 and 152 years old. Old wood is dry and porous; it would absorb fluid readily, and ignite easily. Schlosser and Gebbia say nothing about the source of the wood they used, but it was probably fairly new, fairly green, and much less flammable than a century-old stair tread.

Another problem with their experiment is that they did not account for the presence of carpeting on the stairs. According to the web site for the Ronson Corporation, Ronsonol lighter fluid, which is still in production, is "best for all wick-type lighters" ("Ronson Flame Accessories"), i.e., lighters that hold the fluid in a reservoir and channel it to the ignition device through a fiber wick. If this fluid were poured over carpeted stairs, the carpet would absorb the fluid and function as a wick, causing a slower burn in the initial stages. Ultimately, the carpeting itself would—and did—ignite, creating another source of fuel for the fire.

The third flaw is that they were working in an empty lot, and the fire at the Up Stairs originated in a closed stairwell. As the Up Stairs fire spread, both the lighter fluid and the burning carpet would have released combustible gases that would rise with the heat and collect near the second-floor entrance. William McCrossen, the city's fire chief, believed that these fumes ignited when introduced to fresh air, causing a flash fire.[47] The initial rush of rising air when Luther Boggs opened the door to the lounge might well have caused this ignition, with the open door funneling fire and combustible gases inside.[48] Once the fire and gases entered the lounge, they found fresh oxygen in the air space above the dropped ceiling of acoustic tiles, and even more as desperate people broke the windows.[49] Schlosser and Gebbia, working in an open, empty lot, had no way to recreate the effect of accumulated combustible gases suddenly exposed to multiple fresh sources of oxygen.

Still, Schlosser and Gebbia at this point were willing to admit that their tests were inconclusive, and their work in the coming days was based upon the possibility of arson. In fact, that very day, evidence surfaced that seemed to support the possibility.

The Up Stairs was at the intersection of Chartres and Iberville. One block away, at the intersection of Royal and Iberville, was a Walgreens drug store (it is still there). Police detectives Marshall and Strada, working on the case under Schlosser and Gebbia, had been searching the neighborhood for witnesses or other people with relevant information. A sales clerk at the Walgreens tobacco counter, Mrs. Claudine Rigaud, recalled having sold three cans of Ronsonol lighter fluid the previous day. One was to a woman who was part of a tour group, and who had commented that many items in Walgreens were less expensive than where she lived. Mrs. Rigaud sold another can to an elderly white man; though she did not know his name, she recognized him as a regular customer. She sold the third can to a white man with medium-length dark hair, wearing a white or light-colored shirt. She estimated his age to be about 24, and thought that he was probably 5'2" to 5'3" tall.

According to Schlosser and Gebbia's report:

> Mrs. Rigaud stated that this subject appeared to be "Gay" as he was soft spoken and the way he carried himself and had feminish [sic] traits. Mrs. Rigaud added that this subject appeared to have been drinking and was very upset as his hands were visibly shaking and he seemed to be emotionally upset [47].

A white man in his early twenties, with medium-length black or dark brown hair, wearing a white or light-colored shirt; these characteristics had all been used to describe one of the men thrown out of the bar.[50] He had been the one annoying people in the restroom as he sat in one stall, staring and making comments about the people in the other. When he had followed Michael Scarborough to Scarborough's table, Scarborough had hit him, knocking him to the floor. As he lay on the floor, this man had said something to Scarborough before being thrown out of the bar by Buddy and his assistant, Hugh Cooley. Those events could all account for his being shaken and emotionally upset. But was the man that Mrs. Rigaud sold the lighter fluid to the same man who had been thrown out of the Up Stairs? And did he buy it with the intention of setting a fire as an act of revenge?

Mrs. Rigaud estimated that she sold the fluid to this customer between 4:30 and 5:55. The late end would still be about an hour too early for the generally accepted chronology of what had happened at the Up Stairs. Still, the physical description fit well, and other people had shown a similar inaccuracy in estimates of time. When a person routinely sells lighter fluid as part of her job, how aware of time will she be during each transaction? The information Claudine Rigaud gave to the police detectives definitely qualified as a lead, but Schlosser and Gebbia still needed a name.

The next morning, at nine, Wednesday, June 27, Schlosser and Gebbia met with Major Henry Morris and Captain Milton Cox to discuss the tests that the crime lab had performed on various specimens found at the scene, including flooring and carpet samples removed from the stairwell, and the empty can of Ronsonol. The can had proved negative for fingerprints, and the flooring and carpet samples had tested negative for volatile materials.[51]

At 12:45 they went to Charity Hospital to interview survivors, but none was in a condition to speak to the police detectives. The assistant administrator, John Anderson, asked that the police go through him before attempting future interviews.[52]

From three until 10:30 they tried to locate and interview several people known to have been in the bar when the fire broke out. They learned little, because most of the people they were looking for had died in the fire. The few people the detectives were able to locate didn't know much more than the police.[53]

On Thursday, June 28, James Hambrick died of his injuries, raising the death toll from twenty-nine to thirty. That afternoon, Schlosser and Gebbia went to the headquarters of the MCC, hoping to find more survivors and to gain new information. "This is the congregation," they wrote, "that most of these homosexuals belonged to" (51).

During their visit, Schlosser and Gebbia spoke to a man named Frank Dean, who had escaped by following Buddy Rasmussen. Frank Dean said the fire looked like it had been shot from a flame thrower. He said that by the time he neared the door between the lounge and the theater, the inside of the Up Stairs was full of flames and heavy black smoke. Asked who else was in the bar, Frank Dean gave the detectives a list of names that, again, was not very useful, because most were people who had died in the fire.[54]

On July 2, eight days after the fire, Schlosser and Gebbia were called to the 600 block of Iberville Street by the fire marshal investigators, William Roth and Edward Hyde. Roth and Hyde had just interviewed someone named Allen Guidry. Police had spoken to him the night of the fire. He told investigators that one of the men thrown out of the Up Stairs had been someone named Gerry or Johnny, and that he lived in the 2700 block of Esplanade. Both the names and the address had been lies, and eight days after the fire, Allen Guidry told Roth and Hyde the truth. They asked Schlosser and Gebbia to meet them at 606 ½ Iberville Street, which was in the building next door to the Up Stairs. There, Schlosser and Gebbia "observed a white male subject, 25–26 years old, 5'8" tall, medium build with black medium length hair which appeared to be dirty" (54). This man, they learned, was Rodger Nunez.[55] When they arrived, Nunez's behavior was odd, leading them to believe he was drunk. He wasn't. Roth and Hyde told the police detectives that Rodger Nunez was disoriented because he had just had an epileptic seizure. Two patrolmen brought Rodger Nunez to Charity Hospital for treatment. Once he was at Charity, doctors discovered that in addition to the seizure, Rodger was suffering from a broken jaw; since the man Schlosser and Gebbia sought was one Michael Scarborough had punched in the jaw, this was a suggestive injury. Charity physicians operated on Nunez to repair his jaw, and insisted on holding him for several days for treatment and observation. Detectives agreed, and left Nunez at Charity, under the care of the doctors. Amazingly, since they wanted to question Nunez about the possibility that he started a fire that killed thirty people (to date), they did not assign a police guard to watch him. All Schlosser and Gebbia asked of the hospital staff was that they notify the police department upon completion of the surgery and again prior to release. They wrote a note to this effect and put it in Rodger Nunez's route sheet.[56]

The next morning, July 3, Schlosser and Gebbia returned to Walgreens to speak to Claudine Rigaud. They brought with them eight mug shots from the police Bureau of Identification (B of I). One of them was of Rodger Nunez and another was of Mark Allen Guidry, both of whom had prior police records. Schlosser and Gebbia presented these photographs to Claudine Rigaud and asked if she could identify the man who had purchased the lighter fluid from her on the day of the fire. She was unable.[57]

Later that day, Schlosser and Gebbia returned to Charity to speak to Rodger Nunez. Doctors told them that Nunez was resting comfortably, but he would be in the hospital for an undetermined time. Schlosser and Gebbia left, reiterating in the report that they informed hospital officials that Nunez was not to be released unless the police received prior notification.[58]

The report indicates that over the course of the next several days, Schlosser and Gebbia retuned to Charity several times. Each time they were told that Nunez was doing well, but was still unable to speak because of the operation on his jaw.[59] In the meantime, they interviewed several other witnesses, including a man named James Peterson, who had been at the Up Stairs. He estimated that he left at 7:45. He said he had walked from the corner of Iberville and Chartres to the corner of Chartres and Canal, one block away. He was on Canal, standing on the neutral ground,[60] when he heard the sounds of screaming and turned around to see smoke coming from the lounge. He said that only a few minutes had passed since he had left the Up Stairs,[61] and, in fact, the walk he described would have taken only five minutes, at most.

On July 7,[62] Schlosser and Gebbia returned to Charity to try once again to speak to Rodger Nunez. Upon arrival, they learned that Nunez had been released from the hospital earlier that morning, despite the note in his file that he was not to be released without police detectives being notified. The report says nothing about how Schlosser and Gebbia felt when they learned that Rodger Nunez was gone, but it does say that they spent July 7–9 trying to locate Nunez, as well as trying to learn from the coroner's office the identities of several other victims.[63]

On July 9, Schlosser and Gebbia spoke to Gene Davis, a man who owned two bars on Iberville Street. Wanda's was in the 700 block of Iberville, a block away from the Up Stairs. A rough place, it had a mixed (straight and gay) clientele, and was a known hangout for male hustlers in search of a john. About a year before the fire, Gene had purchased a bar which he named Gene's Hideaway, though people usually just called it the Hideaway.[64] Like Wanda's, the Hideaway had a mixed clientele and was a place where hustlers could ply their trade.

The Iberville entrance of the Up Stairs had a street address of 604 Iberville. The Midship was next door at 606. Next to the Midship, at 606 ½, was the street entrance for some cheap apartments, including the one where police had found Rodger Nunez. The Hideaway was at 608.

Gene Davis had spent a lot of time outside his bar the evening of the fire, sitting on the fender of a car parked at the curb. Because the fronts of buildings on that part of Iberville Street are narrow, Davis's perch gave him a clear view of the entrance to the Up Stairs. According to the police report, he even admits to speaking to people entering and leaving the Up Stairs, some of whom were friends or customers. Davis told the police that he didn't see anyone go into or out of the entrance for the Up Stairs for "ten or fifteen minutes before the

Gene Davis (center) was the owner of Gene's Hideaway in the same block as the Up Stairs, and he also owned Wanda's down the street. He almost certainly knew more about the fire than he revealed to police (photograph courtesy Johnny Townsend).

fire." Later, he amended his statement slightly, saying that he didn't see anybody go into or out of the entrance for "ten to fifteen, maybe even twenty minutes before the fire" (Schlosser and Gebbia 58–59).

This is difficult to believe. Stewart Butler remembered leaving the bar with his lover, Alfred Doolittle, and says that almost as soon as they arrived at Wanda's, a block away, they heard that the Up Stairs was on fire. Regina Adams remembered leaving the Up Stairs to go get a checkbook and Jean Gosnell's hat, and returning ten or fifteen minutes later to find the bar already in flames. Eddie Gillis, who was caught in the fire and got out through the Iberville fire escape, said that he had only been in the bar for about ten minutes before the fire started. William White and Gary Williams, two tourists from Pineville, remembered entering the stairwell and debating whether or not to go inside. They decided against it, and by the time they were a block away, they turned back to see the Up Stairs in flames. James Peterson, who had been at the Beer Bust, left the bar and walked to Canal Street—a journey of five minutes at most—only to turn back when he heard the screams from people on the street who had just seen the fire bursting through the windows.[65] It is likely, perhaps even probable, that one or two of these witnesses incorrectly estimated the time lapse. It is unlikely that all of them did, and that only Gene Davis was correct.

Once the fire started, Davis told police that a man "came from around the corner from towards Royal Street or from Canal Street, through Exchange Place. This subject went into the bar and Davis followed him" (Schlosser and Gebbia 58). The name of this person and the significance of his entering the Hideaway are oddly not included in the NOPD General Case Report; either Schlosser and Gebbia, in summarizing the facts of the case, neglected to include the information, or they deliberately excluded it. In the transcript of Davis's statement, however, this unnamed person is identified as Rodger Nunez. Davis went on to say that Nunez said, "Thank God I made it out of the fire," creating the impression that he had been inside the Up Stairs when the fire started (Davis Statement to Criminal Investigation 2; Schlosser and Gebbia 58). However, none of the multiple witnesses who saw a man fitting the description of Rodger Nunez being thrown out of the bar mentioned him re-entering it later, and if he approached Gene's Hideaway from the direction of Royal Street or Exchange Place, he was coming from the wrong direction to have been in the Up Stairs when the fire started.

Following the synopsis of Gene Davis's statement is a paragraph summarizing several days' worth of unproductive labor, saying that between July 9 and 13, Schlosser and Gebbia interviewed numerous subjects, but learned no new information, and that they tried to locate Rodger Nunez, but to no avail.[66] During those days, Luther Boggs and Larry Stratton died of their injuries, bringing the death toll from the fire to thirty-two.

A gap of several days exists between July 13 (a Friday) and July 17 (a Tuesday), with apparently no activity taking place on the investigation. During that gap, on the night of Sunday, July 15, the NOFD's Chief McCrossen went on the local television show *Newswatch, Newsmaker* and spoke about the Up Stairs Lounge, voicing the opinion that the fire was arson. His appearance was covered in the newspapers the next day, and though McCrossen stressed that he was voicing his own opinion, he felt that the speed of the fire and the fact that so few people made it to safety were both telling points.[67]

On Tuesday, July 17, Schlosser and Gebbia resumed work on the case, and two important things happened.

One was that Schlosser and Gebbia received a report from Captain Milton Cox of the NOPD. He had just received the results of flammability tests conducted by the office of the state fire marshal, which employed what was—and still is—the standard test for carpet flammability: the so-called "pill test."[68]

According to the 1971 Flammability Fabrics Act, which is still in effect, all machine-made carpets in the United States are required to pass the pill test. In it, an aspirin-sized piece of a chemical called Hexamine (also known as Methenamine) is put on a 9" × 9" piece of carpet, ignited by a match, and allowed to burn for two minutes. The carpet fails to pass the test if the resulting burn extends more than three inches.[69] Since it was legal to smoke in bars in 1973, the carpet in the Up Stairs had been burned many times. In his statement to investigators, the owner, Phil Esteve, had noted that customers had often dropped cigarettes on the floor with no real consequences.[70]

The official flammability tests yielded an interesting result. The lab investigators for the state fire marshal tested three nine-inch squares of carpet taken from the Up Stairs. With the first square, the resulting burn was only three-quarters of an inch in diameter. The second and third squares, however, were consumed, and "completely burned to a black residue" (Schlosser and Gebbia 62). Lab investigators then submitted the first square to a second test. This time, it, too, burned to a black residue.

The pill test produced very different results from Schlosser and Gebbia's experiment in which they poured lighter fluid over bare wood in an empty lot. It also produced a different result from the NOPD crime lab's experiment, which examined the carpet and flooring samples and failed to find volatile materials. However, it is worth noting that the contents of a seven-ounce can of lighter fluid would cover only a very small area. Witness reports and the fire marshal investigation all suggested that the fire started on the second and third steps of the staircase. The stairs and the carpets covering them were seriously burned, with part of the second step charred through.[71] Whatever samples Schlosser and Gebbia were able to retrieve for the NOPD might never have been in contact with volatile materials.

What the pill test demonstrated was that the carpet itself, installed before the 1971 Flammability Fabrics Act, was highly flammable under the right conditions, and that a small flame could quickly result in a huge fire. When such a carpet had been installed in a stairwell, it would be particularly hazardous, because the steps would facilitate the natural tendency of heat and flame to rise, and the structure of the stairwell itself would act in much the same way as a chimney flue.[72]

On July 17, detectives Schlosser and Gebbia also received a call from the fire marshal investigators, who had interviewed Michael Scarborough the day before. They suggested that Schlosser and Gebbia do the same.

Michael Scarborough had punched the man bothering patrons in the bathroom, and had managed to escape the Up Stairs by squeezing through the narrow spaces between the window bars. He was burned severely; his injuries left his face and head heavily scarred, and six fingers and both thumbs had to be amputated at either the first or second joint.[73] He had been brought to Charity Hospital the night of the fire, where he was listed in serious condition. As soon as he was stabilized, he was sent to West Jefferson Hospital.[74] Still later, he was transferred to Baton Rouge General Hospital, about ninety miles away from New Orleans. More than three weeks had passed since the fire. Michael was so isolated that, although he knew his lover, Glenn Green, had died,[75] and although he had received a card from Phil Esteve, he told investigators "most of the people that I know that were there are dead now.... I really don't know who's alive" (Scarborough 3).

Michael Scarborough told the familiar story of that night. The Beer Bust had been crowded and everyone was having fun. A man positioned himself in one of the restroom stalls, where he was bothering people. Michael reported him to Buddy and Hugh, who made this man get out of the restroom. Angry at being reported, the man approached the table where Michael sat and harassed him. Michael then stood up and punched the troublemaker in the jaw, knocking him to the floor. Soon afterward, Buddy and Hugh made the man leave the bar.

Then Michael supplied a new detail that nobody else could have supplied: before the man got up from the floor, he looked up at Michael and said, "I'm gonna burn you all out" (Scarborough 2).

Michael Scarborough did not know the man's name. Asked to pick him out of a group of eight photos, Michael picked photo number six.[76] This was a picture of Rodger Nunez.

At this point in the investigation, the case against Rodger Nunez appeared strong. Angry at Michael Scarborough for hitting him (and probably breaking his jaw in the process), and angry at the Up Stairs staff, Rodger threatened to burn them out. After being evicted from the bar, he went to Walgreens, where he bought the lighter fluid from Claudine Rigaud. Returning to the bar, he doused the second and third steps of the entrance staircase with lighter fluid and threw a lit match on the soaked carpet. Then he ran away.

Although Scarborough's testimony and his identification of Rodger Nunez both seem to be breakthroughs in the case, detectives Schlosser and Gebbia did not renew their efforts. In fact, their interview with Michael Scarborough was the effective end of their investigation. They record no further attempts to find Rodger Nunez, and Michael Scarborough was the last witness they questioned. The case report, dated August 30, was filed more than six weeks after they spoke to Scarborough on July 17.

The brief synopsis at the end of Schlosser and Gebbia's report states that there had been two subjects in the case: David Dubose, who had been cleared, and Rodger Nunez, who "since his release from Charity Hospital after undergoing surgery could not be located for interview" (63).

"However," the synopsis continues, "it should be noted, that with all the persons interviewed, none observed anyone leaving or entering the stairwell just prior to or after the discovery of the fire" (63). This was followed by a handwritten notation, "See statement of Floyd Villareal—page 28." Floyd Villareal was the man who recalled seeing someone running out of the stairwell just before the fire started, though the description he supplied was of a person more closely resembling David Dubose than Rodger Nunez.

The final page of the report reads:

> The majority of the statements contained in this report are conflicting in content. In as much as numerous persons stated that they have seen different things at the same time and same location which proved impossible.
>
> Although there is speculation of arson, as of the writing of this report, there is no physical, evidence [sic] to indicate anything other than this being a fire of undetermined origin.
>
> Any interviews not covered in this original report, as well as any future developments in this matter will be covered in a Supplemental Report [64].

Though a few supplemental pages are included with the case report, they tend to be random notes, listing, for example, leads regarding people who might have died in the fire, or information regarding which victims were sent to which funeral homes. Nothing in the supplement indicates any further investigation of the case.

The New Orleans Police have often been cast as villains in this episode. Many people, then and now, felt that investigators just weren't doing their job. Unfortunately, the official case report supports this perception. The fact that Schlosser and Gebbia ended their investigation at the very moment Michael Scarborough's statement strongly implicated Rodger Nunez is troubling. The official explanation that the witness testimony was "conflicting in content" (64) is a weak defense, because eyewitness testimony is, more often than not, conflicting in content, and that explanation ignores the fact that the testimony regarding Nunez and his actions that night was overwhelmingly corroborative.

The assumption among many gay and lesbians in New Orleans is that the police were never particularly interested in solving the case and did not want to spend any more time or resources investigating the possible murder of people they perceived as undesirable, or even expendable. Certainly the language of Major Henry Morris, who characterized the Up Stairs as a hangout for thieves and queers, was hostile in nature, and many sections of Schlosser and Gebbia's case report betray a certain unease with, or distaste for, the people with whom the investigation brought them into contact. Consider the passage (cited above) in which Schlosser and Gebbia described David Dubose as someone who "frequented homosexual bars and usually lived with homosexuals," and who "was living with a homosexual by the name of Francis Barker, alias 'Pepper'" (35). Or consider their description of the MCC as "the congregation that most of these homosexuals belonged to" (51), rather than the one "that most of the victims belonged to" or "that most of the bar's patrons belonged to." The difference in tone is rather extreme.

Still, Schosser and Gebbia had put several weeks' worth of work into the case, only to suddenly drop it. Why did Schlosser and Gebbia cease their investigation after Michael Scarborough identified Rodger Nunez as a man who has threatened to burn out the people in the Up Stairs Lounge? Did they sincerely think that they didn't have a case to pursue? Or did they simply not care about the lives of thirty-two people who had the bad luck to die in a gay bar?

Sam Gebbia was contacted by certified mail and asked to be interviewed for this book. Through a third party, he consented to a telephone interview, but he did not answer his telephone at the agreed-upon day and time, nor did he respond to multiple subsequent voicemail messages. In 2013, as the fortieth anniversary of the fire approached, Sam Gebbia granted an interview to *TIME* magazine. He objected to charges that the police bias played a role in the failure to solve the crime. He claimed that Major Morris' statement about thieves and queers had been taken out of context (though he did not explain what context would have made the remark less objectionable), and said that in his entire career in the homicide division, anti-gay bias had never been a factor in an investigation. He said that in the Up Stairs investigation, the police "pulled out every stop" (Dias and Downs), and pointed out that arson cases are notoriously hard to prove.

Admittedly, the case against Rodger Nunez as it emerges in the NOPD report is circumstantial. It would have been much stronger if Rodger Nunez had left fingerprints on the can of lighter fluid, if Claudine Rigaud had been able to identify him in the photo line-up, or if there had been a witness to say, "I saw him do it."

Still, it is hard to reconcile Gebbia's 2013 interview with the written record he left behind. Speaking to *TIME*, Gebbia said, "There are a lot of times you'll know, you as an investigator will know what happened, and you know who did it. But legally, if you don't have any teeth to sink in to arrest someone, you'll just have to wait. I'm sure in my heart of hearts this is the guy who set our fire" (Dias and Downs). If what Gebbia said in 2013 is true, it is far from clear why he and Schlosser dropped the case immediately after Michael Scarborough told them that Rodger had threatened to burn out the occupants of the lounge. It is far from clear why the written report dismisses the witness reports as conflicting in content. And if Schlosser and Gebbia truly believed the fire was arson and they knew who did it, it is far from clear why they closed the report by describing the fire as being of "undetermined origin" (64).

Though Schlosser and Gebbia terminated their investigation after only a few weeks, the arson investigation team for the state fire marshal labored on for years. They were never able to make an arrest, either, but the surviving documents from their investigation shine a different and more complex light on the Up Stairs Lounge fire than the case report from the NOPD.

VI

"A terrible cross"

The Fire Marshal
Investigation and the
Death of Rodger Nunez

— · — · — · — · — · — —

William Roth and Edward Hyde, investigators for the state fire marshal, began looking into the fire on the morning of Monday, June 25, receiving at least occasional assistance from another fire marshal officer, John Fischer, who eventually took over for William Roth. Although NOPD detectives Schlosser and Gebbia terminated their investigation in mid–July, Roth, Hyde and Fischer continued much longer and their case report is much more detailed than that of the NOPD. Now on microform at the Louisiana State Archives in Baton Rouge, their file occupies ten microfiche slips and contains many supporting documents, including the texts of multiple witness statements, internal memos sent through the office of the fire marshal, correspondence with lawyers and family members of the Up Stairs victims, police records of several persons of interest, and a final letter stating the office's official conclusion.

In the early stages, the investigation conducted by Roth, Hyde and Fischer largely mirrors that of police detectives Schlosser and Gebbia, though one gets the sense that Hyde and Roth were a bit more aggressive in their questioning, a bit less nervous about the gay community, and much more dogged in their pursuit of the case.

For example, in the days immediately after the fire, they questioned many of the same witnesses as Schlosser and Gebbia, including Claudine Rigaud, the sales clerk at Walgreens, who told Hyde and Roth about selling the Ronsonol lighter fluid to a young man who was "on the gay side, brownish hair, nervous type" (Hyde, Roth, and Fischer 15). Unlike Schlosser and Gebbia,

Hyde and Roth did not capitalize the word gay, nor did they put it in quotation marks. While their report, like Schlosser and Gebbia's, is written in the seemingly objective passive voice, they are more likely to include some occasional slang, and unlike Schlosser and Gebbia, they do not make obsessive note of who is "homosexual."

Among the witnesses interviewed by both the police and fire marshal teams was Mark Allen Guidry (usually known as Allen), who deliberately misled Hyde and Roth—as he had done the police—by saying that the man thrown out of the bar for bothering patrons in the restroom was someone named Jerry[1] or Johnny who lived in the 2700 block of Esplanade. The police detectives never pursued this lead, but Hyde and Roth did, going to Esplanade and knocking on all the doors in that block.

When none of the neighbors recognized the description of the man allegedly named Jerry or Johnny, Hyde and Roth went to see Allen Guidry at his room at the Savoy Hotel in the 100 block of Royal, and they asked him to show them where this Jerry or Johnny lived. Put on the spot, Guidry admitted that the man's name was not Jerry or Johnny, but was Rodger Nunez. Guidry further told them that Rodger Nunez did not live on Esplanade, but was staying in an Iberville Street apartment that belonged to a woman named Cynthia Ann Savant, known as Cee Cee.

Cee Cee's apartment was at 606½ Iberville Street, virtually next door to the entrance of the Up Stairs Lounge and above Gene's Hideaway.[2] Because of their work, Hyde and Roth were the first to find Rodger Nunez, who was asleep on the sofa when they knocked on Cee Cee Savant's door on the morning of July 2, eight days after the fire. They noticed Rodger's swollen jaw and, undoubtedly recalling the fight in the bar shortly before the fire broke out, they asked Rodger how he had become injured. He claimed "that he had had a fight with three negroes on Iberville Street the night before who took his wallet and knocked him down" (Hyde, Roth, and Fischer 20). He admitted that he was in the Up Stairs the night of the fire, but denied being in a fight with anyone or having any trouble. Rodger agreed to go to the police station and give a statement, and while Hyde and Roth called Schlosser and Gebbia to alert them, Rodger began to dress. That's when he had an epileptic seizure.[3]

When the police detectives arrived, the four investigators agreed to take Rodger to the emergency room to be treated for his seizure. The doctors discovered that Rodger had a broken jaw and admitted him for surgery. Schlosser and Gebbia left Rodger Nunez in the hospital without a police guard, but with a promise from the hospital that they would notify the police before discharging Rodger.[4]

Nine days passed, during which Hyde and Roth continued to interview witnesses and to pursue leads. On July 11, Hyde learned that Rodger Nunez had been released from the hospital several days earlier. Though detectives Schlosser and Gebbia had been in the habit of sharing information with Hyde and Roth, they neglected to pass this piece along. In their official report, Schlosser and Gebbia explain their failure to get a statement from Rodger Nunez by saying that officials at Charity Hospital failed to follow their promise to contact the NOPD before releasing him.[5] However, Hyde and Roth's report indicates that Sergeant John Perino, head of Charity's security division, had, indeed, phoned the Detective Bureau of the NOPD to tell them about Rodger's impending discharge, and that the police department neglected to send anyone to take his statement.[6]

A comparison of the fire marshal's case report with the NOPD case report suggests multiple ways that Schlosser and Gebbia might have done a more effective job. Fire marshal investigators Hyde and Roth, for example, learned at Charity Hospital that Rodger Nunez was scheduled for outpatient treatment on the 13th. They went to Charity that day so they could speak to him if he showed up. He did not keep his appointment, but going to Charity in case he did was certainly worth a try.[7]

Schlosser and Gebbia do not seem to have made that minimal effort. They record spending several days trying to find Nunez, but not getting any results, and they state that they were never able to locate him for questioning.[8] However, this seems unlikely, because by the afternoon of July 13, Hyde and Roth had gotten a lead: Rodger Nunez had been briefly detained by the police in Morgan City, a small town in the southeastern part of the state. He had been driving a black Plymouth Fury registered in his name and to an address in Abbeville. The officer who detained Rodger had not known he was wanted for questioning in New Orleans, and was unable to connect him to criminal activity in the Morgan City area, so he had to let Rodger go.[9] Nothing in the NOPD case report indicates that Schlosser and Gebbia were even aware of the Morgan City incident, despite the fact that the information was clearly available to law enforcement officials.

On July 13, Hyde and Roth also learned that Michael Scarborough, the man who had punched someone in the jaw on the night of the fire, had been transferred to Baton Rouge General Hospital. Though recovering from severe burns, he was conscious and able to walk around, and a nurse told them that he would be able to answer questions.

On Monday, July 16, they visited him in the hospital, and this is when he was first able to give his story to investigators. He told them about the man who had been aggravating him, first in the restroom and then at his table, until Michael stood up and punched him in the jaw. Michael told Hyde and Roth that as the man was on the floor he looked up and said, "I'm going to burn you all out" (Hyde, Roth, and Fischer 24). Hyde and Roth showed Michael a photo line-up with pictures of eight men. Michael identified Rodger Nunez. Hyde and Roth contacted Schlosser and Gebbia, urging them to visit and question Michael Scarborough. The police detectives did so the next day, with Michael repeating the same story and once again identifying Rodger Nunez as the man who had made the threat.[10]

As noted in the prior chapter, this effectively ended the police department's involvement in the case; Schlosser and Gebbia documented no further efforts to find Rodger Nunez, and they interviewed no more witnesses. Six weeks later, when they filed their final report on August 30, they claimed that he "could not be located for interview," and they ultimately dismissed the fire as being one of "undetermined origin" (Schlosser and Gebbia 63–64).

On the other hand, the statement given by Michael Scarborough seems to have energized the fire marshal's arson investigation team; in the coming months, Hyde, Roth and Fischer would continue to interview witnesses and collect documents. Their efforts, the documents they collected, and the witness statements they took help answer many questions surrounding the case, including who Rodger Nunez was and what might have happened on June 24, 1973.

Rodger Nunez, born February 22, 1947, was twenty-six at the time of the fire. His parents were divorced, and his mother and stepfather lived in Abbeville, a small town in Vermilion Parish, an area of southwestern Louisiana that was—and still is—overwhelmingly Catholic. A cathedral dominates one entire side of Abbeville's principal town square, setting the tone for the community. His father lived in Grand Chenier, an area of Cameron Parish further to the west.[11] Both Vermilion and Cameron parishes are near the coastal mashes that border the Gulf of Mexico, and they are both full of tiny communities like Forked Island and Cow Island where the Nunez family had ties. Most people in this part of the state are of Cajun French descent, with some Spanish lineage thrown in for good measure. In Rodger's youth, it would have still been common to hear people speaking French as their first language. Many people in the area support themselves through fishing for shrimp or oysters. Others raise sugar cane. Still others work in the oil industry, often staffing offshore rigs or the boats that service them.

This part of the state is charming in many ways, but with its culture largely determined by agricultural labor, extended family and Catholicism, it was not a place where an effeminate young gay man was likely to feel comfortable, especially in an era in which the unrelenting message from peers, the media and the Catholic church was that homosexuals were sick at best, and sinfully depraved at worst. Most men in Rodger's shoes would either work very hard to remain closeted, perhaps marrying or entering the priesthood to provide cover, or they would leave and move to a big city at the earliest opportunity.

Rodger moved to New Orleans in about 1970, and his life there was not enviable. Though his police file indicates he worked, at least at some point, as a nurse, Rodger Nunez was probably really only a nurse's aide. The other jobs he held suggest he had no education beyond high school, and it is not clear that he even graduated.[12] While in Abbeville, he sometimes worked as a deck hand on the crew boats that serviced oil rigs.[13] A job like this required little education and would pay something beyond the $1.69 hourly minimum wage that existed in 1973, but conditions would be hard, and there wouldn't be much possibility for advancement. When not working on crew boats, he reportedly did construction and janitorial work, including janitorial work for Gene Davis, owner of Wanda's and The Hideaway.[14] In the early 1970s, Rodger was arrested several times for fairly minor offenses: he was caught driving while intoxicated in Texas in 1970, and was arrested in New Orleans in December of 1972 and April of 1973 for unauthorized use of a credit card. Interestingly, shortly before that first New Orleans arrest, he applied to be a member of the New Orleans Police Department, though that application does not seem to have gone very far.[15]

During the early seventies, friends reported that he worked at least part time as a hustler.[16] If this is true, it helps explain his friendly relationship with Gene Davis. Larry Raybourne, who worked as a bartender at Wanda's, remembers Gene knowing all the male hustlers in town. Gene would sometimes have sex with one in his home and then send him to Wanda's with instructions to tell the bartender on duty to give him money out of the till. This system, which allowed Gene to employ hustlers without putting money in their hands himself, had been devised to circumvent prostitution laws.[17] Neither Wanda's nor the Hideaway was specifically a gay bar, both attracting a "mixed" clientele,[18] but they both had reputations for being hangouts for male hustlers looking for work.

That seems to have been taking place on the twenty-fourth of June. At about two that afternoon, Rodger Nunez went into the Hideaway in the company of a much older man by the name of Donald Landry. Gene Davis observed them sitting together until another young man joined them. This man was Allen Guidry. While Rodger Nunez was a reported hustler, Allen Guidry was an admitted one, telling fire marshal investigators that he routinely had sex with men for money, earning anywhere from $15 to $50 each encounter.[19] Rodger Nunez, Donald Landry and Allen Guidry drank together for a while before walking down to Wanda's and eventually returning to the Hideaway. Shortly thereafter, Allen Guidry left with Donald Landry. Though nobody overtly said so, Donald Landry was apparently a client that Rodger had found, and that Allen lured away. Rodger Nunez was twenty-six. Allen Guidry was nineteen. Donald Landry, elderly and wearing a colostomy bag, would not have been physically attractive to these much younger men, yet Gene Davis said—more than once—that Rodger sat in the Hideaway drinking and brooding, visibly upset because Allen had gone home with the older man.[20]

Shortly before five, Allen Guidry and Donald Landry returned. Landry only lived a couple of blocks away, and presumably he and Allen had slipped away for a quick trick. They rejoined Rodger, but he remained in a bad mood, which didn't fully lift even when Donald Landry, apparently trying to smooth things over, gave Rodger a $20 bill.

At five o'clock, Rodger proposed that the three of them go to the Up Stairs for the Beer Bust. Gene Davis, inside the bar then, objected to the proposal. In telling the story to fire marshal investigators, Davis said,

> I says [to Landry] no, I'll give you, I'll cash your check. I'm not afraid to take your check but I will not let you go up because you're too loaded, I said, you'll fall down those stairs and break your neck, which he couldn't even walk. We had to all most, [sic] he fell off the stool two or three times and we picked him up and that's why I wouldn't let the old man go, so Rodger disappeared and went upstairs by hisself [Davis Statement to Arson Investigation 2].

According to Davis, Rodger had been drinking steadily throughout the afternoon, so he probably was drunk, and probably still in a bad mood when he went to the Up Stairs.[21] Allen Guidry left the Hideaway with Donald Landry. When Allen returned to Iberville Street by himself about ninety minutes later, he went to the Up Stairs at 6:30, but left about twenty minutes after the Beer Bust ended. In that brief period, the fight between Michael Scarborough and Rodger Nunez took place; though Allen Guidry denied seeing the fight itself, he did admit to seeing Rodger being put out of the bar.[22]

Right about five o'clock—the time that Rodger left the Hideaway to go to the Up Stairs—Gene Davis began spending time on the street, sitting on the fender of the parked car, watching the people and traffic move along Iberville Street. In speaking to police, Davis claimed to have been outside all evening, sitting on the car, "from about 5:00 p.m. until about 7:30 p.m. that being about the time of the fire," and said that he didn't see anybody enter or leave the Up Stairs, "ten to fifteen, maybe even twenty minutes before the fire" (Davis Statement to Criminal Investigation 1; Schlosser and Gebbia 58). In speaking to the arson investigators, he said that he spent two and a half to three hours outside watching the street that night, "right by the bar in and out. I wouldn't say I was on the street all the time. I was in and out" (Davis Statement to Arson Investigation 1). Taken together, the statements mean that he had his eyes on the street all evening. Except when he didn't. And he can verify that nobody entered or left the Up Stairs for twenty minutes before the fire. Unless it was ten. Davis also said that he did not see Rodger Nunez leave the Up Stairs, which would have happened while Davis watched the street action. Gene Davis conceded, however, that it was possible he missed seeing Rodger's departure.[23] Undoubtedly this would have been during one of the intervals when Gene was inside the Hideaway. This excuse would also presumably account for Gene's failure to see Stewart Butler, Alfred Doolittle, Regina Adams, William White, Gary Williams, Eddie Gillis and James Peterson, all of whom said that they either entered or left the bar within twenty minutes of the fire.[24]

It should be mentioned that Gene Davis had a prior history with the law. In 1958 he had been arrested for taking obscene photographs of teenage boys, and was later charged with having sex with one of them.[25] More notably, he had actually been drawn into Jim Garrison's investigation of the Kennedy assassination. As mentioned in the third chapter, Garrison had difficulty believing that a lone gunman like Lee Harvey Oswald could successfully shoot a man in a moving car several hundred feet away. Garrison eventually developed a theory that the assassination and cover-up had been engineered in New Orleans, and that a successful local businessman named Clay Shaw was involved in the plot.[26] Shaw was gay, reportedly with a fondness for young male hustlers, and Gene Davis was drawn into the investigation because of alleged connections with Shaw through neighborhood associations and through the gay bar and gay hustler scenes. In the Garrison investigation, Davis displayed a talent for giving evasive, confusing or contradictory answers to what seemed to be straightforward questions. During testimony to the Orleans Parish grand jury, for example, Davis was asked the relatively simple question of whether he had ever recommended a particular lawyer to gay men in legal trouble. Davis replied, "If I did, I don't know about it. I won't say for sure, 'cause I am not positive, but I don't think I ever did." When the question was rephrased, his answer remained, in essence, the same: "I don't remember, but I don't believe I ever did. I won't say for sure" (Davis Proceedings 4).

Davis's technique had become a bit more subtle by the time of the Up Stairs investigation. When Davis told police and fire marshal investigators about what he saw on the evening of the fire, claiming that he was on the street, but was in and out, and that he hadn't seen anyone enter or leave the stairwell for twenty minutes, unless it was fifteen, or unless it was ten, his responses seem to be designed to give the impression of being extremely helpful even as everything he said created the possibility for reasonable doubt.

Hyde and Roth were aware of this. At one point they gave Gene Davis the Dektor PSE-I stress evaluation, an alternative to the standard polygraph lie detector test, which measures vocal stress when a person being questioned is not telling the truth. When asked if he saw Rodger Nunez leave the Up Stairs on the day of the fire, Davis said no, but his voice indicated stress. Later he was asked if Rodger Nunez told him anything about the fire, and he answered no. His voice, once again, indicated stress, and the person conducting the test wrote, "He is lying here" (Davis Dektor PSE 2). Later he was asked if he knew of his own knowledge if Rodger Nunez set the fire. Davis said no, and the person conducting the test wrote, once again, "He is lying" (2). The test further indicated lies when Davis gave negative answers to the questions regarding whether he saw anyone come out of the lounge prior to the fire, whether he had knowledge of a fight between Michael Scarborough and Rodger Nunez, whether he knew if Rodger Nunez set the fire, and whether he knew of anyone who had set the fire. When he was asked, "If you knew who set the fire, would you tell us?" he answered, "I sure would." The person conducting the test wrote, "Stress indicating that he is lying. Lots of nervous tension" (2).

Gene Davis's testimony during the Dektor PSE and Rodger Nunez's actions on June 24, however, are two entirely different things, and Rodger's actions are the issue. Between five o'clock, when he went to the Up Stairs, and seven o'clock, when he was thrown out, his actions are well known. Between seven and eight is a missing hour. With the possible exceptions of Claudine Rigaud, the Walgreens clerk whose time estimates didn't match, and Gene Davis, whose testimony investigators found questionable, nobody knew where Rodger Nunez was or what he was doing.

In their summary of Gene Davis's statement to the police, which he made on July 9, Schlosser and Gebbia wrote, "Just after the smoke started going out of the stairwell and the fire escape, one person came from around the corner from towards Royal Street or from Canal Street, through Exchange Place. This subject went into his bar and Davis followed him" (58). Schlosser and Gebbia neither name this person in the report nor explain the significance of his going into the Hideaway with Gene Davis following him.

These questions are answered in the transcript of the statement that Davis actually gave to the police,[27] however, and they are repeated in the statement he gave to the arson investigators three months later on October 1. The very date of that statement reveals that the fire marshal's team continued working on the case long after Schlosser and Gebbia gave up. In the statement to the fire marshal's team, which is more detailed than his earlier statement to the police, Gene Davis described hearing and seeing the fire burst out of the windows of the Up Stairs, the flames so large that they touched the buildings all the way across the street. Davis told investigators:

I was standing in the door at that time, watching the fire trucks come and I saw Rodger coming around the corner, not from the corner, he was right at the corner and I can't say if he come around or not. He was right by the corner. It's possible he come around that corner on Exchange Place or he could have come from Royal Street. I don't know, but he was coming that way.... When Rodger come in [to the Hideaway], Jackie was still on the phone, calling the police and fire department yet and he sit down next to her and told the barmaid, give me a beer quick. Then he says, Thank God, I just made it, from the fire. And that was, I think that's the exact words [Davis Statement to Arson Investigation 4].

Davis went on to describe Rodger as winded from running, and later reiterated that Rodger claimed to have just made a narrow escape from the fire. Once Rodger got inside the Hideaway, he sat at the bar quietly nursing a beer instead of going out onto the street to watch the action.[28]

Rodger Nunez's story about a narrow escape from the fire is suspicious for two reasons. In the first place, multiple witnesses would ultimately identify Rodger as the man who was thrown out of the bar at seven o'clock, about an hour before the fire started. It is unlikely, to say the least, that Rodger could have re-entered without anybody noticing him, or without Buddy or Hugh telling him to leave again. In the second place Gene Davis said Rodger Nunez was coming from the direction of Exchange Place or Royal Street. If this is true, Davis's testimony both establishes Rodger's alibi and provides a clue that the alibi was bogus; quite simply, Rodger was coming from the wrong direction.

There were only four ways out of the Up Stairs once the fire started. The first was the stairwell from which the flames bellowed. Only Eugene Thomas and Fred Sharohway escaped this way. The second was the Iberville Street fire escape, a route taken by Eddie Gillis, Jean Gosnell, Luther Boggs and Steven Whittaker. All six people who used these two exits were burned in the process, most of them quite severely. This fire escape was directly in Gene Davis's line of vision, and he described watching the people who got out this way.[29] Not only didn't he see Rodger Nunez come out on the fire escape, but Rodger had no burns.

The third route of escape was through the theater. Buddy Rasmussen led about twenty people out through the fire door onto the roof of a neighboring building, and then down to the street through the stairwell of the next building over. They came out onto Iberville Street in between the Hideaway and the entrance to the Up Stairs. Again, this would have been directly in Gene Davis's line of vision. Remarkably, Gene Davis said that he didn't see anyone making it to safety this way.[30] Admittedly, Davis said that as soon as he saw the fire, he went inside and called out to his barmaid, urging her to phone the fire department. Buddy's group of twenty people might have reached the street during this interval. Still, for a man who claimed to have had his eyes on the street for two to three hours, he seems to have missed a remarkable number of events.

The last route of escape was through one of the front windows overlooking Chartres Street, or the intersection of Chartres and Iberville. Rusty Quinton, Michael Scarborough, and Francis Dufrene were among about a dozen men who made it out through these windows, squeezing between the narrowly-spaced bars. While some, like Michael Scarborough and Francis Dufrene, were badly burned, others, like Rusty Quinton, sustained either only minor injuries or no injuries at all. It is possible that Rodger Nunez was one of these men. It is possible, too, that after he reached the street, he then ran a block to Canal Street, took a right, ran a half a block (to Exchange Place) or a full block (to Royal Street), took another right, ran back to Iberville, then took a third right so that he could approach Gene Davis from behind. All of this is possible, but none of it is probable. It bears repeating that nobody remembered Rodger Nunez re-entering the bar after he was thrown out at seven o'clock, and that while running all the way around the block would account for Rodger being winded, there would have been no reason for him to make this circuitous journey to the Hideaway; it would have been much easier—and much quicker—to walk a few steps down Chartres to Iberville, turn left and walk a few more steps to the Hideaway.

Rodger's behavior the night of the fire remained suspicious. When he finally finished his beer in the Hideaway and went out to the street, Buddy Rasmussen saw him and grabbed him by the arm, asking him where he had been. Rodger said he had been at Wanda's.[31]

Rodger could not have been at Wanda's, as he told Buddy, if he had been in the Up Stairs, as he told Gene Davis. Moreover, Allen Guidry, who had spent much of the afternoon with Rodger in the Hideaway, actually went to Wanda's that night, arriving shortly after seven, remaining there until news of the fire brought him onto the street, and then returning to Wanda's, where he stayed until two or three the next morning. He told investigators that he did not see Rodger in Wanda's at all during that time.[32]

Of course, the only person who knew with absolute certainty where Rodger was between seven and eight o'clock was Rodger himself. Arson investigators continued looking for clues, interviewing multiple witnesses over the next few months, and slowly but steadily building a case against Rodger Nunez. On July 18 they took a statement from Buddy Rasmussen and showed him the photos that they had shown to Michael Scarborough. Buddy identified Rodger Nunez as the man who had fought with Michael, as well as the man Buddy had apprehended on the street and brought to a police officer for questioning before the police officer made him let Rodger go.[33] Hyde and Roth questioned Allen Guidry again, and although he denied seeing the fight, he did admit to seeing

Rodger in the bar before the fire and to seeing Buddy apprehend Rodger in the street after the fire.[34] Hyde and Roth questioned Courtney Craighead, who had witnessed the fight, although he hadn't been able to hear what words were exchanged. Courtney identified Rodger Nunez as being in the fight and being made to leave by Buddy and Hugh. Courtney also further corroborated the story that Buddy had apprehended Rodger Nunez on the street during the fire and had brought him to a police officer who made Buddy let Rodger go.[35]

Rodger Nunez had not returned to New Orleans, but because he had been briefly detained by police in Morgan City in July, and because he had been driving a car registered in Abbeville, Hyde and Roth suspected that he might still be in the southwestern portion of the state. In September they contacted the Abbeville sheriff to ask for assistance. William Roth issued a subpoena, and Criminal Deputy John Landry of the Abbeville sheriff's office brought Rodger Nunez in for questioning on September 18. After the first session, they decided to give him a lie detector test, and he agreed, but that technology was not available in Abbeville, so they brought Rodger Nunez back to New Orleans that same day.[36] They interrogated him in a room in the Detective Bureau of the New Orleans Police Department.

In the closing lines of the NOPD case report, signed less than three weeks earlier, detectives Schlosser and Gebbia wrote, "Any future developments in this matter will be covered in a Supplemental Report" (64). Now the man upon whom their investigation had focused was in their own headquarters. However, the transcript of the session indicates that the only people present were Rodger Nunez and the fire marshal's arson investigators, Edward Hyde and John Fischer.[37] The NOPD case report does not contain so much as a note indicating that Schlosser and Gebbia were aware of this interrogation.

Some of the questions that Hyde and Fischer asked Rodger Nunez account for his disappearance from New Orleans after being discharged from Charity Hospital. His mother, Rose Sale, and his stepfather, Gene Sale, had driven in from Abbeville, had him released, and brought him home. He had lived with them for about six weeks, until a move took them to Houston. Rodger remained in Abbeville without them. He had only left Abbeville twice in the prior two months: once to go to Kaplan, where an orthodontist removed the wire braces Charity surgeons had used to repair his broken jaw, and once to go to a religious meeting in Grand Coteau,[38] a tiny town where religion was the major industry, as it was then home to both a convent school and a Catholic seminary.

Rodger had been supporting himself by working as a deckhand. The rough work had been hard on him. Though Rodger had long suffered from epilepsy, a workplace accident had made it worse. When his boat was suddenly jolted because a heavy load of equipment fell on the deck, Rodger had fallen, hitting his head against the side of the boat. He told investigators, "That's what started me having more frequent seizures than normal" (Nunez Statement 6).

On fairly safe, innocuous questions like these, Rodger's memory and answers were clear. The only sign of nervousness was a verbal tic: he frequently included the meaningless sound "er" in his responses:

> Q: What is your mother's name?
> A: My mother's name is Rose er ... Sale, S-a-l-e.
> Q: What is your father's name?
> A: Er ... Mansel [Nunez Statement 1].

When the questions turned to the fire at the Up Stairs, Rodger said nothing about making a narrow escape or about talking to Gene Davis in the Hideaway as the fire raged the night of June 24. He only admitted to discussing the fire with Gene about ten days later,[39] when Rodger was in Charity recovering from jaw surgery, unable to speak to police because of his condition. It is possible, of course, that Gene somehow got through to Rodger in the hospital; it is also possible that Gene spoke to Rodger shortly before he was hospitalized or shortly after his release. One wonders if, during this conversation, Gene Davis gave Rodger any pointers for dealing with investigators. In the Garrison investigation, Gene Davis had responded to fairly simple questions by saying that he couldn't answer because his memory could be flawed, and he might not remember key details. When questioned by the fire marshal's investigative team, Rodger Nunez responded in a remarkably similar way.

Though Gene Davis said that Rodger claimed he had been in the bar at the time of the fire, and that he had barely escaped, when Hyde and Fischer asked Rodger if he was in the Up Stairs at about 7:56 on the night of June 24, he said, "I don't know" (3).

Asked if somebody that night had grabbed him in the street outside of the Up Stairs, he said, "I don't know" (3).

Asked if he had a fight with somebody in the Up Stairs, he said, "I don't think so. I could have. I don't know for sure" (2). A variation of the question came later, when investigators asked if he had had a fight with Michael Scarborough. Rodger answered, "I don't know, sir. I don't think so. I could have though [...] cause they said I did" (3). When investigators asked for a third time if he had been in a fight, he said, "I don't know, sir. I really don't. I don't think so. I, it's not my nature to fight. I never fight" (11).

Rodger displayed a similar ignorance of the facts of his own injury. Questioners asked if he had suffered a broken jaw, and Rodger said, "I have had a broken jaw, sometime later. Yes, sir. About a week later, I think. I don't know for sure" (4). Later, they asked if his jaw broke when someone in the bar knocked him down. Rodger said, "No, sir. I don't think so because it was a week between this Sunday that you're talking about and when I was in the hospital and I couldn't have possibly gone more than a few hours with a broken jaw" (11). When Rodger had been located at Cee Cee Savant's apartment by Hyde and Roth the week after the fire, he claimed that he had been beaten up the night before by "three negroes" (Hyde, Roth, and Fischer 20). That event (or that story) apparently slipped his mind in the two months that had passed since then, because he never mentioned being beaten up by three black men, nor did he ever explain exactly how his jaw broke, implying only that it happened in some unspecified way at some unspecified time between the night of the fire and the time investigators found him and brought him to Charity Hospital.

When he was asked, point blank, if he set the fire at the Up Stairs, he replied, "No, sir" (11). To the final question, "Is there anything else you could tell us about the fire in the Upstairs Lounge?" Rodger replied, "No, sir" (13).

The transcript of this statement is thirteen pages long, and it is clear that investigators were doing all they could to ratchet up the pressure, hoping that Rodger Nunez would make an admission. This never happened.

Rodger Nunez never took a polygraph test, in part because it was thought that the drugs he took for his epilepsy would contaminate the results.[40] Instead, like Gene Davis, Rodger Nunez took a Dektor Psychological Stress Evaluation (PSE), though that did not take place until October 9, and it was administered in Abbeville. Like Gene Davis, Rodger showed a great deal of stress when he denied knowledge of the fire in several different questions. Most important, when he answered no to the question, "Did you set the fire at the Upstairs Lounge," the test administrator noted, "Stress indiacting [sic] that he is lying. He does have knowledge of the crime" (Nunez Dektor PSE 1). When he also answered no to the question, "Did you set the fire in the stair way?" the test administrator noted, "Stress indicating that he is lying. Hard Stress" (1). Gene Davis answered twenty-six questions when he took the Dektor PSE, but Rodger Nunez answered only thirteen; he was advised to stop by his attorney lest he incriminate himself.[41]

Still, one would think that the results of the questions that he had answered would have been enough to result in an arrest. They certainly seemed to confirm the theory that Rodger Nunez set the fire. The problem, however, was that results of both the standard polygraph test and the Dektor PSE were difficult to admit in court.

The polygraph is popularly called the "lie detector test." That is a misnomer, because the test does not measure the truthfulness of a statement, but merely the physiological state of the body as the statement is being made. In the standard polygraph, the subject is connected to sensors that measure breathing, pulse, blood pressure and perspiration or skin conductivity. The subject is asked a series of innocuous questions to establish a base line for these vital signs. Later, as more substantive questions are asked, the sensors are supposed to indicate variations in things like the breathing and pulse if the subject is telling a lie. These variations need to be interpreted by a trained reader, who must distinguish, for example, between a rise in pulse rate due to falsehood, or a rise in pulse rate due to fear and stress.[42] This element of subjective judgment is simply not present in many other crime tests, and so some states won't admit polygraph evidence in court at all, and other states only do so if all parties involved agree. The U.S. Supreme Court has historically viewed polygraph evidence as suspect, ruling so as early as 1923 in *Frye v. United States*, and much more recently in the 1998 case *United States vs. Scheffer*, in which the majority concluded that there was no consensus on the reliability of polygraph evidence.[43]

The Dektor PSE, developed in 1969, does not measure multiple physical responses, such as respiration, pulse and blood pressure. Instead, it relies solely on the level of stress communicated through the voice of the subject as he or she answers questions. Like the polygraph, the measurements of vocal stress must be interpreted by a trained evaluator,[44] and like the polygraph, the test lends itself to subjective interpretation. Hence, Dektor PSE results are also difficult to admit in court, though the recorded interrogations may be.[45]

While polygraph and Dektor PSE results may be useful as interrogation tools, and while they may help investigators determine who may or may not be lying, they are, to say the least, problematic in terms of solidifying a case. This is the issue the arson investigators faced in trying to solve the case of the Up Stairs fire. Though they had a likely suspect, in the absence of a confession or a credible witness, and with no fingerprints on the empty can of lighter fluid, there was no way to prove that Rodger Nunez set the fire.

Still, Hyde, Roth and Fischer persisted, even as other duties and other cases drew them away. Their case report stops measuring incremental progress in terms of days, and starts doing so in terms of weeks, or even months. Their October 1973 interview with Gene Davis made it clear that Davis knew something, even if he wouldn't reveal what that was, so they continued to interview survivors and Iberville Street habitués, hoping that one of them would provide a crucial missing piece.

In October of 1973, four months after the fire, *The Times–Picayune* reviewed Troy Perry's first memoir, *The Lord Is My Shepherd and He Knows I'm Gay,* which had been published the year before. The belated attention from *The Times–Picayune* may have been the result of Troy Perry's local presence in the aftermath of the fire. This memoir, a history of Troy Perry's spiritual journey, and a description of the genesis of the Metropolitan Community Church, has proved over the years to be an important spiritual document for thousands of gays and lesbians trying to reconcile their sexuality to their spirituality.[46]

The Times–Picayune covered another important event two months later, when the trustees of the American Psychiatric Association passed a resolution stating that homosexuality should no longer be considered a mental disorder. This vote followed a ten-year effort by psychiatrists and gay activists, who believed that classifying homosexuality as a mental illness was "oppressive and discriminatory" ("APA" 43). Recognizing that some gays and lesbians still had problems accepting themselves, the APA took homosexuality out of their diagnostic manual and replaced it with sexual orientation disturbance, a disorder "for individuals whose sexual interests are directed primarily toward people of the same sex and who are bothered by, in conflict with, or wish to change their sexual orientations" ("APA" 43).

It is possible that Rodger Nunez read both these stories, though there is no way to know for sure. He had moved to Abbeville following his release from Charity Hospital, but at some point in the last months of 1973, he returned to New Orleans. He lived for a while at the Imperial Hotel in the 600 block of St. Charles Avenue. This hotel had seen better days, and when Rodger was living there, it was functioning as a halfway house, funded in part by the archdiocese.[47] While living there, Rodger made two important friendships.[48]

One of these friendships was with Ralph Forest, who moved into the halfway house in January of 1974. Like Rodger, he was gay, and for a while they had a sexual relationship that had some potential to become a romantic one.[49] The other friendship was with Sister Mary Stephen Ledet, a nun who had no official connection with the halfway house at the Imperial Hotel, but who visited there during the Mardi Gras season in February of 1974, and who became a friend and confidant to Rodger. Though they saw each other only about ten times, Rodger telephoned her when he was upset or in emotional distress, which seemed to happen fairly often.[50]

Meanwhile, the site of the Up Stairs remained without a tenant, its broken windows and smoke-stained walls giving mute testimony to the fire as they would for many years.[51] By December of 1973, Phil Esteve opened a new bar called The Post Office. A press release in the *New Orleans Causeway*, a new alternative paper for gays and lesbians, compares The Post Office to the Up Stairs, noting, "Much of the same kind of funky décor ... is in evidence at The Post Office. Carrying on the best traditions of the Upstairs, The Post Office retains a genuinely friendly and family-like atmosphere" (Parker 2). Buddy continued to work for Phil at The Post Office, though he eventually quit, leaving the bar business behind.[52] Many of The Post Office customers were former patrons of the Up Stairs. Even some of the same traditions remained. For a year or two after the fire, it was customary to close at the end of the evening by having everybody form a circle, hold hands and sing the old Up Stairs anthem "United We Stand." Formerly, this song had been sung joyously, an affirmation of friendship and solidarity. After the fire, the song became more of a dirge, sung in recognition of all who had died.[53]

Not all of the survivors or old regulars became customers at The Post Office. Some went through long periods when they were too mournful, or too frightened, to go into another bar. Some never returned to the bar scene at all.[54] Others kept a low profile and, not wanting to have their fears confirmed, avoided the newspaper accounts of who had lived and who had died.

Napoleon and Stanley had moved out of the city a few weeks before the fire. They returned about a year later, and discovered that several people who hadn't seen them in a long while had just assumed that they had died in the Up Stairs Lounge. One man ran away in fear when he saw them, convinced that they were ghosts.[55]

On June 24, 1974, a year after the fire, there was an informal memorial that escaped public attention. A group of people assembled at the Candlelight Lounge on North Rampart. They lit candles and walked in formation from the Candlelight up North Rampart to Iberville, then walked on Iberville to the site of the Up Stairs Lounge. Marcy Marcell remembers participating in the memorial, but she does not recall who organized it, and it does not seem to have received press coverage.[56]

Also in the summer of 1974, arson investigators Hyde and Fisher, continuing their investigation, took a lengthy statement from Cee Cee Savant, the woman on whose sofa Rodger had slept the week following the fire. They suspected that Cee Cee, like Gene Davis, knew something about Rodger's actions, but Cee Cee was similarly adept at navigating investigations. For example, she readily told Hyde and Fischer detailed stories about how, in the week following the fire, Rodger woke up from nightmares in which he was being accused of setting the fire. When it came to questions of his actual culpability, her testimony became laced with statements that gave her an element of plausible deniability.

> Q. Did he tell you that he had anything to do with setting this fire?
> A. No. Not that I can honestly remember, he didn't [Savant 3].

Most people would "honestly remember" whether or not a friend said he had set a fire that killed more than thirty people.

In some ways, the most interesting thing she said had little to do with Rodger's actions, and a great deal to do with his personality. In trying to learn how well Cee Cee and Rodger were acquainted, the investigators asked how and why he came to be sleeping on her sofa.

Q. Where did you meet Roger [sic]?
A. At the bar.
Q. I mean prior to that, how long have you known him?
A. I didn't really know Roger. Nobody did [Savant 7].

Among the people who "didn't really know" Rodger Nunez was his wife, Elaine Wharton Basset Nunez. They had met early in 1974, and were married in May.[57] Perhaps, in marrying a woman, Rodger was trying to cure himself of his homosexuality, as so many gay men have done, before and since. Perhaps it was only a marriage of convenience, because he needed care, or a place to live, or a dependable income. His epileptic seizures were getting worse, and he had surgery in 1974 to remove a brain tumor.[58] It isn't known whether this tumor had caused the epilepsy, whether it increased the incidence of seizures, or whether it was an entirely separate disorder. It is clear that he needed help. Elaine had a house and more money than the $146 per month[59] that Rodger received as a disability benefit.[60] He had been writing bad checks, some on his wife's account, and he wasn't paying his bills.[61]

Theirs was almost certainly not a love match, at least as far as Rodger was concerned. When they married, Rodger was twenty-seven and Elaine was forty-nine. The age difference was significant by any standard. Elaine herself said that she and Rodger never consummated their marriage. He disclosed to her after the wedding that he was gay, and he said that he was impotent, too. Though officially his address was the same as hers, they effectively lived apart; Elaine slept in the house, and Rodger in a small trailer in the back yard.[62]

That's where Elaine found his dead body on the morning of November 15, 1974.

In the trailer with Rodger were three empty bottles for recently filled prescriptions, and six empty beer cans. The autopsy revealed that he had taken the pills and drunk the beer. Among the multiple causes of death were partial aspiration of gastric contents and cerebral edema related to the ingestion of barbiturates. Though there was no note, the coroner ruled his death a suicide.[63]

After Rodger's body was discovered, Elaine Nunez phoned Ralph Forest, the gay man Rodger had befriended in the halfway house. He was devastated by the news, and like many people, he dealt with his grief by going out for a drink. The bar he chose to go to was Phil Esteve's new bar, The Post Office.

Michael Scarborough was in The Post Office that day. He had spent nine months in hospitals and in his hometown recovering from the injuries he sustained in the fire. His head and face bore visible scars, and many of his fingers had been partially amputated because of the burns he received while escaping from the Up Stairs. Michael had a very slight acquaintance with Ralph Forest, who had asked, and been told, where and how Michael had been injured. That was as much as the two men knew about each other.[64]

Michael was talking to Phil Esteve when Ralph came in, crying and in obvious distress. They asked what was wrong, and Ralph told them that his best friend had killed himself. Trying to be sympathetic, Phil asked who Ralph's friend was. When Ralph said his friend had been Rodger Nunez, Michael Scarborough started to laugh. Phil tried to get Michael to stop laughing because he was upsetting Ralph, but Michael said, "That is the one that set the fire to the Up Stairs Lounge, you know?" (Forest 5–6).

Under pressure from Phil, Ralph admitted that Rodger had told him that he had indeed set the fire. Phil insisted that Ralph call the authorities, and soon Ralph was giving his account to the arson investigation team from the office of the state fire marshal.

Ralph Forest's story was that on three or four occasions in the previous year, Rodger Nunez had told him that he had set the fire in the Up Stairs Lounge. According to Ralph, Rodger said it was because he was mad at being thrown out of the bar. Once Rodger had even said he had started the fire with a can of lighter fluid he purchased at Walgreens. Rodger was always drunk when he told the story. When he sobered up, if Ralph asked about it, Rodger would say, "You must be kidding! Me do that?!" (Forest 1).

Edward Hyde, conducting the investigation, wanted to know why Ralph Forest had not come forward with this information before Rodger's death. Ralph said, "One, I thought he was lying, and two, I was very fond of him at that time [and] didn't want him to get into trouble" (Forest 2). Later, Hyde asked the question in a slightly different way:

> Q: Prior to Roger's death, did you ever tell anyone that Roger told you that he had set the fire at the Upstairs Lounge?
> A: No, I did not.
> Q: Was there any reason for you not telling anyone?
> A: Possibly because I didn't believe that he had done it and also because I still had feelings toward him [8].

These were remarkable admissions for Ralph Forest to make. During this investigation, many other intimate relationships between men had been effectively whitewashed. Even Buddy Rasmussen and Michael Scarborough had edited and virtually erased their relationships by describing their deceased lovers as their "roommates" when they gave official testimony.[65] Alone among the witness reports, Ralph Forest's statement gives testimony of one man having tender feelings for another.

The point does not seem to have been lost on Edward Hyde, who, like the police detectives, Schlosser and Gebbia, seems to have had a slightly grotesque fascination with the gay subculture into which this crime had led him. In the middle of a discussion of issues far more pertinent to the fire, Hyde suddenly asked:

> Q: Have you ever committed any sexual acts with Roger?
> A: Yes, I have.
> Q: In what way? What I mean, who was the man and who....
> A: Fifty-fifty proposition.
> Q: Was this an unnatural copulation you're talking about?
> A: Yes.
> Q: And you took turns, is that right?
> A: Yes.
> Q: Now, getting back to the statements that Roger made to you about the fire...[8].

In the course of the interrogation, Ralph Forest spoke of Sister Mary Stephen Ledet, the nun who had befriended both Ralph and Rodger, and to whom Rodger had become particularly close. Ralph said that he had called Sister Stephen before going to speak to the arson investigators, and said he had asked her if she knew anything about Rodger's involvement with the fire.

This simple headstone marks the grave of Rodger Nunez, the principal subject of the investigations. He committed suicide in November of 1974, about 17 months after the fire (author's photograph).

According to Ralph Forest, she admitted that Rodger told her about being a suspect in the case, but said he had not told her that he had set the fire.[66] She was called in by Hyde and Fischer, and she repeated much the same story. Ledet said that she hadn't quite believed Rodger when he said he'd been a suspect, and thought that he had been trying to impress her with his masculinity (suggesting that he himself was insecure on that point). She clearly recognized him as troubled, and said, "he didn't, he didn't like to er, to be gay and that er, threw him. That was, I think, his, stemmed, his problems all stemmed from that, you know, he couldn't, he, he reached the point where he couldn't accept himself for what he was" (Ledet 3–4).

Even with Rodger dead and with Ralph Forest's statement, the investigators for the fire marshal would not give up, and they continued to question people they felt might have some knowledge of the fire, apparently wanting—or needing—to get some corroboration of Ralph Forest's statement in order to bring the case to a close. They questioned Rodger's widow, Elaine Nunez, in December of 1974, just a few weeks after his death. Though she was able to tell them about their brief, bleak marriage, she said she had no knowledge of whether he had set the fire.[67]

The investigators continued, interviewing Jacqueline Bullard and Dorothy Rikard as late as March of 1975—four months after Rodger's suicide. Both women knew Rodger, and both were employed by Gene Davis at the Hideaway at the time of the fire. Again, it seems as though they might have known something, but that they were determined not to cooperate with the police, either because of a sense of loyalty to Rodger or Gene Davis, or because of a distrust of police authority. In their testimony, phrases such as "I don't know," "I don't remember," and "Not that I recall" occur with regularity. Jacqueline Bullard repeats the story that Rodger claimed to have been in the fire and to just have gotten out in time.[68] Dorothy Rikard seems to have been not just disingenuous, but obstinate, causing even the transcript of the session to give the impression that her questioner was losing his temper:

> Q. Did you have a conversation with Gene Davis about this fire?
> A. ... I had conversations with almost everybody about it.
> Q. Did Gene Davis tell you to keep your mouth shut about the fire?
> A. No.
> Q. Did you threaten Mark Allen Guidry about this fire?
> A. No.
> Q. Did you tell Mark Allen Guidry he ought to keep his big mouth shut ... in my presence?
> A. No, not....
> Q. You didn't say something to that effect?
> A. Not that I can remember.

Q. Is there any reason for you making that remark?

A. No, not that I know of.

Q. Do you know who set the Upstairs Lounge fire?

A. No, I don't.

Q. Do you know if Rodger Nunez set the Upstairs Lounge fire, er, on fire?

A. No, I don't. I really don't think he'd, did. You never know people [Rikard 6].

And so yet another witness who might have known something avoided any unqualified admissions. At the end of the statement, Rikard was asked to affirm that she had told the truth. She replied, "Yes, I have; to my knowledge" (10).

Investigators officially presented the case to the New Orleans district attorney in July of 1975, hoping that the case would be considered complete enough for the D.A. to accept it and give it official closure. This did not happen, and correspondence in the official case file indicates that Hyde, Roth and Fischer fought to keep the case open, filing extension after extension for another five years, apparently hoping that one day someone would say something to corroborate their theory and Ralph Forest's account. Finally, in 1980, Frank J. Locascio, Jr., who was chief of the Arson Division for the Department of Public Safety, filed an internal memo addressed to the investigative team of William M. Roth, Jr., and John M. Fisher regarding the fire at the Up Stairs Lounge. It includes the words:

This report [on the investigation of the fire] was submitted to the Dist. Att'y... N[ew].O[rleans].La. The suspect at the time, Roger [sic] Nunez, has since committed suicide. There was no other evidence or information pointing to anyone other than the above mentioned person. The investigators were completely satisfied that he was the person who set the fire. No charges were ever accepted by the D.A., N.O. La. It is requested that this file be closed....[Locascio].

The corroboration of Ralph Forest's statement that might have led to the D.A. accepting the case could quite probably have come from Sister Mary Stephen Ledet. Though when she spoke to arson investigators, she denied knowledge of whether Rodger had set the fire, she may not have been telling the complete truth.

In 2003, a memorial service was held in a Canal Street hotel to commemorate the thirtieth anniversary of the fire. Following a prayer service, participants silently marched down Iberville Street where a bronze plaque was placed in the sidewalk outside of what had been the entrance to the bar. One of the people participating in the event was fire chief William McCrossen, who had been on the scene in 1973, and who supervised the removal of the dead. He was elderly and frail by 2003, and the march to the site tired him, but when everyone returned to the hotel, he sat in a chair in the front of the room, encouraging the assembled crowd to ask him anything they wanted to about the fire.

Of course somebody asked him if he knew who was responsible. McCrossen told about a visit he had received from a woman many years earlier. She had been a nun and had left her order. She was preparing to move away, but before leaving, she wanted to tell Chief McCrossen that she once heard a confession from a young man who had said that he started the fire in the Up Stairs Lounge, and who had since taken his own life.[69]

Though McCrossen did not name the woman, and though McCrossen has since died, the details are suggestive: a young man confessing to a nun and later committing suicide; a former nun speaking to the Fire Chief before moving away. Sister Mary Stephen Ledet left her order in 1974. She eventually moved to Florida where she married a man and lived the rest of her life as a layperson. She died in 2007.[70]

Technically, or theologically, what she heard was not a confession; only priests are empowered to perform the Sacrament of Reconciliation, and only priests are legally empowered to withhold from the law the details of what they hear in the confessional. Still, this nun, having promised to keep the secret of a distraught young man, would not have broken her vow lightly.

Another person later came forward with a similar story. Early in 1973, some months before the fire took place, Rodger was in Orleans Parish prison where he met a drag queen who had also been arrested on a minor charge. Miss Fury, a New Orleans personage for many years, was known for having flaming red hair and a temper to match.[71] Many years after the fire, she told Johnny Townsend, a New Orleans writer, that Rodger had once admitted to her that he had burned the Up Stairs Lounge. Rodger's confession to Miss Fury took place on Christmas Eve 1973, six months to the day after the fire had taken place. Once again, Rodger made the confession under the influence of alcohol. Though Ralph Forest had indicated that Rodger had shown no signs of remorse,[72] Miss Fury said that Rodger wept as he told her what he had done. According to Miss Fury, "He'd only meant to cause a little fire and some smoke.... He'd only meant to scare everybody. He didn't realize the whole place would go up in flames" (Townsend 219).

It's possible, of course, that during this confession, Rodger was drunk and having a crying jag, behaving like a young child who says, "I didn't mean to do it." But the claim that he had only wanted to scare people actually receives partial corroboration from the statement given to police by Claudine Rigaud, the clerk from the tobacco counter at Walgreens. She had told police that, on the evening of the fire, the "feminish" (her word) young gay man with dark hair entered the store and walked directly into the aisle where the lighter fluid was kept. After looking around, he approached her and asked for assistance. At that time, Walgreens stocked Ronsonol lighter fluid in three different sizes:

a 4½-ounce can, a seven-ounce can, and a twelve-ounce can. The young man was looking for the smallest size, but Claudine Rigaud told him that they were out of stock. Unable to purchase the smallest, he purchased the next smallest.[73]

Of course, these confessions by Rodger may all have been false, as the confessions of Raymond Wallender, David Dubose and the putative member of Black Mama, White Mama had been. But Raymond Wallender had a clear motive for lying: he was apparently afraid of being killed in his California jail, and saw extradition to Louisiana as a way to save his life.[74] David Dubose, probably both drunk and stoned, and definitely under pressure as he was questioned by police, may have wanted to relieve the pressure by telling police what he thought they wanted to hear. As for Black Mama, White Mama, police often receive false confessions to high-profile crimes, and the people making those confessions are generally looking for a chance to be in the spotlight, if only by proxy, and if only for their fifteen minutes of fame.

Rodger Nunez did not have Raymond Wallender's clear motive for a false confession. Unlike David Dubose, he had proven himself more than able to resist the pressure of an official interrogation. Far from seeking the spotlight by phoning television stations with his claims, Rodger Nunez confessed only secretively, and only to close friends.

He told his story to Ralph Forest three or four times, at least once to Miss Fury, and probably at least once to Sister Mary Stephen Ledet. With the exception of his possible confession to Sister Mary Stephen, he was always drinking when he confessed, and seems always to have retracted the confession as soon as he was sober. Since his drunken and sober statements contradicted each other, we have to wonder when he was telling the truth.

Aaron Edwards, a licensed addiction counselor, was asked when people were more likely to tell a lie: when sober, or when under the influence? Although Edwards could not commit to a categorical answer, he did cite the old aphorism *In vino veritas*, and say that there is something about intoxication that makes people want to unburden themselves. He also said that people are more likely to tell a *coherent* lie when sober, because the cognitive processes necessary to do so are impaired by alcohol.[75] Rodger's drunken confessions seem to have been consistent in their details and seem to have aligned with the known facts.

But what about his suicide? Is that evidence of guilt? Perhaps. But Rodger left no note to explain why he killed himself, and his life had not been a good one. He had no money, no real skills, and worked menial jobs, apparently augmenting that income by turning quick tricks. He had many health problems related to his epilepsy, and apparently had issues with substance abuse as well. On top of all that, the words of Sister Mary Stephen Ledet and his marriage to Elaine Nunez both suggest that he was suffering from sexual orientation disturbance as it had been newly defined in 1973: he was a gay man bothered by, or in conflict with, his attraction to other men. Any—or all—of these factors might have given him a reason to want to end his life, whether or not he had set the fire.

Still, many people in New Orleans are familiar with the story of the fire being set by an angry young hustler who later killed himself.[76] Though few know the name of the hustler or why he was suspected of the crime, most assume that he killed himself out of guilt, and most now regard him with pity instead of anger. "I don't think he had any *idea* or notion *whatsoever* that what he was doing would have that kind of outcome," Stewart Butler says today. "What a terrible cross he must have borne!"

VII

Southern Stonewall?
Or Rehearsal for a Plague?
The Social and Political
Legacies of the Fire

It has been said that the fire is the New Orleans equivalent of the Stonewall riots that took place in New York four years earlier, giving birth to a local gay rights movement. Language to this effect is on the bronze memorial plaque that is now embedded in the sidewalk near the former entrance to the Up Stairs Lounge. Marcy Marcell and Toni Pizanie,[1] who have spent their adult lives living and working in the New Orleans gay and lesbian community, both take this view. Asked in 2009 about the long-term positive effects of the fire, Toni Pizanie said, "It had a tremendous effect! It changed so many things." In another interview, Marcy Marcell rhetorically asked, "How could it not?" But when asked for specific long-term changes attributable to the fire, both Pizanie and Marcell were hard-pressed to name any.

At the other end of the spectrum are New Orleans residents such as Robert Batson, an historian specializing in gay and lesbian issues. When asked today whether he sees the fire at the Up Stairs as a Southern equivalent to the Stonewall riots, he says, "The fire did not produce any substantial changes in the lives of gay people in New Orleans. Our 'Stonewall' was the protest against Anita Bryant four years later."[2]

Early, in 1977, Dade County, Florida, passed an ordinance that prohibited employment discrimination based on sexual orientation. Anita Bryant was a devout Christian who did not want homosexuals in the classrooms. She was known for saying that because homosexuals couldn't reproduce, they were forced to recruit. She had been a fairly successful singer in the 1950s and early

1960s, scoring a number of hit records. By 1977 her star had dimmed, and she was mostly known for being the celebrity spokesperson for the Florida Citrus Commission. Still, she had national name recognition. She and her husband used her fame in an effort to overturn the Dade County ordinance, which they accomplished by voter referendum on June 7, 1977. Their success in this area led them to participate in several other campaigns against gay rights, most notably the Briggs initiative in California, where Bryant and other anti-gay activists were defeated in 1978.

While Anita Bryant was pursuing her anti-gay political agenda, she continued her career as an entertainer. By coincidence, even before her opposition to gay rights in Florida put her in the middle of a national political discussion on homosexuality, she had been booked to perform in New Orleans as part of the 1977 New Orleans Symphony Summer Pops Concert series in Municipal Auditorium. The date of her scheduled performances—Friday, June 17, and Saturday, June 18—came less than two weeks after her Dade County success. The timing couldn't have been better for her supporters to show their loyalty, or for her opponents to display their ire.

A group called Christians Behind Anita held prayer meetings in her support and staged a "Rally for Righteousness" in front of the Municipal Auditorium before her Friday evening performance. Their spokesperson, Danny Bryant (no apparent relation to Anita), said that the rally was meant to "get Christian people to reach out in love" so that they could help homosexuals out of their "trap" ("NOPD Pledges to Prevent Confrontation" 7). Meanwhile, the police department, attempting to forestall any threats, made it known that they would give Anita Bryant all available protection.[3]

The other side was organized and represented by two local gay rights organizations: The Gertrude Stein Society and Human Equal Rights for Everyone (HERE). They held a rally featuring Air Force Sergeant Leonard Matlovich, who had been discharged from the military for being gay in a high-profile case from 1975. HERE also planned a march down St. Ann Street to protest Bryant's performance, and was bringing in other activists from Atlanta, Jackson, New York and Chicago.[4]

During Anita Bryant's first performance, about 200 protesters stood outside of the Municipal Auditorium, lining Rampart Street and holding flickering matches.[5] Bill Rushton, speaking for HERE, assured *The Times–Picayune* that they wanted a peaceful rally, and Sergeant Matlovich said he was happy that Anita Bryant was speaking out against gays and lesbians so vociferously. He believed that her opposition to gay rights galvanized gay people to action while also making straight people question anti-gay prejudice. "Our greatest fear is God will tell Anita to stop," he said. "She gives us credibility and is our road to liberation" (Citron "Anti-Anita Forces" 14). Meanwhile, inside the auditorium, Bryant performed wearing a silver sequined dress. Although she sang a few Christian-themed songs, her performance as a whole was reminiscent of a night club act in Las Vegas, and most of the numbers were showbiz standards like "The Boy Next Door," "Singin' in the Rain," and "Somewhere Over the Rainbow."[6] In retrospect, this last song choice is a bit ironic, as it is normally associated with gay icon Judy Garland, and in 1978 a San Francisco artist adopted the rainbow as a symbol of gay pride.[7]

There were a few boos during her show, and a handful of people exited the auditorium in clearly staged protest, but the audience was generally respectful, and references to the tension outside were largely absent. One of the few occurred when, during an interactive portion of the show, an audience member asked if she could call Bryant by her first name. "I've been called a lot of things," Bryant said, "but I prefer Anita" (Citron "Anita Sings" 14).

On Saturday the anti–Anita crowd had swelled to about 1,500 people, a number that completely dwarfed the 25 to 40 people who turned out to support Bryant. Gathering first at Jackson Square and marching through the French Quarter before reaching Municipal Auditorium, protesters chanted, "Hey! Hey! Ho! Ho! Anita Bryant has got to go!" (Beaulieu 3; Killgore). Although the demonstration remained peaceful, it was clear that the gloves had come off. A man named Ike Nahen, speaking for the anti–Anita contingent, said, "Our out-mobilizing the pro–Anita protesters by a hundred times proves that the majority of the country will support human rights for everyone" (Beaulieu 3). In an accompanying story, reporter Alan Citron called the anti–Anita protests "the biggest gay rights protests in the city's history" ("Out of the Closets" 3).

Meanwhile, the pro–Anita forces held what amounted to a pep rally, spelling out the name of Jesus in orchestrated cheers (*Give me a J...!*), and holding up signs saying, "Jesus Means Liberation" (Grady 3). Anita Bryant did not take part in the outdoor demonstrations herself, but she granted an interview to *Times Picayune* reporter Millie Ball. During this interview she attempted to downplay the controversial nature of her crusade. "I have no hate," she said. "I have no vendetta. My concern is for our children and us as a nation. If we don't turn around soon, we will have to face the judgment." Modeling herself as a paragon of maternal empathy, Bryant filled her interview with statements like "When I think of young people of America today accepting this as an alternative lifestyle, it breaks my heart." She was photographed wearing a gold pin in the shape of a fish hook, which symbolized her Christian mission as a fisher of men's souls. However, her aura of calm spirituality and loving concern completely dissipated in at least one key moment, which Ball chose to use as opening line of the story: "Anita Bryant leaned forward, her elbows on her knees, and said, 'I'd rather my child be dead than homosexual'" ("I'd Rather My Child be Dead" 3).

There is no question that the 1977 protests against Anita Bryant constituted a high-water mark in New Orleans gay activism. But were those protests the effective beginning of a gay rights movement in New Orleans? Or were they the continuation of an activism that began following the fire at the Up Stairs Lounge?

To answer the question we have to go back four years before the anti–Anita protests, to the July 1, 1973, memorial for the victims of the fire. This memorial at St. Mark's Methodist Church had an attendance of between 200 and 300 people. At the end of the service, word arrived that, despite a prior request for privacy, television crews were waiting outside to photograph and interview people as they left. As reported in Chapter 3, Troy Perry announced that there was a side exit from the church and that people who didn't want to face news cameras would be escorted out that way. After a tense and anxious moment, an unidentified woman stood up and shouted, "I'm not afraid of who I am and I'm not afraid of who my friends are. I came in the front door, and I'm going out that way." And so everyone exited the front doors, ready to face the cameras.

But did it happen that way? Although the overwhelming majority of accounts support the story,[8] a few state that some people, indeed, used the side entrance, and some sources are ultimately contradictory.[9] But most participants clearly went out the front, and Troy Perry believes that this event dates the birth of the gay rights movement in New Orleans.[10]

If that's true, the city's LGBT community owes a debt of gratitude to that one courageous woman. But who was she? Though many people recall her words, nobody, then or now, seems to know who she was.[11] And at least one person has claimed that it wasn't even a woman. The Reverend Paul Breton, one of the MCC ministers who came to town after the fire, believes it was the young African-American man who accepted Breton's invitation to attend the memorial, not the white woman that most people remember.[12] So was it the older white woman, or was it the young black man? In some senses, it scarcely matters; the effect upon the crowd was the same.

Then there is the final question of whether the television crews were actually outside; nearly every account ends with people walking out the front door to meet the cameras. Some accounts say that by the time people left the church, the cameras had already gone away. Stewart Butler doesn't think that alters the importance, saying, "We knew they had been there. And we all went out to face them." This is echoed by Troy Perry, who said in a telephone interview,

"In a very real way, it doesn't matter that there were no cameras. People had believed they were there, and they were willing to go out and face them, anyway. That's what was important."

At least one person who had been at the service recalls that there was, indeed, a television crew with a camera, and that Troy Perry, leading the congregation out of the church, saw the camera and walked right up to it so that the focus would be on him rather than the other people leaving the church. "I don't want to be quoted saying this," the witness said in 2009, "but Troy Perry never saw a television camera he didn't like. And I know this happened, because I remember going home and watching the story on WWL's ten o'clock news." Unfortunately, WWL no longer has its archives from the early 1970s; it has sent them to the Louisiana State Archives in Baton Rouge, and the State Archives has no record of broadcasts concerning the Up Stairs Lounge. If there was one television crew present, WWL is the likeliest; its headquarters are on North Rampart Street just one block up the street from St. Mark's Methodist Church where the memorial was held.

On the night of the fire, the few survivors willing to speak to television journalists would only do so if their faces were not filmed. The risks of being publicly identified as possibly homosexual were too great. A week later a church full of mourners decided to walk out in public together. "That was such a wonderful moment," Toni Pizanie said in 2009. "We went from being hated, to showing a sense of pride and unity." Soon there was a flurry of gay activism.

One of the most visible local effects of the fire was the founding of a group called the Gay People's Coalition (GPC), a group which, for some members, represented "a personal story moving across the history of their lives and culminating in a commitment growing out of the fire tragedy at the Up Stairs" ("Who is the GPC?" 1). Hoping to be a "stronger link in an old chain" previously forged by the activity of earlier, short-lived groups such as the Gay Liberation Front and the Daughters of Bilitis, the GPC threw itself into its work. Within a month of the fire, the GPC announced the opening of a gay V.D. clinic on North Rampart "with the help of Head Clinic" ("Who Is the GPC?" 1). Harkening back to a time before HIV and AIDS, when STDs were referred to more commonly as venereal diseases, and when syphilis and gonorrhea were the most dreaded infections, the clinic was designed to help gay people who were afraid to go to their regular physicians because it could mean outing themselves to a potentially unsympathetic doctor.

The GPC helped establish a gay counseling committee and a gay information switchboard committee "to aid gay brothers and sisters with their personal and social problems" ("Who Is the GPC?" 1). It also started a gay news outlet, *The New Orleans Causeway*. This punning title has a reference to the local geography; Lake Pontchartrain, one of the boundaries of the city, connects to parishes to the north by a 24-mile-long bridge called the Causeway, which was for many years the longest bridge in the world. The title of the paper refers to this bridge, but also alludes to the mission of the paper, which was to be a way for gay and lesbian causes to be advanced. It had been preceded by a small paper called *The Sunflower*, distributed by the Gay Liberation Front (GLF), which had a brief existence in the city in 1970–71.[13] An editorial in the second issue of *The Causeway* claimed that *The Causeway* was "the first Gay newspaper to originate in the New Orleans area" (Estavan and Hargrove 5), but it really seems to have picked up where *The Sunflower* had left off.

The Causeway is very much a product of its time, filled with references to gay brothers and sisters, notices about the formation of "rap groups" (i.e., discussion groups), articles about the progress of the Equal Rights Amendment (ERA), and advertisements for gay bars such as The Grog, which featured "Dancing in the Psychedelic Room." The New Orleans chapter of the MCC and the congregation of St. Mark's Methodist were both heavily involved with the GPC and feature prominently in articles in *The Causeway*. The MCC headquarters in Bill Larson's former home on Magazine Street housed the gay information switchboard, and St. Mark's Methodist donated space to Head Clinic and the gay V.D. clinic.

The GPC and *The Causeway* gave a face to the gay community at a time when it was important that the community have one. Mayor Moon Landrieu, who had been criticized for his silence and inaction in the aftermath of the fire, apparently tried to make amends by taking belated action and giving support to the gay community in a tangible, public way. In early August, just six weeks after the fire, Mayor Landrieu met with the GPC and appointed gay and lesbian representatives to his own Human Relations Committee (HRC),[14] a body that existed to make sure the needs of the city's various constituencies were being addressed.[15] Previously it had been primarily concerned with race relations. Addressing the concerns of gays and lesbians constituted a real shift in its mission. A spokesperson for the mayor stated that "the idea is to get people to see that homosexuals are not just freaks they see on the street, but people they work with and respect" ("HRC to Attack Gay Problems" 17). An article covering the announcement noted that "the [Gay People's Coalition] has worked with the HRC staff since the Up Stairs fire on how city government can best respond to the problems confronting homosexuals" ("HRC to Attack Gay Problems" 17). The first gay and lesbian appointees to the HRC were the Reverend Lucien Baril, the MCC minister who became acting pastor after Bill Larson's death; Bill Rushton, the journalist for the *Vieux Carré Courier* who had criticized both Mayor Landrieu and Archbishop Hannan for their silence in the weeks immediately following the fire; and Celeste Newbrough, director of research for an organization called Total Community Action, Inc. In a little more than a month, the HRC prepared a list of recommendations for actions the city could take. These included ongoing meetings and cooperation between the GPC and the HRC, referrals to GPC services by the city switchboard, and issuance of a full report on the problems faced by the local gay community, though the HRC's deputy director, Bill Stewart, noted that the HRC really did not have adequate staff to meet all those needs.[16]

Although getting even this far was an impressive step forward, there were already signs of trouble. Even before the GPC and HRC issued their joint recommendation, Celeste Newbrough was announcing her intention to separate from the GPC. She said, "I feel the things I, as a lesbian, want can be gained through women's liberation. I feel the aims of the Coalition will be of benefit to men. I don't disagree with this, but I will put my energies where they will help me" (Treadway "A Walk on the Gay Side" 8). Newbrough went on to explain that many of the members of GPC were interested in changing laws that resulted in men being arrested while looking for sex partners, which was of much less concern to lesbians, who tended not to engage in those behaviors, and were, therefore, rarely arrested by the vice squad.[17] This would be far from the last time that the aims and goals of gay men and lesbians were either unrelated to or in conflict with each other.

There were other conflicts as well. One of the early goals of the GPC was to get as many gays and lesbians to come out of the closet as possible. "This will either cause a great deal of embarrassment or cause them to be accepted," a GPC spokesperson said ("HRC to Attack Gay Problems" 17). A 2009 study suggests that, even in the twenty-first century, a majority of gays and lesbians still prefer to remain closeted in the workplace,[18] so the GPC's strategy, in 1973, was more than some people could take; a man speaking to *The Times–Picayune* on condition of anonymity was soon quoted as saying, "The Coalition and other similar organizations too often parade [homosexuality] in the wrong way; I'm not for parades" (Treadway "Walk on the Gay Side" 8).

With so many conflicting goals and points of view, it isn't surprising that the GPC and its news venue, *The Causeway*, didn't last much longer than the Gay Liberation Front had earlier in the decade. The eighth issue of *The Causeway* was published in August of 1974, and both the newspaper and the GPC disappear from view shortly afterward. It would be a mistake, though, to assume that efforts such as the GPC and *The Causeway* bore no fruit. Descendants of *The Sunflower* and *The Causeway*, for example, include *Impact*, a gay and lesbian alternative paper that ran from 1977 to 2000. For nearly twenty years it was one of two New Orleans-based gay newspapers, the other one being *Ambush*, which started running in 1982 and is still being published. Larry Raybourne, a former Up Stairs patron, is proud of the fact that he has written articles for all three publications.[19]

Similarly, while the GPC faded, its lasting legacy was getting the mayor to publicly acknowledge the GLBT community and to appoint its members to a standing city hall committee. Gay and lesbian liaisons have served every mayor since Moon Landrieu, either as citizen appointees of the HRC or in another capacity. For many years, one such representative was Toni Pizanie, who, along with Carol Tully, developed a course of training sessions to acquaint police, firefighters and EMTs with gay and lesbian concerns. She and Tully soon learned that the firefighters weren't particularly interested in learning from them, and that the EMTs didn't really need the training. During the sessions, the EMTs would laugh as if to say, "We already know this," and in a 2009 interview, Pizanie said, "My gaydar went off pretty loudly in a room full of EMTs." Pizanie concentrated, then, on training the police, where she could do the most good. Unfortunately, Pizanie said, such training stopped under Mayor Ray Nagin,[20] despite the fact that it was mandated by city ordinance.[21] Pizanie died in 2010. She would have been happy to know that in 2012, Mayor Mitch Landrieu (son of Moon Landrieu), along with Barack Obama's attorney general, Eric Holder, unveiled "a bevy of sweeping reforms" intended to address civil rights violations by the New Orleans police, including "measures dealing with how police investigate and handle sexual assault and domestic violence cases, as well as how officers deal with lesbian, gay and transgendered people" (McCarthy).

Even though the GPC did not last long as an entity, other groups soon took its place. Three of these are the Gertrude Stein Society, which formed in 1975, the Louisiana Gay Political Action Caucus (LAGPAC), which formed in 1980, and the Forum For Equality, which established a New Orleans chapter in 1989. Together with other long-lived groups such as the MCC, NO/AIDS (founded in 1982), and the New Orleans chapter of P-FLAG (also founded 1982) there has been no shortage of "homophile" organizations in the city for many years.

In some ways, the most important political activity connected to the fire wasn't local at all; it was a brief, national project intended to provide aid and support to survivors of the Up Stairs, both those who were injured by the blaze, and those who lost loved ones in it. This was the creation of the National New Orleans Memorial Fund.

Credit for this can be given to the activists who had been called the "fairy carpetbaggers." Troy Perry announced the formation of the fund during that week in New Orleans, and trustees included all of the MCC ministers and gay activists who had come to the city after the fire. The Reverend Lucien

Baril, who took over the New Orleans MCC after Bill Larson's death, was also a trustee (though he was later replaced by Chris Gamble, a member of the New Orleans Gay People's Coalition). An important addition to the group was Dick Michaels, who lived in Los Angeles and was the owner of *The Advocate*, then as now one of the nation's premier news publications for gay and lesbian readers. *The Advocate* acted as custodian of the fund,[22] and it regularly reported both on the amounts coming in and on how those funds had been disbursed. By August 1, the fund had topped $1,400. Soon, *The Advocate* reported it had reached the $5,000 mark, then $7,200, then $15,500, then $16,500. In the end, it collected nearly $18,000.[23]

The records from the fund are currently in the ONE National Gay & Lesbian Archives. The list of donations received shows that they started coming in as early as June 30, 1973, and were received as late as October of 1974, though the vast majority of them were made within four months of the fire. In a 2010 telephone interview, Troy Perry said, "I've also had lots of people come up to me and say, 'You know, I made a $5,000 donation to the relief efforts after the fire,' and I've thought, "If only that were true!'"[24]

Most of the donations came from individuals and were for very small amounts. Gifts of $5 or $10 far outnumber those of $25 or more. Of those donations that were $100 or more, most came from the various branches of the MCC and were clearly the result of fundraising activities. In July of 1973, for example, the New York chapter donated $237, the San Jose chapter donated $276, and the Tampa chapter donated $334. Smaller amounts came from chapters of Dignity, an organization for gay and lesbian Catholics, as well as from Integrity, a similar organization for Episcopalians. Only four donations were more than $500, and they were all from businesses: Club Miami Baths and *The Advocate* both donated $500, the Warehouse VIII in Miami donated $1,000, and the Up North Bar in Chicago donated $1,500. Although most of the checks were not very large, there were a lot of them, and they came in from all over the country: New York, Boston, Philadelphia, Baltimore, Atlanta, Jacksonville, Detroit, Chicago, Houston, Phoenix, Denver, Boulder, San Jose, Los Angeles and San Francisco.

A small portion of the money went to reimburse Troy Perry and the other activists for their travel costs after the fire or to pay administrative costs of the fund, but these were meager amounts. Larger sums went to help bury the dead. The Memorial Fund helped defray the funeral and cremation costs for Bill Larson, for example, and also to help pay for the funeral of Clarence McCloskey.

Much of the money went to people who were injured in the fire to cover medical expenses or living costs while they recovered from their injuries. Grants were given, for example, to Earl Thomas and Fred Sharohway, lovers who escaped by going directly into the flame-filled stairwell and running through the fire to the street. Other grants were given to Roger "Dale" Dunn, Sidney Espinache, Eddie Gillis, and Michael Scarborough, all of whom had significant injuries, leaving them with large medical expenses and limited or no ability to work in the months after the fire.[25]

A grant of a very different sort went to a woman named Jane Golding. She was the widow of John Golding, who had died in the fire. She had previously known about his homosexuality, and the two of them had worked out a relationship that allowed him a certain amount of freedom. They kept both his sexuality and their arrangement quiet, and few, if any of their friends knew about it.[26] When John was identified in the newspapers as a casualty of the fire, his sexuality and the nature of the Golding marriage were both effectively "outed." Jane was not only left to live on a small Social Security survivor's benefit of $275 per month, but when the summer ended, her twelve-year-old son was bullied at school because of John's homosexuality. The harassment he experienced was so severe that the fund sent her money to put him in a private school where, Morris Kight was able to report, "he is happy for the first time" (Records, National New Orleans Memorial Fund).

Another of the beneficiaries of the fund was Jean Gosnell, one of the two women in the bar when of the fire broke out. The other woman, Inez Warren, had died along with her two sons, Eddie and James. Jean, a straight woman, had been in the bar partially because she lived across the street, and partially to meet Luther Boggs, one of her gay friends who frequented the Up Stairs.

In March of 1974, Jean Gosnell was the subject of a feature story in *The Advocate*, titled "Yesterday's Dreams, Today's Ghosts." She talked about her life in the French Quarter and her friendship with Luther Boggs (who escaped the bar only to die later of his injuries). She also discussed the difficulties of trying to rebuild her life after spending months in the hospital, much of it in the intensive care unit, as she received multiple skin grafts and other treatments for her injuries. She talked about being discharged from the hospital, of not being able to work, and spoke enthusiastically of her appreciation for the assistance she received from the fund.[27]

Later that year, the memorial fund paid to fly her to Los Angeles, where she took part in that year's Gay Pride celebration. An unsigned article with the title "Survivor Discovers Her True Friends" describes her riding down Hollywood Boulevard as a featured guest in the Gay Pride parade, and addressing a crowd in a park at Sunset and Cherokee, telling them, "I'm straight—I can't help it—I was born that way" (8). The same article also describes Gosnell relating how many of her straight friends jumped to the conclusion that she was a lesbian when it was discovered that she had been in the fire, and then deserted her as a result of their prejudice. She said, "I think I understand some things better" (8).

A short article just beneath the profile of Jean Gosnell noted that the fund had, at that point, received donations totaling $17,900, and had disbursed $13,800. Morris Kight, speaking as a trustee, noted that "most of the $13,800 spent so far has gone for hospital and medical bills, plastic surgery, burial costs and survival needs" ("Fire Fund Gives $13,800" 8). Records of the National New Orleans Memorial Fund, currently in the ONE National Gay & Lesbian Archives, show that Jean Gosnell and several other survivors continued to receive necessary financial assistance throughout 1974 and even into 1975.[28]

Just as the most important political activity that resulted from the Up Stairs fire may have had less to do with local activism than it did with a national relief effort, the most important media activity had less to do with the genesis of sustained New Orleans gay news outlets than it did with a shift in how local mainstream news outlets began to treat gay and lesbian issues.

This is easiest to gauge in looking at *The Times–Picayune*, the only one of the three local daily papers from 1973 that is still in existence, and the only one that was indexed in the early 1970s, making it a useful tool for media research. A signpost indicating a new direction came with a six-part series on homosexuality run by *The Times–Picayune* in September of 1973, explicitly in response to the fire at the Up Stairs lounge. The series is very much of its period. In the first installment, for example, staff reporter Joan Treadway felt compelled to write that as a result of the fire "people across the country and New Orleanians themselves were confronted with the fact that the city has an active homosexual community which does not magically appear on Mardi Gras, but which exists year round" ("Gay Community Surfaces" 13). Today it is hard to imagine even the most conservative resident of a major city needing a journalist to explain that there are, in fact, gay people in town. Treadway's series put an abrupt end to an informal policy of "Don't Ask, Don't Tell"[29] that had existed in the New Orleans press for many years.

The Times–Picayune and other local papers had written about gays or lesbians before, but the coverage tended to be rather incurious and unsympathetic, despite the fact that *The Times–Picayune*, like other local news outlets, had a number of gay and lesbian staff members. In a 2013 interview, longtime New Orleans journalist Clancy DuBos said, "We knew who the gay people on the newspaper staff were, but nobody talked about it."[30] In addition, *The Times–Picayune*, like other newspapers of the period, often avoided controversial stories and hard-hitting editorials. Clancy DuBos says today that *The Times–Picayune* "was a crappy paper back then, but it wasn't crappy because it was anti-gay. It was crappy because it was crappy."

What was its typical coverage of gay issues like in the early 1970s? In the eighteen months leading up to the fire, there were only a handful of articles dealing with homosexuality, and the coverage in the first six months of 1973 is representative. The first of these was only tangentially about homosexuality, part of a series on the use of electroshock and chemical therapies in the treatment of alcoholism. With these two forms of treatment included under the umbrella of behavior modification therapy, the article in question quoted Dr. James T. Henry of Charity Hospital as saying that electroshock and chemical therapies also held great promise for other character disorders, "such as habitual criminal tendencies and homosexuality" (Lee "The Way Back" 15). A few days later, *The Times–Picayune* published a letter from a James H. Patterson who wrote, in protest, "There is much recent literature on the subject of homosexuality, but your paper chooses to ignore it while perpetuating the irrational social prejudice against homosexuals"(8). As if this letter had never been published, *The Times–Picayune* soon ran a story featuring an interview with Catholic theologian the Reverend Christopher J. O'Toole, C.S.C. The entire point of this article was to give Father O'Toole an opportunity to state that there was no place for homosexuals in the Catholic church. O'Toole wrote that it was "a contradiction" to believe that a person could be a homosexual and a practicing Catholic at the same time" ("Position Taken" 20). O'Toole went on to say that the church's position did not rule out friendships between two men or two women, but that it did "utterly rule out the developing of such friendships into a style of life which is so plainly condemned by Revelations[31] and the Church" ("Position Taken" 20).

The next two *Times–Picayune* stories both concern male rape in prison, a serious problem to be sure, but one which has less to do with sexual orientation than it does with rape being a tool for inspiring fear and maintaining control over others; many prison rapists are, in fact, heterosexual, and these particular stories detail a pattern of rapists choosing victims specifically because they were of a different race, suggesting that domination and humiliation were the goals of the attacks.[32]

Another story, which came through the AP wire services, was just over 50 words, and refers to activities of the MCC in California (although the name of the organization is incorrectly reported). The story documents SCOTUS Justice William O. Douglas refusing without comment to lift a ban that prevented the MCC from going into California prisons for the purpose of ministering to gay inmates.[33]

This brief sampling suggests how homosexuals and homosexuality were normally treated in New Orleans newspapers prior to the fire at the Up Stairs Lounge; gays and lesbians were assumed to be people with character disorders and criminal tendencies. They were potential rapists, unworthy of participation in mainstream Christian churches, and sometimes legally disallowed from participating in the churches that would accept them.

Other than James Patterson's letter in response to Dr. Henry's remarks, there is only one exception to this pattern. On May 14, just over a month before the fire, *The Times–Picayune* ran a photo of someone who appears to be a large-eyed, dark-haired woman wearing a glittering tiara and a pearl necklace. She was actually Lady Baronessa, a drag queen from Chicago who had just been crowned Miss Gay America, and who said that one of her goals was to use the title to try and unite gay people with straights.[34] Immediately next to Lady Baronessa's picture is a story announcing that Archbishop Hannan would be saying the commencement mass for the graduating class of St. Mary's Dominican, a private Catholic college for women. One suspects that both the decision to run the coverage of Lady Baronessa and the decision to place it next to a story mentioning the archbishop were made by one of the closeted gay staffers.

With the pre-fire coverage of homosexuality having been both sparse and overwhelmingly negative, Joan Treadway's six-part series in response to the fire almost certainly had to be an improvement. Today, Clancy DuBos says, "If *The Picayune* was running a six-part series on homosexuality, by the standards of the time, they were really stepping out."[35]

The first installment, which ran on September 13, is titled "Gay Community Surfaces in Tragedy of N.O. Fire." The article both confirmed that the Up Stairs fire served as a catalyst for an increasing sense of community among gays and lesbians, and acknowledged the role of the "nationally known gay liberation leaders who arrived in the city soon after the fire" (13). Treadway talked about the activities of the GPC and the MCC, and she detailed some of the problems faced by the city's gays and lesbians, particularly those whose appearance or behavior didn't conform to gender norms, or those whose sexuality was discovered: employment and housing discrimination, blackmail, violence, the ever-present threat of arrest. Treadway also discussed the recent inclusion of openly gay and lesbian people in the mayor's Human Relations Committee, noting the strong contrast with the actions of city officials and police officers who met in 1958 to discuss the best methods for reducing the city's gay and lesbian population.

Treadway's second article was titled "A Walk on the Gay Side: Independent Route Taken for Personal Objectives." It basically acknowledged the diversity of goals and points of view among the city's gays and lesbians. It is in this article that Treadway reported Celeste Newbrough's decision to leave the GPC and concentrate on women's liberation because of the differing concerns of gay men and lesbians. It is also in this article that Treadway quoted the anonymous man who was highly critical of the GPC, saying that the organization was making itself too public, and in the process, making a "parade" of homosexuality (8). Treadway revealed another line of division among gays when she quoted a man who carefully separated himself from people who do not conform to gender expectations: "I'm not a screaming faggot who dresses in women's clothes. Those people are sick!" (8).

When Treadway raised the question of possible conversion to heterosexuality, Newbrough and one of the anonymous men said that they believed conversion was possible, although they also said that they weren't particularly interested in trying to convert; the second anonymous man talked about seeing a psychiatrist who advised him that his best bet for happiness was to accept himself as he was.[36]

Part three of the series ran under the headline "Homosexuals Disagree on Behavior's 'Sickness,'" suggesting that Treadway would examine the different views gay people had regarding whether homosexuality was a disease. In point of fact, she contrasted how some gay people viewed homosexuality with what three local psychiatrists thought. It is important to recall that this appeared in September of 1973, three months before the trustees of the American Psychiatric Association would pass a resolution stating that homosexuality should no longer be considered a mental disorder,[37] which means this article appeared at a particularly sensitive moment in time, one during which mental health professionals were debating the very issues Treadway's article raised.

Treadway opened by asking Celeste Newbrough and Morty Manford if they thought homosexuality was an illness or a disorder. Newbrough and Manford both described it in morally neutral terms, saying that it was merely a behavioral variant as old as human behavior itself.[38] When Treadway turned her attention to the views of the psychiatrists, she noted that two of the three men she interviewed considered homosexuality a sexual deviation as defined by the then-current (but soon to be outdated) diagnostic manual. When Treadway concluded that "a majority of the more vocal homosexuals hold the same opinion as only a minority of American psychiatrists" (2), she appeared to be taking a side. And it wasn't Manford's and Newbrough's.

The article is a time capsule of late twentieth-century stereotypes and misinformation. Dr. John Paul Pratt, former head of the Louisiana Psychiatric Association, stated that homosexuality was only "a component" of his gay patients' problems. Although he acknowledged that, for some, homosexuality was an incidental factor in why they sought treatment, he also said that "all male homosexual relationships are 'fragile' and riddled with fear and suspicion" (Treadway "Homosexuals Disagree" 2). Dr. Arthur Epstein, a professor of psychiatry at Tulane, said that the general professional consensus was that homosexuality was a "failure in psycho-sexual maturation" (2). Dr. C.B. Scrignar, also of Tulane, gave rather ambiguous (and grammatically challenged) responses. He first said, "I disagree that it's a disorder, under the condition that it's a real relationship, and it's the same situation with heterosexuals." He then went on to say:

> There is a lot of promiscuity among homosexuals, and that kind of thing I think is sick, in contrast with two people who meet and decide they want to live together to share not only sex, but their lives. This is an individual choice [2].

The issue of conversion to heterosexuality was raised, of course, because whether homosexuality was a "disorder" or merely "a failure of psycho-sexual maturation," conversion would amount to a cure. Dr. Pratt said he thought conversion was possible, and mentioned that he knew of several men who had cured themselves, married, and had families. Therapy to achieve such goals, known as reparative therapy or conversion therapy, has long since been abandoned by the APA as ineffective, at best,[39] and so potentially harmful in its assumptions and effects that the state of California recently passed a law making it illegal for a parent to seek out such therapy for a minor child.[40]

Treadway questioned the psychiatrists about possible causes of homosexuality. Dr. Epstein acknowledged that genetics, hormonal factors, or even the brain itself might play a role (views that are generally accepted today), but he also spoke of homosexuality being caused when men had "an early traumatic experience with a female" (2). Dr. Pratt said that "the weak or absent father and dominant mother family background is typical among homosexuals," though he was careful to note that "there are many exceptions" (2). Addressing these exceptions, Dr. Scrignar discussed how it was possible that homosexuality might be cured by "a good experience with the opposite sex during adolescence" (2). Causes and potential cures for lesbianism were never addressed.

Installment four, "Psychiatric and Clerical Views—A Wide Spectrum," shifted the focus of the series from what psychiatrists thought to what local priests, ministers, and rabbis thought.

The Reverend Lucien Baril, who had assumed Bill Larson's post after Larson died in the fire, was allowed to speak about the views of the MCC. However, Baril's gay-inclusive views were starkly contrasted with those of another man[41]: the Reverend Bob Harrington, a Baptist evangelical minister based in the French Quarter, known since 1963 as "the Chaplain of Bourbon Street." Though Treadway had been careful to note in this article that none of the three psychiatrists she had interviewed thought that there was anything *evil* about homosexuality, the Rev. Harrington disagreed. He launched into an attack on the MCC position, saying that if the preachers in such a church condone homosexuality, "they're anti–Christs, enemies to God in clerical garb" (18). The Reverend Hilton Rivet, a Catholic priest and prison chaplain, described homosexuality as a moral failing, but conceded that other sins—like hatred—might be worse. Regarding possible conversion to heterosexuality[42] (a question which was clearly on Treadway's mind, as she raised it in five of the six installments), Rivet said, "There's nothing someone can't do if they want to; the means are something else" (18). Means that he thought might be useful were psychiatry, counseling, "or just moving out of a neighborhood like the Quarter" (18).

Other than Lucien Baril, the two most gay-inclusive clergy were also the only two non–Christians. Rabbi Benjamin Kroner said there was no way to tell if homosexuality was inherently sinful; he described it (as Manford and Newbrough had) in terms of being a behavioral variant. He was echoed by Rabbi Leo Bergman, who said that consenting adults had the right to determine the course of their own lives.[43]

Part five, "It's Not Illegal to BE Gay—Certain Acts Are Criminal," focused on legal concerns. Treadway interviewed a variety of policemen, city officials and judges. Police Chief Clarence Giarrusso described homosexuality as a "social as well as a police problem" (14). Giarrusso's concern was that if an adolescent were to be seduced by an older man, it might "deprive the child or adolescent at a later date of the right to make a mature decision on what he personally wants to be" (14). If psychiatrist Dr. Scrignar believed that a single well-timed sexual experience could turn a gay adolescent into a straight one, Giarrusso seemed to believe that a single, ill-timed experience might turn a straight adolescent gay. While Giarrusso suggested that he did not *personally* have a problem with sexual activity between two consenting adults of the same gender, he also favored keeping homosexual activity illegal, because if it were to become legal, "someone would build a glass house" (14).

Chief Assistant District Attorney John Volz addressed gay men being entrapped by police and arrested for sexual activity. He denied that entrapment took place, but admitted that it had in the past. Addressing current police practices, he said that recent arrests on charges related to homosexuality were, at most, "borderline entrapment" (14). Treadway neglected to ask for a definition of what "borderline entrapment" might be. Nor did she report the fact that morals laws had recently been broadened so that police did not have to catch someone in a forbidden sexual act to make an arrest; instead, all police had to do was be able to show "criminal intent" ("The Law" 5). In other articles in her series, Treadway had been careful to reflect a spectrum of points of view, interviewing, for example, multiple members of the clergy ranging from the gay-friendly Lucien Baril to the anti-gay "Chaplain of Bourbon Street." For this article, she did not interview people who had actually been arrested on morals charges to ask what had happened during the arrest, or whether they had considered their arrest to be a case of entrapment.

In fairness, Assistant District Attorney Volz did voice support for modifying existing so-called "crimes against nature" laws to allow two adults to engage in consensual sexual behavior in private, saying that enforcement of existing laws couldn't take place without infringing on a person's right to privacy. And, in point of fact, at this time the "crimes against nature" laws in Louisiana applied, in theory, to all citizens, whether straight, gay, lesbian or bisexual. All non-procreative sexual activity was technically illegal, and Treadway's article pointed out that a New Orleans criminal judge, Charles Ward, had recently opined that the law was, or should be, unconstitutional. For a while, some gays and lesbians thought that this meant their sex lives would be decriminalized,[44] until Judge Ward clarified that he felt that laws should be repealed only as they applied to heterosexual couples.[45] Another judge, Bernard Bagert, said that he had noticed a decline in homosexuals being brought to court on charges related to consensual sexual activity, which he thought was good, as the police had more important things to do than arrest people for consensual sexual activity. When asked how he approached such crimes in court, he said that rather than send someone to jail, he preferred to order the offender to get psychiatric treatment. Bagert was careful to state that he thought that if someone were to propose a nondiscrimination ordinance to protect gays and lesbians, he felt it should have limits, saying, for example, that he wouldn't want a homosexual leading a troop of Boy Scouts.[46] Judge Bagert, like police chief Giarrusso, was clearly conflating homosexuality with pedophilia, a confusion that persists today, and that has, in fact, traditionally been part of the reason that the Boy Scouts of America has refused to allow openly gay troop leaders—or openly gay members. The BSA recently seemed to be softening this position, announcing in 2013 that it was giving consideration to allowing troops to either drop or maintain the ban on an individual basis.[47] Later in the year, the BSA voted to allow gay scouts, but said that gay scout leaders would still be banned.[48]

The last article in the series bore the title "50s 'Climate of Hostility' to Gays Gone—What Now?" Treadway opened by referencing an initiative the city had taken in 1958 to rid the city of homosexuals. She noted that in 1973, just fifteen years later, official municipal will to continue the effort had largely dissipated. Attorney Jacob Morrison, who had once headed a citizens committee to help rid the city of gays, expressed sadness that the city had become more tolerant, saying that he thought New Orleans was in danger of becoming "the queer capital of the U.S." (Treadway "50s Climate" 21). Treadway noted that in past years complaints about homosexuals had come from the View Carré

Property Owners and Associates, who were now just as likely to field complaints about hippies and Jesus freaks. The association's president, John Dodt, said that some of the complaints about gay men might be misdirected, with many people reflexively associating long hair with homosexuality. Dodt conceded that the Quarter and the city as a whole were probably home to many law-abiding gays and lesbians. Moving even further toward a position of tolerance, Harry J. Blumenthal, Jr., a member of the city's HRC who was working with the committee's recently-appointed gay representatives, said that he felt the city needed to give serious attention to the complaints that gays and lesbians faced discrimination in housing and public accommodation.[49]

The article closed by talking more about the cooperation of the HRC and the GPC, as well as about the attempts of students at Tulane University to get official recognition for a gay students union, an effort that had started a year earlier, and that would continue for several more. The article—and the series—ended with the rather equivocal statement, "It is apparent that some New Orleanians no longer feel that the homosexual subculture is hidden and is itself a community problem, but that it is surfacing and that it has its own problems" ("50s Climate" 21).

News coverage of the fire had prompted a lively exchange of letters to the editor two and a half months earlier, but the response to this series was considerably more subdued, generating only four letters. One came from James Patterson, who, earlier in the year, had objected to an article in which a Charity Hospital physician had included homosexuality in a list of mental illnesses that could be cured through electroshock and chemical therapies.[50] Patterson complained (with justification) that the Treadway series was a compilation of anti-gay stereotypes. He wrote at length about the misguided and inaccurate portrayals of homosexuality advanced by the psychiatrists, and criticized the emphasis on conversion therapy as well. Addressing Treadway's interview with police and criminal judges, he criticized police chief Giarrusso and Judge Bagert for their conflation of homosexuality with pedophilia, arguing that such misconceptions served to create and reinforce discriminatory law enforcement practices. In a reference to how the people interviewed in the Treadway series often demonized or pathologized gays and lesbians, Patterson wrote, "People who see homogoblins need help" (14).

A few days later, *The Times–Picayune* ran a letter by the Reverend Richard C. Arceneaux, Jr., who responded by attempting to explain to Patterson, "a few pertinent facts" (12), most of which had to do arguing that certain biblical passages amounted to God opposing homosexuality and lesbianism.[51]

The third letter generated by the series was by Etienne Somme, who said that the Reverend Arceneaux's letter was "an example of the thinking that has driven so many people away from the organized church" (10). Somme pointed out that many issues of translation and transcription open even seemingly clear Bible verses to interpretation and conjecture. Identifying himself as a member of the Gay Liberation Front (though that organization seems to have been dormant in 1973), Somme actually spoke out in favor of the Treadway series, focusing not so much on its content as on its intent: a genuine (if heavily flawed) effort by Joan Treadway to understand a complex set of social, cultural and psychological issues, and to transmit that understanding to a reading public that, for the most part, had no knowledge of homosexual behavior outside of stereotyped media portrayals. If her series is occasionally myopic, naïve, or cringe-inducing, it is perhaps because a layperson's understanding of forty years ago is being judged by twenty-first century standards.

It's important to remember that uncloseted gays or lesbians were very much a rarity in the 1970s. Many well meaning, well educated people didn't know any GLBT people—or at least they didn't know that they knew any. Sigmund Freud famously believed that all women were neurotic and maladjusted because he was unable to distinguish between his female psychiatric patients (a group who, by definition, *were* neurotic and maladjusted) and the female population at large. The psychiatrists interviewed by Joan Treadway probably had a similar experience in relation to homosexuality; the only gay and lesbian people they knew were their unhappy patients. Therefore, it made sense to them to think that all gay and lesbian people must be unhappy. Similarly, many police officers and judges probably didn't know any openly gay or lesbian people, save for the ones that they encountered in their work.

Gay writer Dan Savage grew up in the 1960s and 1970s the son of a policeman. Writing about the anti-gay attitudes his father harbored then, Savage states that the attitudes came from "ignorance, not malice," and adds,

> It didn't help that my dad was a Chicago homicide detective whose beat included Chicago's gay neighborhood. In the seventies, gay neighborhoods were not filled with trendy restaurants, pricey condos, and rainbow geegaws. They were filled with sleazy bars, male hustlers, and violent predators. Before I came out to my father, most of the gay men he'd met were murderers [168].

Gay writers today frequently argue that the single most important political act an LGBT person can perform is to come out to family, friends and coworkers; it is easy to believe negative stereotypes about homosexuals when the people they apply to remain abstract, but it is much harder to harbor such views about one's brother, son, daughter, niece or colleague. If psychiatrists and law enforcement personnel in the 1970s neglected to get to know LGBT people other than those they encountered in their work, LGBT people were actively working toward the goal of not being known. In remaining closeted, they became complicit.

A final letter written in response to Treadway's series pointed in the direction in which social views of homosexuality would move in coming decades. It is assigned the title "Souls Laundered," and is signed "A Square Grandma." The letter speaks both about the love God has for all people, and the power some churches have of turning people away from organized religion. The letter also says, "My grandchildren are all wonderful; whatever life-style they choose when they grow up, they'll still be wonderful" (14).

Did the Treadway series have any lasting effect? Did it signal a shift to a new way of covering gay issues in what is, effectively, the single most important New Orleans newspaper?

In 1974 there were only four articles specifically related to gay issues in *The Times–Picayune*, and all presented homosexuals and homosexuality in a positive light. One was a brief story from the AP wire services about a court ruling in favor of an attempt to form an organization for homosexual students at the University of New Hampshire.[52] Two were letters to the editor protesting a recent statement of Archbishop Hannan (not published in *The Times–Picayune*) in which he had referred to homosexuals as enemies of the family.[53] The fourth article, and the only one actually generated by a staff reporter for *The Times–Picayune*, ran under the title "Church Strives Following Fire." This unsigned article is a respectful profile of the efforts of the local chapter of the MCC to rebuild after losing much of its membership "in the tragic Upstairs Lounge fire" (4).

In some ways, this article is most interesting for what it does not include. It does not include interviews with clergy of other denominations who debate the sinfulness of homosexuality or the appropriateness of a church for homosexuals. It does not include discussions of whether homosexuality is more accurately classified as a disease, a disorder or a natural variant of human behavior. It does not raise the question of whether conversion to heterosexuality is possible, practical, or even desirable. Instead, it merely documents a recent change in leadership and ongoing efforts to boost membership and raise funds. The article appears on a page devoted to religious news, quietly included among articles detailing the recent activities of local Baptist, Presbyterian and Catholic churches. Other than a brief, closing reference to its mission as promoting "a greater understanding and acceptance of the homosexual lifestyle as a valid way of life" (4), the MCC is not described as exceptional in any way, and that, perhaps, is what makes this article so exceptional.

In 1975, twenty-one articles on gay issues ran in *The Times–Picayune*. Many of these were related to the national coverage of the case of Sergeant Leonard

Matlovich who that year fought a valiant, but ultimately unsuccessful battle to remain in the military after disclosing to his commanding officer that he was gay. Other articles concerned local events.

One covered a colloquium at Tulane University in which Dr. Stephen F. Morin from the psychology department at California State College in San Bernardino discussed gay issues. The problem he identified was not homosexuality, but homophobia. He said, "People hate gays not so much for what they do as for their violation of traditional roles" ("Homophobia Causes Told" 15). His message was that we would all be better off if society allowed for more variation in human behavior.

Another covered the activities of Mary Morris, the worship coordinator of the New Orleans chapter of the MCC, who was giving pastoral counseling to gay and lesbian couples. Though the reporter, Nancy Weldon, referred to these couples as married, and though the article referred to the MCC performing ten such marriage services in the past year, Weldon was also careful to point out that these relationships had no legal standing, as they were not (and still are not) licensed or recognized by the state of Louisiana. Some of the marital issues Morris discussed were specific to gay and lesbian couples, such as how to communicate with a child from one partner's former "straight" marriage. Other issues, like the equitable division of housework, were "the kinds of situations that cause trouble in any marriage" (Weldon 40).

In 1976, *The Times–Picayune* indexed twenty-three articles on homosexuality, with an additional four under the subject heading "Gay Liberation." By 1977, the number had jumped to eighty. Many of these stories concerned national issues: the first inclusion of recurring, openly gay characters in television series, for example, or the recognition by businesses that gays represented a niche demographic that could be targeted through advertising.[54] Other stories covered the ongoing battle between Leonard Matlovich and the Air Force, and Anita Bryant's campaign in Dade County. Both of these stories acquired a local angle in June of 1977 when Anita Bryant came to perform in New Orleans, and when Sergeant Matlovich took part in the protests against her. While the coverage of the event was outwardly respectful of Bryant, it was equally respectful of the protesters. And when a quotation from Millie Ball's interview with Bryant was slightly paraphrased to serve as the title "'I'd Rather My Child Be Dead Than Homo,'" there was no escaping the implied criticism of the Bryant campaign.

Based on the paper trail left by *The Times–Picayune* in the years 1972–1977, then, it seems clear that the Up Stairs and the coverage it received, including the controversial Treadway series, did result in a shift in coverage of gay issues. Stories about homosexuality following the fire are not uniformly positive, but then neither was the behavior of gays and lesbians. A 1976 article, for example, noted a police crackdown on gay cruising in City Park, necessitated because parents were tired of not being able to take their children there without their kids seeing sexual activity.[55] Still, the greatest part of the coverage—and by a large margin—was respectful of gays and lesbians, and made an effort to go beyond stereotypes involving sin, mental illness and prison rape.

In regard to media coverage, then, there can be no doubt that an important corner had been turned, and the continued cooperation of the mayor's office and the LGBT community via the Human Relations Committee cannot be overlooked. Whether the fire served to implement a sustained gay activism is a much more open question. There is a gap between the dissolution of the GPC, which seems to have occurred in late 1974, and the Anita Bryant protests in 1977. Even the Gertrude Stein Society, which formed in 1975 and was instrumental in organizing the Anita Bryant protests, was not active in a noticeably public way in its first two years. The group most likely to attract attention was the MCC, which was more concerned with the spiritual than the political.

Ultimately, the gay activism stemming from the fire that is easiest to trace is the activism that memorialized the fire itself. In 1991–92, for example, the Louisiana State Museum put on an exhibit titled "Devouring Element," which commemorated notable fires in the city's history. Stewart Butler is a former Up Stairs patron who had been in the bar on the night of the fire, though he had been fortunate enough to leave before the fire started. He went to see the exhibit and was both angry and appalled to see that, while other fires received extensive coverage, the fire at the Up Stairs was completely ignored. "It did not include one mention of the Up Stairs Lounge!" Butler says today. "Not one! Rich Magill and I had gone to the exhibit, and we were horrified to see how that fire had been completely erased! It was the deadliest fire in the history in New Orleans, and it didn't get one single mention!" Butler and Magill complained to museum officials, and today Butler says, "They tried to excuse the omission by saying there wasn't anything about the Up Stairs in the exhibit because they had nothing to include." Butler pauses before adding, "It seems unlikely that this was true."

That is an understatement. If the museum staff were able, for example, to uncover documentary accounts of the two great fires in the city that occurred in the eighteenth century, they should have been able to dig up a few news clippings and archival photographs of the Up Stairs fire, which had occurred less than twenty years before. Speaking about the omission, Butler says, "I wouldn't be surprised if the museum had actively rejected any suggestion of including the Up Stairs Lounge."

Throughout most of the twentieth century, it was common for publishers, authors and museum curators to eliminate gay-themed topics or works from books, articles or exhibits, and to expunge or whitewash even passing references to homosexuality, referring to two cohabiting men, for example, as "confirmed bachelors," and sometimes embellishing or even inventing romances with women.[56] There is no way to tell the story of the Up Stairs without talking about homosexuality.

The museum's official position was and still is that they did not include the Up Stairs because they had not been able to find sufficient material.[57] Butler's and Magill's complaint had some effect though, and they and others kept the Up Stairs in the consciousness of the museum staff. As a result, in 1998 the museum staged an exhibit devoted solely to the Up Stairs fire as a commemoration of its twenty-fifth anniversary. As part of the exhibit, the museum hosted a panel discussion. The panelists included NOFD fire chief William McCrossen, who assisted in putting out the fire and removing the bodies; Courtney Craighead, a local MCC member who had been in the bar and managed to escape; Clancy DuBos, a journalist who reported from Charity Hospital the night of the fire, describing in detail the suffering experienced by survivors who had been brought there for treatment; and Johnny Townsend, then a New Orleans–based writer who had interviewed many of the survivors, and whose work later culminated in the only other book ever published about the fire, *Let the Faggots Burn*.[58] There were other commemorative events, including a memorial service organized by the MCC, which was conducted by the Reverend Troy Perry, who flew into New Orleans for the occasion.

There had already been multiple memorials for the fire—on the twentieth anniversary and the twenty-second, for example[59]—and there would be more in the future. In advance of the thirtieth anniversary, the Reverend Dexter Brecht, then the pastor of the New Orleans MCC, worked with Toni Pizanie and Donald St. Pierre. Together they raised funds to place a memorial plaque in the sidewalk on Iberville Street, right outside of what had been the entrance to the Up Stairs. To get municipal permission to place the memorial, they worked with Larry Bagneris, then the executive director of the mayor's Human Relations Committee.[60] Speaking about the plaque, he said that it was significant "because it not only marks history, but also makes a statement for the future. It is [Bagneris said,] one of only a few monuments in the country dedicated to the gay rights movement, a place where people can go to remember what was and what can be" (O'Brien E2). A large square of bronze, the plaque has a dark triangle motif in the center, the triangle a symbol both of homosexuality and of the oppression of homosexuals.[61] Above the triangle, an inscription reads, "At this site on June 24, 1973 in the Upstairs Lounge, these thirty-two people lost their lives in the worst fire in New Orleans. The impact

Today, a plaque in the sidewalk outside of the building that housed the Up Stairs Lounge commemorates the fire. When this photograph was taken, a recent pilgrim had decorated the plaque with two stickers denoting equality. The inscription at the top says, "At this site on June 24, 1973, in the Upstairs Lounge, these thirty-two people lost their lives in the worst fire in New Orleans. The impact went far beyond the loss of individual lives, giving birth to the Lesbian, Gay, Bisexual and Transgender rights movement in New Orleans." The names of the dead border the three sides of the triangle. Three are listed only as "Unidentified White Male" (author's photograph).

went far beyond the loss of individual lives, giving birth to the Lesbian, Gay, Bisexual and Transgender rights movement in New Orleans." The names of the dead follow the borders of the triangle.

Regarding the memorial plaque, local gay historian Robert Batson said, "The plaque is not accurate. The fire did not galvanize large numbers of gay people into activism. We have Anita Bryant to thank for that." Even if this is true, it is still undeniable that the Up Stairs had an effect on the city's culture. It was directly responsible for Mayor Landrieu's decision to enlist gay representatives to the city's Human Relations Committee, and that single act started a dialogue between city hall and the LGBT population that has never been brought to a close. It was directly responsible for the Treadway series, flawed in itself, but a clear indication that the city's newspaper of record would, in the future, work toward fair coverage of gay concerns. People like Stewart Butler and Paul Killgore, Toni Pizanie, and Marcy Marcell, who would all go on to become politically active members of the city's LGBT community, would all later say that they were first inspired toward activism by the fire.[62]

When the fortieth anniversary of the fire came around in 2013, there was no question about the mark the fire had made on the history and consciousness of the city. Playwright and composer Wayne Self premiered a musical, *Upstairs*, at Café Istanbul in the Bywater area; it became the must-see media event in the city, with additional performances being added as quickly as the already-scheduled ones sold out. All the local television stations ran commemorations of the fire, and Royd Anderson's documentary, *The Upstairs Lounge Fire*, received repeated broadcasts in south Louisiana television markets. At the Historic New Orleans Collection (HNOC), a privately-run museum and archive, artist Skylar Fein and writer Clayton Delery-Edwards spoke to an audience that filled a room designed to seat nearly two hundred, with dozens more people standing against the back wall and in open doorways. Following this event, a jazz funeral procession left from the front steps of the HNOC and meandered through the French Quarter, eventually arriving at the former door of the Up Stairs Lounge where a prayer service was held and the names of the dead were read aloud. In what were perhaps the most healing moves, Mayor Mitch Landrieu, son of the 1973 mayor, Moon Landrieu, issued a proclamation in which the city officially recognized the fortieth anniversary of the fire, and sitting archbishop Gregory Aymond finally offered an apology on behalf of the archdiocese for not offering a statement at the time of the fire (though Aymond remained silent on whether there had been a prohibition of Catholic burial).[63]

Whether the fire became the cause of sustained activism, or whether it was ultimately the beneficiary of the activism resulting from the Anita Bryant protests, is, at this point, something of a chicken-and-egg question, and a point that is ultimately moot. It is true that the GPC and the gay activism following the fire had a fairly brief initial existence, but perhaps one problem had been trying to unite the LGBT community under a single umbrella. Celeste New-brough felt as though the GPC was not meeting the needs of lesbians, and an anonymous man quoted by Joan Treadway felt as though the GPC wanted people to be too public. Yet another man quoted by Treadway was reluctant to be linked to "a screaming faggot who dresses in women's clothes" ("A Walk on the Gay Side" 8). The solution to bridging these divides wasn't to dissolve an organization; it was to start more. In an interview in 2009, Toni Pizanie compared the activism of LAGPAC to that of the Forum for Equality. She described the Forum as being an "uptown crowd," meaning they were polite, well-heeled and genteel. LAGPAC was more of a downtown crowd, willing to be more activist and assertive. She regretfully noted that LAGPAC was no longer very active, saying, "Frankly, I think we got a lot more done in the early days."[64]

If the fire was not directly responsible for a sustained gay activism (beyond that which is required to memorialize the fire itself), if it did not truly become a Southern Stonewall, perhaps that is because of fundamental differences between the two events.

Stonewall had, after all, been a moment of victory, a battle in which angry street kids, drag queens and bar patrons fought back against arbitrary and discriminatory laws that put people in jail for no crime other than that of socializing with each other in a place of public accommodation. The Up Stairs fire was not, by any conceivable definition, a victory; it was unquestionably a moment of loss.

At Stonewall there had been a clearly identified antagonist: a bullying and abusive police force. There was no such antagonist for the Up Stairs. It was not a hate crime. There was no clearly identified bully. Instead, a young hustler, definitely angry and probably drunk, struck out against people who had tossed him out into the street. While the police force was periodically abusive and undeniably homophobic (as evidenced, for example, by Major Morris's remarks about thieves and queers, and Giarrusso's fear that predatory homosexuals were out to seduce straight kids), they were not defeated in any recognizable way and evidence suggests that any attempt to identify and prosecute the arsonist was prematurely abandoned by the NOPD. It's easy to build a political movement to oppose a fundamentally unfair legal system, or even to oppose a B-list celebrity on a campaign to pass anti-gay legislation. It's much harder to generate a sustained movement against one angry man striking out—especially when the crime remains unsolved, and the criminal remains officially unidentified.

However, while the fire may not have represented a gay and lesbian political coalescence in the city of New Orleans in the 1970s, in a very real way, it prefigured another crisis—the AIDS crisis—that would take place in less than a decade.

The situations in many ways are analogous. Both the fire and the AIDS crisis resulted in the loss of many gay lives. The governmental and spiritual people who should have become leaders were either silent or hostile. Ronald Reagan was elected president in 1980, when the first cases of a strange "gay cancer" were being reported. In 1982 the CDC announced that AIDS had become an epidemic among gay men. During a press conference, Reagan's White House spokesman, Larry Speakes, was asked about the president's response to this news. Speakes didn't even know what AIDS was. By the time Reagan first mentioned AIDS in public in 1987, he was more than six years into his eight-year presidency and 20,000 gay men had already died.[65]

Figures as diverse as conservative commentator William F. Buckley, prominent medical researcher Richard Restak, Klansman and perennial politician David Duke, all made public statements indicating that they believed that people with AIDS should either be tattooed for ready identification, put into quarantine camps, or both.[66] Meanwhile, the Catholic church continued to speak out against condom use (the most effective means of preventing transmission). Then-cardinal Joseph Ratzinger described homosexuality in 1986 as being "objectively disordered" and homosexual acts as "intrinsically evil" (Ratzinger). Despite the fact that the Catholic church was and continues to be one of the largest providers of care to people with AIDS (and despite an emerging epidemic of AIDS among Roman Catholic clergy[67]), the church's public pronouncements during this era basically amounted to blaming both the victims and those gay men who were taking responsible steps toward preventing transmission.[68]

With many straight Americans worried about whether they could get AIDS from bodily fluids such as sweat, and afraid of what would happen if a gay person sneezed on them, and with Reagan's silence a tacit judgment upon, and condemnation of, gays who might have the deadly disease, America's gays and lesbians joined ranks. Their activities bore a striking resemblance to many that took place in New Orleans following the fire: they organized to raise funds; they coordinated to provide medical care for each other; they started organizations such as ACT-UP to raise consciousness; they established centers that would provide safe, confidential testing for those who feared they had this new sexually transmitted disease; they started hotlines to provide medical information and emotional support. A detailed history of the AIDS-related activism of gays and lesbians during the 1980s and 1990s falls far outside of the realm of this book, but has been documented in many other sources, such as the recent documentary by David France, *How to Survive a Plague*, as well as Randy Shiltz's classic book, *And the Band Played On*. Rejected and ignored by society during one of the most dire health emergencies of the 20th century, America's gays and lesbians turned to each other.

This was foreshadowed in an article published in *The Advocate* in August of 1974. The title of the article was "Memorial Fund Coming to an End," but the title ran underneath the banner "We'll Know Next Time." Discussing the history of the National New Orleans Memorial Fund, the article says, "It was the first time that the gay community in America had been asked to respond collectively in an emergency situation.... Now we know we have that capability"(24). The capability was needed with the advent of the AIDS crisis. In retrospect, it seems clear that, whether or not the fire represented a Stonewall moment for New Orleans, it was, in a very real sense, a rehearsal for a coming plague.

Afterword: "Anecdote of the Jar"
Final Remarks

Allow me to do something I have so far resisted doing: allow me to speak in the first person.

In my day job, I'm an English teacher. I sometimes have my students read a poem by Wallace Stevens titled "Anecdote of the Jar." Its opening lines are:

> I placed a jar in Tennessee,
> And round it was, upon a hill.
> It made the slovenly wilderness
> Surround that hill.

My students find this poem baffling. There are several ways to read it, but one that I present to them is that it is a poem about how we create order—and sense—out of the wilderness of experience life puts in our way. Once that jar is in the wilderness, it becomes a referent. Everything else is either near the jar or far away, but the jar itself has become an organizing principle.

So now I'd like to address two questions that have come up when I have given presentations on the Up Stairs Lounge: how did I first become interested in it, and what have I learned in my research?

In June of 1973 I was living in Metairie, a suburb of New Orleans. I was just a few weeks away from my sixteenth birthday. I was also about to enter my third year of a Catholic high school for boys, and I was dreading it. Although I had absolutely no sexual experience whatsoever, I was effeminate enough to set off alarm bells in the other students (never underestimate the gaydar of adolescent boys). Called "Gay Clay" on campus by both students and faculty, I was frequently mocked, physically harassed, and occasionally made the subject of restroom graffiti. Continually punished for crimes I had not yet committed, and continually punished for crimes I did not yet even know how to commit, I had spent the first two years of high school in deep denial. *I'm not gay*, I would tell myself; *I'm not. It's just these stupid, bigoted people around me. All they know how to do is stereotype. They're wrong!*

But as time passed and the accusations kept coming, my adolescent hormones kicked in. I began to notice *who* I noticed when I was riding my bike in the suburbs or walking through shopping malls. It wasn't the girls. I was therefore forced to grapple tentatively with the question, *What if they're right about me?*

With no clue as to what that would mean for my future, and no clue how to figure that out, I sat down one evening to watch television. We had only one set in the house, and my family had seven people in it, so while I don't remember who was with me in the room, I'm fairly certain that I wasn't alone. And suddenly the program we were watching was interrupted by a news report: there had been a fire in a French Quarter bar. The bar was frequented by homosexuals. Arson was suspected.

As I watched the television news coverage and followed the story during the next few days in the newspaper, I remember thinking, *Oh my God, they're going to kill me!*

The horror I felt was only the tiniest fraction of what the people at the scene must have felt, but in some ways this was a defining experience for me as a young gay man wrestling with issues of self-acceptance. I spent a lot of time on my bicycle in those days, taking long, circuitous rides through the suburbs and into the city. I would sometimes go into the French Quarter and lock my bike up somewhere, exploring the area on foot. It didn't take me long to find the site of the Up Stairs Lounge, which became a reference point for me. It was recognizable by its boarded-up, broken windows and smoke-stained walls, and I walked past it frequently, saying a silent prayer for all those who had died.

I went away for college, but came back fairly regularly for weekends. I had begun the process of coming out by that time, and because the legal drinking age then was only eighteen, I spent many nights at gay bars that were near the tourist-friendly area of Bourbon Street: Le Bistro, The Pub, The Parade, Café Lafitte in Exile. If I found myself alone at the beginning or the end of the night, I would walk back up to Iberville Street and pass the Up Stairs. The building still looks much the same as it did then, although in 1989 it received a new owner who finally repaired the broken windows and painted over the smoke stains on the stucco exterior. The ground floor still houses the Jimani Bar and Grill, which was operating in 1973, when the fire happened. The flophouse rooms on the third floor have been empty for many years, looking dusty, lonely, and forlorn. The second floor, which once housed the Up Stairs, has never again had a regular tenant. It is currently used by James Massaci, Jr., as storage space for the Jimani, which he inherited from his father.

As I started working on this book and began speaking to people who either used to frequent the Up Stairs, or who had some historical interest in it, I was amazed by how many people told me that they, too, had developed the ritual of visiting the building and saying prayers for the dead. Sometimes on June 24 they will quietly assemble on the sidewalk just before eight o'clock, drinking beer out of plastic cups. At eight, they will join in a chorus of "United We Stand."

One of the people who walked past the Up Stairs for many years is Lawrence Raybourne. He was in the bar the night before the fire saying goodbye to his "Midnight Cowboy," Leon Maples, who would be dead less than twenty-four hours later. Lawrence Raybourne and I were sharing these stories during a telephone call when he described the sidewalk outside of the Up Stairs as, "a sacred spot."

I first conceived the book in 2003, when I read a story in *The Times–Picayune* about the placement of the memorial plaque in the sidewalk outside of the bar's entrance, but for a variety of reasons, I did not start the book until 2009. Over those six years, several people I would have liked to speak to died, and several others moved away, scattered by Hurricane Katrina or by the shifting demands of time, age, and family obligations. Of the people I found, many were no longer willing to speak of their experiences because they had already been interviewed in the past and they were tired of reliving the memories. Others did share their stories with me, but acknowledged that they did so at great emotional cost, because the memories are painful even after forty years.

I went into the project full of preconceptions and bits of received wisdom. One was that the police didn't try very hard to solve the case. I wanted to be able to reject that preconception. I wanted to believe that the police did all they could. I have reluctantly come to the conclusion that they did not. Despite Sam Gebbia's assertion in 2013 that the police "pulled out all the stops" (Dias and Downs), they never even questioned Rodger Nunez after Michael Scarborough not only identified him, but stated that he had threatened, "I'm gonna burn you all out!" When the evidence seemed strongest, the police stepped back.

The best indicator of how much more the police could have done was how much more the investigators for the State Fire Marshal actually did. This was something I had not expected to find, because, frankly, I hadn't known of their involvement. It had never occurred to me that an investigation would be conducted by an agency other than the NOPD. In reading the case files that Hyde, Roth, and Fisher left behind, I was continually impressed with how doggedly they tried to bring closure to the case. They investigated more aggressively than the police, interviewed more witnesses, and continued working on the case for years after the NOPD had given up. Still, they were thwarted by the circumstantial nature of the evidence, and after Rodger Nunez's suicide, there was never really any way to bring the case to a satisfactory conclusion.

I'd heard reports of the indifference or hostility of government leaders, and these all turned out to be accurate, though some of these people later showed evidence of growth in their attitudes toward gays and lesbians. Mayor Landrieu and Governor Edwards, for example, both refused to issue any statements at the time of the fire, but it wasn't long before Mayor Landrieu appointed gay and lesbian representatives to his Human Relations Committee. In his last term in office, Governor Edwards signed an executive order making it illegal for state agencies to discriminate against gay and lesbian people in hiring and providing services. Unfortunately, since this was an executive order and not a legislative act, the policy did not bind his successor, Governor Mike Foster, who allowed the Edwards order to lapse. A similar policy was enacted by an executive order of Governor Kathleen Babineaux Blanco, but that, too, was allowed to lapse under the current governor, Bobby Jindal.

The reports of the indifference or hostility of religious leaders were also accurate—to a point—but they were incomplete. The cold silence of Archbishop Hannan and the rancor of Bishop Noland do not tell the whole story, which includes the bravery and compassion of the Reverend Bill Richardson, who hosted a memorial in his church the night after the fire, as well as that of Edward Kennedy, the Methodist minister who made St. Mark's available for the July 1 memorial, and his bishop, Finis Crutchfield, who not only attended the service himself, but encouraged young seminary students to attend. Interestingly, both Bill Richardson and Finis Crutchfield reportedly came out as gay in their later years. A cynic would be tempted to say this explained their compassion for the Up Stairs victims and their willingness to support Troy Perry and the MCC in the week after the fire. Perhaps this is true, but homosexuality among Catholic priests is both commonly known and amply documented, and that did not lead to any official or individual demonstrations of support from local Catholic clergy during the same period.

Some of the stories I'd heard turned out to be wildly inaccurate; there was no shirt soaked with gasoline found at the base of the stairs, nor was there any evidence of Molotov cocktails. Additionally, other preconceptions I had when I went into the project were groundless. Like many people, I had assumed that the fire had been a hate crime. I did not initially know if I would ever learn who had been responsible, but in my mind, I envisioned a quiet man of a certain age with a house in the suburbs and a room full of Klan robes and Nazi memorabilia. That man does not exist. Or, if he does, he had nothing to do with the fire.

One of the first people I interviewed when I began work on the book was Stewart Butler, a surviving patron of the Up Stairs. He dismissed the possibility of the fire being a hate crime, yet qualified the statement by adding, "But you *do* have self-hatred. I mean, look at Roy Cohn!"

We went on to discuss Roy Cohn, who never publicly came out during his life, but who is now generally believed to have been a closeted gay. Cohn first rose to national attention as an aide to Senator Joseph McCarthy. McCarthy, it should be remembered, persecuted and blacklisted not only communists, but homosexual men. Roy Cohn was willing to assist in those persecutions, damaging people guilty of no other crime except for that of being like himself. Stewart Butler later told me a story (possibly an urban legend) about Roy Cohn making out with a male lover in the back seat of a chauffeured limosine, but having to stop to get out of the car and speak at an anti-gay rally.

Self-hatred is still a problem among gays and lesbians, and it manifests itself in many forms, including substance abuse. Jon E. Grant of the University of Minnesota Medical Center, and director of the Pride Institute, a residential treatment center for LGBT people, estimates that gay and bisexual men are two to three times more likely to have problems with substance abuse than the general population, and that lesbians are at even greater risk.[1] Anti-gay activists will sometimes cite statistics like these to prove that homosexuality is in itself a mental illness (a position that the APA rejected in the same year as the fire). It is more likely, however, that the high rates of substance abuse are symptomatic of the mental and emotional strain of living in a culture in which LGBT people are still all too often stigmatized, marginalized, bullied, harassed, fired, assaulted, and even murdered just for being who they are.

This was reinforced to me during the four years I worked on this book; I kept a file of prominent news events that either reflected advances in gay rights or continued animus against the LGBT population. Over time, the file became quite thick.

Most of the news was good. As of May 2014, gays and lesbians have won the right to marry in nineteen states, court challenges have been filed in many other states, and the Supreme Court has overturned the part of DOMA that prohibits the federal government from recognizing marriages between two people of the same sex. The Internal Revenue Service recently announced that it will recognize same-sex marriages in tax returns, whether couples live in marriage-equality states or not. In 1973, Steven Duplantis would make the long drive from Randolph Air Force Base in San Antonio to New Orleans so he could go to the Up Stairs and enjoy a sociable evening without having to worry about the military police who would monitor local gay bars and discharge any service members they found. Now, gays and lesbians can serve openly and honorably in the military, they can legally marry their same-sex partners, and those partners are eligible to receive spousal benefits. In popular culture, movies and televisions shows often (not always) feature positive portrayals of LGBT characters instead of using them as objects of pity or as the butt of cheap jokes. Thousands of high schools around the nation now have a Gay-Straight Alliance, or safe zones where LGBT students can find refuge from bullies.

Other stories I filed away contained news that was not so good, and many of these described events that could have taken place before the Stonewall riots. One set of stories concerned a 2009 police raid on a gay bar called the Atlanta Eagle. The reason for the raid was not clear, because, when asked, the police kept changing their story. What is clear is that patrons were forced to lie face down on the floor while police said derogatory things about them and searched them without warrants.[2] In that same year, plainclothes officers in New York were arresting gay men for the crime of indicating an interest in consensual sex. The anti-sodomy laws the police were attempting to enforce had been declared unconstitutional by New York's supreme court in 1981 (not to mention being declared unconstitutional by the Unites States Supreme Court in *Lawrence v. Texas* in 2003).[3] This story replayed in Baton Rouge in 2013, shortly after the 40th anniversary of the Up Stairs fire, with police illegally arresting men for the crime of indicating an interest in consensual sex in private homes.[4] LGBT people are still being demonized and pathologized by religious and political leaders whose words could echo some of the most extreme opinions that surfaced in Joan Treadway's 1973 series in *The Times–Picayune*.

For example, the Westboro Baptist Church continues to proclaim "God Hates Fags," and despite the more moderate tone of Pope Francis, the Catholic Church still seems largely guided by the words of Pope Benedict, who called homosexual acts "an intrinsic moral evil" (Ratzinger). Rick Santorum, a 2012 presidential hopeful, has famously compared gay and lesbian sex to bestiality, and said that, if president, he wanted to address the issues of contraception and non-procreative sex (a category that would include all sexual acts performed by gay couples and a great many acts performed by straight ones); in his view, these are not part of God's plan.[5] Michele Bachmann, another 2012 presidential hopeful, once said that homosexuality was "part of Satan" ("Michele Bachmann in Her Own Words"). Her husband, Marcus Bachmann,[6] runs a clinic that is said to specialize in so-called reparative therapy, the aim of which is to turn gay and lesbian people straight.[7] The APA rejected such therapy in 1997,[8] and reparative therapy is so misguided in its assumptions and so potentially harmful to the patient[9] that the state of California made it illegal for a parent or guardian to seek such therapy for a minor child.[10] New Jersey has recently followed suit, with Governor Chris Christie signing the ban in August of 2013.[11] Still, Santorum, Bachmann, and every other candidate in the 2012 Republican primaries (including the eventual winner, Mitt Romney) all promised to reinstate the military policy of "Don't Ask, Don't Tell," all spoke out against marriage equality, and all pledged that, as president, they would support a federal constitutional amendment limiting marriage to one man and one woman.

The negative views of homosexuality voiced by people like this still influence anxious parents who send LGBT children to reparative therapy, or who throw their children out to live on the street.[12] Despite all the social progress, there is still a long way to go. Imagine how much worse it was for people growing up in the 1940s, 1950s and 1960s, when almost nobody was even talking about gay rights, and when broad social acceptance and positive media portrayals of LGBT people were largely nonexistent.

Imagine, for example, Rodger Nunez, a young gay man from the rural isolation of south Louisiana. Although it is speculation, it is not hard to imagine him absorbing the anti-gay rhetoric he unquestionably heard in church, in school, and possibly at home. It's easy to imagine him running away to New Orleans, hoping for something better, and finding a set of supportive (if questionable) friends like Allen Guidry and Gene Davis. It's easy to imagine the ambivalence he must have felt as a young man in a big city. On one hand, he was in a place where there was at least the possibility of living an authentic life. On the other hand, the statement given to investigators by Sister Mary Stephen Ledet, his unconsummated marriage to Elaine Wharton, and what seems to have been a serious case of substance abuse, all suggest that Rodger had internalized the negative messages that told him that, as a gay man, he was a freak. It's easy to imagine him, drunk and angry in the Up Stairs, annoying the patrons, and getting both punched and thrown out. If he indeed set the fire, whether it was meant to cause harm or merely a prank gone wrong, it's easy to imagine him being furious at being rejected by the very people who were supposed to accept him, and subconsciously anxious to punish in them what he couldn't bear in himself.

It's easy for me to imagine all of this, because it very much the story of my own upbringing. Although I was born a decade later than Rodger Nunez, and although I was raised in a suburban rather than a rural area, I'm not certain that either time or location gave me any special advantages. My hometown of Metairie, to pick one not-so-random example, was the one that elected the infamous Klansman, David Duke, to the Louisiana state legislature in the

1980s. Neither diversity nor tolerance was particularly valued when I was growing up in the sixties and seventies, and gay people were so invisible in my world that my entire knowledge of them consisted of the usual media stereotypes from that era: the lonely tortured man who usually either committed suicide or was murdered; the heavy-breathing predator, living alone and forever cruising for sex; the "artistic," comical, but ultimately pathetic queen. A small wave of tolerance came through in the seventies—at least in the popular media—when the television movie *That Certain Summer* and the theatrical film *The Boys in the Band* portrayed gay men sympathetically in feature roles, but films like these ultimately only reinforced the notion that a gay life was destined to be one of loneliness and familial rejection.[13] Always one to look for answers in the printed word, I haunted the local library and read every relevant book and magazine I could get my hands on. While most still discussed homosexuality as a subcategory of mental illness, an occasional book or article suggested that the news wasn't all bad, that some experts considered homosexuality a natural variant of human behavior rather than a disorder, and that there were gay men who lived reasonably happy and fulfilled lives.

When high school was finally over I was free to go to college. Before the end of my first year, I had my first boyfriend. Before the end of my second year, we had gotten together with a group of like-minded friends and founded the university's first gay students' organization; its name was *Alterum*, a Latin term which can be translated in several ways, including *the other*. Neither the romance nor the organization lasted beyond my undergraduate years, but by the time I had my B.A. I had learned quite a bit about gay culture: Stonewall, Walt Whitman, the Metropolitan Community Church, *Christopher Street*, The Theater of the Ridiculous, *Consenting Adult*, Harvey Milk, and disco. I learned that life didn't have to be lived according to the depressing media stereotypes which surrounded me when I was growing up, and that it probably wouldn't end the way it had for the thirty-two victims of the Up Stairs fire.

Still, in the course of writing this book, I sometimes had to confront remnants of my own internalized homophobia. People who oppose gays adopting children or gays being able to marry, for example, sometimes argue that gay and lesbian relationships are inherently unstable. They say that gays and lesbians are just going to break up, anyway, hurting the lives of any children they might have adopted in the process.[14] Even among gays, it is common to joke about the short duration of many same-sex relationships.

Of course, if the possibility—or probability—of a couple breaking up is a reason to deny parenthood or marriage rights, these reasons should logically be applied to heterosexual couples, who currently have a divorce rate hovering around the 50 percent mark for first marriages, and even higher for second and third marriages.[15] My own first committed relationship with another man lasted for twenty years before we broke up in 2000. The couple with whom we socialized most frequently had been together for several years longer than we had, and they are together still. After my partner and I broke up, I spent five years as a single man before falling in love again. Aaron and I regularly socialize with a couple who has been together for more than thirty years. Aaron and I were legally married in 2008, and we are looking forward to many years together. Though this marriage is not recognized by our home state of Louisiana, it is still an advance; marriage was not an option my ex-partner and I ever had.

Despite my experience and observations, I was unexpectedly surprised by the number of long-term relationships I encountered while writing this book; one part of me had accepted the myth that gay relationships don't last. But I kept learning about couples such as Paul Killgore and Frank Scorsone, Jr., who were first friends, then lovers; their relationship lasted more than twenty years, and only ended with Scorsone's death. Stewart Butler and Alfred Doolittle were together more than thirty-five years, until Doolittle's death. Michael Scarborough survived the fire, but his lover, Glenn Green, did not. Some years later, Scarborough settled down with another man and remained with him for decades, until Scarborough died. Similarly, Buddy Rasmussen lost his lover, Adam Fontenot, in the fire. He later found another man. They are both still alive, they are still together, and their union is approaching the forty-year mark. Lawrence Raybourne, unattached at the time of the fire, met his partner in 1980 and they are together still. This evidence—anecdotal as it is—suggests that while many gay and lesbian relationships fail, many others last for durations that marriage-equality opponents such as Newt Gingrich (married three times to date) and Rush Limbaugh (married four times to date) can only envy.

Two other couples deserve special mention: Joe William Bailey and Clarence McCloskey died together in the fire. Duane Mitchell, known as Mitch, and his lover, Horace Broussard, were both in the Up Stairs when the fire broke out. Mitch got out of the bar safely, but when he realized that Horace was still inside, he went back into the flames to try and save his lover. Their bodies were found together. They, along with all the other dead, have been remembered at the various memorials that have taken place over the years.

The memorial on the thirtieth anniversary was especially well conceived. This was the occasion for placing the bronze commemorative plaque in the sidewalk on Iberville Street near the former entrance of the Up Stairs. The plaque lists the names of all the dead, and the ceremony involved identifying each of the dead in a special way. A local ceramics artist had been commissioned to make a jar using the raku process. Originally a Japanese technique, but adapted in the West, raku involves taking a piece from the kiln while still glowing hot and plunging it into a barrel filled with flaming, combustible material. If the ceramic piece survives the process, the result is a crackled glaze in brilliant, glowing colors. The thirtieth memorial started in the Ritz Carlton on Canal Street, about a block away from the site of the fire. During the ceremony, the raku jar, full of water, was brought to the front of the room. One by one, the names of each of the victims was read aloud, and as each name was read, a person chosen to represent that victim placed a pebble inside the jar. Three of the victims were named only as "unidentified white male." When the dead had all been recognized, the participants in the memorial formed a single line and walked silently to the former entrance of the Up Stairs accompanied only by the beat of a single drum. The memorial plaque was dedicated with a prayer, and finally the water from the jar was poured over the plaque.[16] The jar itself was supposed to be permanently housed in the GLBT Community Center of New Orleans.

Of course, sometimes the quest for order eludes us, despite our best intentions, and New Orleans is not known for its orderliness. I contacted the director of the center to ask if I could come see the jar. She said that the center did not have it, and had never had it, but that they would like it very much. I gave her the telephone numbers of several people involved in the memorial in the hope that she might be able to track it down, but she has never been able to locate it.

While I have not been able to see the memorial jar, I have seen the sidewalk plaque many times, and I have even visited the graves of several of the victims. The cremated remains of the Reverend Bill Larson were held for many years at the MCC headquarters in New Orleans. They were kept inside the chapter's principal altar, a table made of oak with gothic arches across the front. For years, every time a service was held at the New Orleans MCC, the minister was literally saying prayers over Bill Larson. Eventually, however, the congregation wanted to move forward, and felt that the altar and the ashes were holding them back.

Larson's cremains are now in a vault at St. Roch Cemetery that was donated by one of the members of the New Orleans MCC. It is a New Orleans custom for nearly everyone to receive above-ground internment in a mausoleum or vault, and also a custom to use each vault multiple times, with the remains of earlier deceased persons pushed to the back to make room for the more recently deceased. Bill Larson shares a vault with several other people, and although some of their names are inscribed on the front, his is not. The oak altar that once held his ashes was donated by the New Orleans MCC to the chapter in Baton Rouge, where it is still in use.[17] I was able to see the altar when I visited the Baton Rouge chapter of the MCC in 2012. The current pastor, the Rev-

This altar, now at the Baton Rouge headquarters of the MCC, was formerly the main altar in the New Orleans chapter. For many years it held the cremated remains of the Reverend Bill Larson, who died in the fire. During each service, congregants were literally saying prayers over him (author's photograph).

erend Keith Mozingo, told me a familiar story. He, too, had been a young gay man with no exposure to a larger gay culture and who first tried to learn about his sexuality through books. "The section of the library with books on homosexuality was full of medical volumes," he said. "They were big, black, forbidding things, and they were under the heading of 'Abnormal Psychology.' But tucked between them was this slim little paperback by Troy Perry with the title *The Lord Is My Shepherd and He Knows I'm Gay*."[18]

I have also visited the grave of Rodger Nunez. If he, indeed, committed suicide out of guilt for starting the fire, he might be said to be its thirty-third victim. I went to his grave site on a day when I had been in New Iberia for the funeral of an old family friend, and I was still wearing the charcoal-gray suit I keep for such occasions. Rodger Nunez is buried near the tiny community of Forked Island, a town so small that my GPS could not locate it, and instead kept insisting that I turn around and go back to Abbeville, the nearest town of any size. To get there, I had to rely on a road map printed on paper. Forked

Island is a low, flat area near the costal marshes fringing the Gulf of Mexico. Many of the houses are raised eight or ten feet above the ground on stilts as a precaution against hurricane-driven floods. Rodger Nunez rests in a small, roadside cemetery that is only partially fenced. This is not good; an old Louisiana superstition says that if a graveyard isn't fenced, the souls will wander.

The Nunez family plot, however, is completely enclosed, forming a small cemetery of a couple of dozen plots within the larger cemetery. Other souls may wander, but Rodger's has found its rest. His simple grave, covered by a marble slab, is near those of both of his parents. Though he has been dead for many years, on the day I went to visit I found a bunch of chrysanthemums near his headstone. They were silk, not natural, but they were not yet faded by the sun or battered by the wind and rain. I said a prayer for him and left my own flowers—a few fresh chrysanthemums in a jar. Then I got back in my car and started the three-hour drive back home, where my husband waited for me.

Chapter Notes

Chapter 1

1. Dias and Downs.
2. Carter 48.
3. These periods of gay-friendliness sometimes led to a backlash, as when, in the early 1970s, a New Orleans attorney and civic leader openly worried that "the influx of these people is making New Orleans the queer capital of the U.S." See Treadway "50s Climate" 21.
4. Treadway "Gay Community Surfaces" 14.
5. Ellis 111.
6. Perez and Palmquist 2; ["Who Is the Gay People's Coalition?"] 1.
7. Frank Scorsone and Paul Killgore would soon become lovers, and they remained together for more than two decades until Scorsone's death in 1992.
8. Nauth B3; Anderson and Frazier A14.
9. Boulard 32–33.
10. Hanley; Houston.
11. "Passing the Buck" A8; Vieux Carré Commission.
12. Townsend 42–3.
13. "Five Story Dive" 3.
14. Esteve 1–4; Townsend 44–45.
15. Schlosser and Gebbia 10–13; Willey 16–20.
16. Fosberg 7; Raybourne; Townsend 44–47.
17. Esteve 1–5; Townsend 44.
18. Hyde, Roth and Fischer 6; Monroe 4; Raybourne.
19. Dufrene; Esteve 1–3; Townsend 46, 52.
20. NOFD Fire Prevention Division: Inspection and/or Investigation Reports: October 9, 1970, October 19, 1970, October 29, 1970, December 4, 1970, March 11, 1971; Townsend 47.
21. Killgore; Townsend 43.
22. Fosberg 7; Townsend 47–49.
23. Newhouse "Smokie."
22. Schlosser and Gebbia 8, 26; Townsend 48–49.
25. Townsend 48–49.
26. Townsend 248.
27. Hiller and Simons.
28. Butler; Marcell; Raybourne.
29. Fosberg 7.
30. Townsend 52–53.
31. Townsend 2, 103–104, 278.
32. "History of the MCC."
33. Brecht telephone interview; Sears 104; Polk City Directory, New Orleans, 1972, 1973.
34. Townsend 35.
35. Perry and Swicegood 81; Polk City Directory, New Orleans, 1972, 1973.
36. Townsend 34.
37. Butler.
38. Brecht Personal Interview.
39. Townsend 34–35.
40. These days, members of same sex couples tend to refer to each other as partners, life partners, or even spouse, husband or wife. In the 1970s, the term lover was commonly used, and I have chosen to retain its use here.
41. Townsend 268, 276.
42. Perry and Swicegood *Don't Be Afraid* 80.
43. Townsend 51–52.
44. Gosnell 2; Townsend 50, 143.
45. Townsend 258–259.
46. Esteve 2–3; Fosberg 7; Townsend 259–263.
47. Townsend 51–52.
48. Townsend 52, 260.

49. Newhouse "Smokie."
50. Esteve 3; Schlosser and Gebbia 13.
51. Townsend 52.
52. Townsend 52.
53. Fosberg 7.
54. Townsend 87–104; 265–270.
55. Fosberg 7.
56. Fosberg. 7; Townsend 262.
57. Townsend 210.
58. Marcell.
59. Raybourne.
60. Adams.
61. Fosberg 7.
62. Raybourne.
63. Scarborough 1.
64. In 1950, 78 percent of all households were headed by married couples, a number that was largely unchanged in 1960, when the percentage was 75 percent. Today, after a long period of decline starting in the 1970s, the percentage of households headed by a married couple is down to 48 percent (Lugalia 15; Tavernise).
65. "Margaret Sanger."
66. The term "outed," meaning to reveal a gay person's sexuality to his or her family, friends or employers, is a bit of an anachronism in stories about the fifties and sixties; according to the Oxford English Dictionary, its earliest uses in mainstream print outlets come in 1990, though it was probably used in conversation or in the gay press for up to a decade prior to that.
67. Raybourne.
68. Townsend 98–101.
69. Townsend 261.
70. Townsend 267–269.
71. Townsend 244–245, 306.
72. Perry and Swicegood 80; Townsend 172–173.

Chapter 2

1. "Premonition."
2. Although about fifty people are known to have cancelled passage on the *Titanic*, many times that number claimed to have done so. In fact, a newspaper account from 1912 satirically estimated that it would have taken two ships the size of the *Titanic* to hold all the people who claimed to have cancelled passage just before the voyage began. See Eaton.
3. Harris.
4. Marcell.
5. Adams; Fosberg 7; Perry and Swicegood 84.

6. Townsend 103–103, 269–270.
7. Butler.
8. Townsend 267.
9. Schlosser and Gebbia 29.
10. Adams; Perry telephone interview.
11. Perry and Swicegood 80.
12. Perry and Swicegood 79–80.
13. "30th Bar Blaze Victim Dies" A3; Perry and Swicegood 82; Townsend 32.
14. Townsend 168, 170–171.
15. Marcell.
16. Schlosser and Gebbia 29.
17. In later years, so many people had claimed to have been in the bar at the time of the fire, or to have left the bar just before the fire started, that Phil Esteve, the bar's owner, sardonically estimated there would have been 500 to 1000 people in the Up Stairs if all the stories were true (Townsend 67).
18. Townsend 209.
19. Townsend 230–238.
20. Townsend 236–238.
21. Townsend 30–31.
22. Dufrene.
23. Duplantis.
24. Name changed by request.
25. Whittaker.
26. Townsend 42.
27. Adams; Frazer A3; Schlosser and Gebbia.
28. Adams.
29. Adams.
30. Esteve 8.
31. Scarborough 1–2.
32. Schlosser and Gebbia 61.
33. Scarborough 1–2.
34. Quinton 3, 8; Schlosser and Gebbia 35.
35. Schlosser and Gebbia 35.
36. Some accounts of the fire claim that it was started by a Molotov cocktail. Nothing in the NOPD or fire marshal's reports substantiates this claim, but the story of the ejected man smashing beer mugs may suggest the origin of the rumor.
37. Schlosser and Gebbia 30, 36–37.
38. Butler; Duplantis.
39. Schlosser and Gebbia 37.
40. Schlosser and Gebbia 50.
41. Adams.
42. Hyde, Roth, and Fischer 28–29.
43. Schlosser and Gebbia 57; Willey 19.
44. Schlosser and Gebbia 53, 57; Willey 19.
45. Rasmussen Statement to Criminal Investigation 1; Schlosser and Gebbia 30.
46. Willey 19n.
47. Willey 19.

48. NOFD Fire Investigation Report Supplemental Information 2.

49. Hyde, Roth and Fischer 18–19; Lind et al. "29 Dead" A1; Philbin "First the Fire" A6b; Townsend 288.

50. Gosnell 3; Hyde, Roth and Fischer 18–19; Lind et al. "29 Dead" A1, 6; Philbin "First the Fire" 16b; Townsend 288–289.

51. Cross 4.

52. Willey 20.

53. Perry and Swicegood 94; Rushton "Fire Three" 7; Townsend 295.

54. Townsend 295.

55. Schlosser and Gebbia 30–31.

56. Whittaker.

57. Willey 17.

58. Willey 17.

59. Willey 17–19. Willey states that fifteen people escaped through windows, but this number would include Eddie Gillis, Jean Gosnell and Luther Boggs, who used the fire escape.

60. Laplace and Anderson "Arson Possibility" 3.

61. Schlosser and Gebbia 8.

62. Scarborough; Townsend 205–206.

63. Adams.

64. Butler.

65. Marcell.

66. LaPlace and Anderson "Arson Possibility" 3.

67. Perry and Swicegood 84–85; Townsend 300.

68. Willey 19.

69. Laplace "Scene of French Quarter Fire" sec. 1: 3.

70. Rasmussen Statement to Criminal Investigation 2; Schlosser and Gebbia 31.

71. Schlosser and Gebbia 31; Townsend 301.

72. Laplace and Anderson "Arson Possibility" 3.

73. Lind "Fire Bares Grisly Face" A6b.

74. Ramussen Police Statement 2; Schlosser and Gebbia 31.

75. Word of this exchange may have spread among local journalists, because at least one newspaper account noted the mannequin-like appearance of the victims. See Lind "Fire Bares the Grisly Face of Death" A6.

76. Rasmussen Statement to Arson Investigation 2.

77. Rasmussen Statement to Arson Investigation 2; Schlosser and Gebbia 31.

78. "New Burn Unit" 16.

79. Schlosser and Gebbia 5.

80. Whittaker interview; Whittaker personal email.

81. Dubos "Blood, Moans" 1, 2.

82. DuBos "Blood, Moans" 1, 2.

83. Whittaker.

84. "'Beer Bust' Erupts into Fiery Trap" 2.

85. LaPlace "Scene of French Quarter Fire" 2.

86. Lind "Fire Bares Grisly Face" A6b.

87. Lind "Fire Bares Grisly Face" A6b; Laplace and Anderson "Arson Possibility" 3; Swindall "Bar Fire" 1, 6; Perry and Swicegood 84; Philbin "First the Horror" A6b.

Chapter 3

1. Ball "Edwards Tours Rault Building" 1, 10.

2. Treadway "Copter Pilot Rescues 8," 16.

3. Lee and Lafourcade 1,5.

4. "Rault Tragedy Claims Sixth Victim" 6.

5. "Landrieu Leaves After Fire News" 1.

6. Ball "Edwards Tours Rault Building" 1.

7. According to the *Official Catholic Directory* (2008 edition), in 1970, the archdiocese of New Orleans included 1,380,400 people, of whom 655,285 were Catholic. It included the city, the suburbs, and many surrounding rural towns. These last, especially if in Cajun areas, were likely to be overwhelmingly Catholic. The city itself would have been more diverse, but Catholics were still the largest single religious denomination, by a wide margin.

8. Hernon 15, 17, 26, 60–61, 80–81, 89–92.

9. Marcell.

10. Segura "100 Policemen Fire At Sniper" 1.

11. Segura "Incident Begins in Chaos and Produces Confusion" 6.

12. Lafourcade "Multiple Rites Arranged for Three Police Victims" 5.

13. Frank Schneider, the assistant manager, died on the scene; Walter Collins, the manager, was severely wounded and lingered in the hospital for several weeks before dying.

14. Lafourcade "Sniper Rifle Same Used in Other Crimes" 1.

15. LaPlace "Endless Lines of Blood Donors Flock to Charity" 2.

16. "N.O. Mourning Is Proclaimed" 9.

17. Lewis 1, 2.

18. Romagosa 1, 3.

19. "Hate Attitude Noted by Cleric: Sniper Became Militant in Navy" 1, 19.

20. Gill.

21. Perry and Swicegood 76.

22. Breton telephone interview.

23. Perry and Swicegood 80.

24. Carter 233–236.

25. Perry and Swicegood 81–86; Breton telephone interview.

26. Perry and Swicegood 86; Gill; Breton telephone interview.

27. Perry and Swicegood 87; Breton journal.

28. DuBos "Blood Moans: Charity Scene"; Lind "Fire Bares the Grisly Face of Death"; Lind, Thomas and Philbin "29 Dead in Quarter Holocaust"; Laplace "Scene of French Quarter Fire Is Called Dante's 'Inferno,' Hitler's Incinerators."

29. Perry and Swicegood Don't Be Afraid 89.

30. Townsend 34–35.

31. Perry and Swicegood 89; Nolan and Segura "Memorial for Fire Dead" 3.

32. Pizanie.

33. Perry and Swicegood 89–90; Nolan and Segura "Memorial for Fire Dead" 3; Sears 104.

34. Rushton "Forgetting the Fire: Who Won't Speak Out" 1, 6.

35. Breton journal.

36. Perry and Swicegood 95–96.

37. It wasn't until 2013 that the archdiocese issued any public response to the fire whatsoever. When contacted by journalists from TIME magazine about a story covering the fortieth anniversary of the fire, the sitting archbishop, Gregory Aymond, replied by email, writing, "In retrospect, if we did not release a statement we should have to be in solidarity with the victims and their families" [Dias and Downs]. While Aymond's email addresses the lack of public statements, it does not address the question of whether or not there was a prohibition of Catholic burial services for the victims.

38. "Passing the Buck" A8; "VCC Blamed" A3.

39. New Orleans Fire Department Fire Inspection, March 11, 1971.

40. Segura "Positive Identifications" 3.

41. Breton journal; Perry and Swicegood 94.

42. Batson personal interview.

43. Rushton "Forgetting the Fire: Who Won't Speak Out" 1.

44. Raybourne.

45. Butler.

46. Kaiser personal email.

47. Carter 140.

48. Perry and Swicegood 88–89.

49. "How the Media Saw It" 6.

50. Rushton "Forgetting the Fire" 1.

51. Lind, Thomas and Philbin "29 Dead" A1; Rushton "Fire Three: Who the Victims Were" 7; Townsend 157.

52. "Upstairs Lounge Fire Network News Coverage."

53. Degrees of Equality.

54. Pela; Rexford.

55. In retrospect, one of the most interesting things about Bewitched is the number of cast members known or suspected to be gay or lesbian, none of whom was out to the public while the show was in production. The list includes Dick Sargent as Darrin, Paul Lynde as Uncle Arthur, Maurice Evans as Samantha's father, Maurice, and Agnes Moorehead as Samantha's mother, Endora. There certainly would have been days when Elizabeth Montgomery was the only straight actor on the set. Ironically, she was the one playing the person with a secret.

56. Raybourne.

57. Though this remark is quoted in several published sources, it is never attributed. A man named Carey Henrdrix, who was then a service member stationed in Biloxi, Mississippi, remembers hearing the fruit jar remark being made by a man named Bob Ruby who had a radio show called "Ruby in the Morning" on WWL radio in New Orleans. Hendrix used to listen to WWL, which then, as now, had an unusually large broadcasting range, and he remembers being appalled when Ruby made the fruit jar remark. Bob Ruby is now dead and cannot comment.

58. Segura "Devastating French Quarter Fire" 3; Segura "Positive Identifications Made for 9 Fire Victims" 3; "Fatal Fire Probe Continues" 5; "Six More Victims of Fire Identified" 9.

59. "Toll of Blaze Here Now Is 32" 22.

60. The list of victims in the NOPD General Case Report records victim #19 as "Joseph Henry Adams, Jr., (Reginald Adams, Jr.), negro male, age 26, residing at 1017 Conti St." Apparently it was thought that the two men were one and the same. Victim 29 is originally listed as "unknown white male," but Reggie's name is penciled in as an addition or a correction. Reggie's autopsy report lists him as N (for Negro), but later describes him as being a "somewhat slender white male" as determined by some patches of unburned skin. Joseph Adams was white. Reggie was black, and surviving photos show him as having very dark skin.

61. Gill.
62. Gill; Breton journal; Perry and Swicegood 95–96; Townsend 38.
63. Breton journal.
64. Breton journal; Perry and Swicegood 93.
65. Kirk A10; Rutland A10.
66. Whether the carpetbaggers actually exploited the region, or whether they enriched it by supplying capital and assisting freedmen, is a subject of academic debate far beyond the realm of this book.
67. "Craighead"; Brecht personal interview.
68. Rushton "After the Fire" 1.
69. Brecht personal interview.
70. Perry and Swicegood 90–91; Rushton "Forgetting the Fire" 6.
71. Garrison wrote about his investigation and prosecution of Shaw in the book *On the Trail of the assassins: My Investigation and the Prosecution of the Murder of President Kennedy.* Garrison's conspiracy theory receives respectful treatment in Oliver Stone's film *JFK*, and in books such as Joan Mellen's *A Farewell to Justice: JFK's Assassination and the Case That Should Have Changed History.* Other people find Garrison's case dubious. See such books as James Kirkwood's *American Grotesque*, Patricia Lambert's *False Witness*, and Milton Brener's *The Garrison Case: A Study in the Abuse of Power.*
72. Perry and Swicegood 98.
73. Breton journal; Perry and Swicegood 90; "Blaze Victims' Memorial Set" 11.
74. Breton journal; Perry and Swicegood 96–97.
75. Perry and Swicegood 97.
76. Winn telephone interview.
77. Winn telephone interview; Dinwiddie; Breton journal; "200 Attend Service" A3.
78. Breton telephone interview.
79. Breton journal; Perry 98–99.
80. Breton journal; Perry and Swicegood 101; Rushton "Forgetting the Fire" 6; Segura "Cleric Says Oppression Problem for Homosexuals" 7; Butler; Killgore; Pizanie; Winn telephone interview.

Chapter 4

1. Reflecting its French and Catholic heritage, Louisiana is divided into parishes instead of counties.
2. NOFD Investigation Report 1n.
3. NOFD Fatality List.
4. NOFD Investigation Report (Supplement) 1; Ussery "Wallender" 1.

5. Willey claims that only twenty-eight bodies were found in the lounge after the fire. A comparison of the diagram accompanying his article with the one in the NOFD report suggests that Willey overlooked body #6.
6. The estimates of the number of people in the bar vary from one report to another. Based upon the known number of dead, the known number of injured, and the estimated twenty led to safety by Buddy Rasmussen, sixty-five seems a better figure.
7. NOFD Investigation Report (Supplement) 3; Willey 17.
8. NOFD Investigation Report (Supplement) 5–6.
9. Some eyewitness accounts indicate that one or more people died of injuries sustained as they jumped or fell from the windows (Laplace and Anderson "Arson Possibility" 3; Perry and Swicegood 83). Willey claims that one of the injured died in the ambulance on the way to the hospital (16). None of the police or autopsy documents support these claims. However, Steven Whittaker recalls finding his friend, Jim Hambrick, lying unconscious on the street after hitting his head when he fell (Whittaker Interview). Although Jim Hambrick lived for several more days, his injury is probably responsible for these reports.
10. Lind, Thomas and Philbin "29 Dead" A1; Nolan and Segura "Memorial" 1; "How the Media Saw It" 5.
11. Townsend 312.
12. Swindall "Blaze Victims Names Sought" 3.
13. "30th Bar Blaze Victim" A3; Townsend 32.
14. Schlosser and Gebbia (appended documents).
15. Brecht "The Upstairs Lounge Fire" 63.
16. Schlosser and Gebbia (appended documents).
17. Perry and Swicegood 93; Brecht personal interview; Brecht telephone interview; Brecht "The Upstairs Lounge Fire" 63.

Chapter 5

1. "How the Media Saw It" 5; Rushton "After the Fire" 5.
2. *Black Mama, White Mama.*
3. Rushton "After the Fire" 5.
4. "How the Media Saw It" 5.
5. "Hate Crimes."

6. "How the Media Saw It" 5; Perry and Swicegood *Don't Be Afraid* 82.

7. Perry and Swicegood *Don't Be Afraid* 68–75.

8. Perry telephone interview.

9. In *Don't Be Afraid Any More*, Perry and Swicegood write that between 1973 and 1990 at least seventeen fires were intentionally set at MCC churches and meeting places (76).

10. Lind, Thomas and Philbin "29 Dead" A1.

11. Lind, Thomas and Philbin "29 Dead" A6.

12. "Chief Feels Fire Arson" 1, 26.

13. Laplace and Anderson "29 Dead" A1; Thomas "Fun, Drinks, Song with Death" A6b.

14. Charred Rubble" A1; Schlosser and Gebbia 31–33.

15. In several places in the NOPD General Case Report, the Jimani bar is misidentified as the Gemini. The name Jimani was given to the bar by one of its two original owners, Jack Curry and Jim Massaci. Jack said that the name meant "Jim-And-I" own this bar (Massaci). Similarly, in at least one place in the case report, the bar named Gene's Hideaway is referred to as Jane's Hideaway. Police working at the scene were recording names phonetically.

16. LaPlace and Anderson "Arson Possibility" 1; Schlosser and Gebbia 33–34.

17. A further error remains on the autopsy report of Reginald Adams; at the top of the form, his racial classification is correctly listed as N, for Negro, but the description below identifies him as "a somewhat slender white male." With severe burns over 95 percent of the body, little of Reggie's intact skin was available for examination, but the report does note "a few portions of the skin of the anterior legs remaining, and being identifiable as white skin." Surviving photographs show that Reggie Adams had very dark skin which would not have been mistaken for white; these errors remain uncorrected.

18. Schlosser and Gebbia 9.

19. Schlosser and Gebbia frequently lapse into the local habit of replacing the cardinal compass points with designations that relate locations to the relative positions of the Mississippi River and Lake Pontchartrain: lakeside, riverside, uptown and downtown. Because the city streets curve to follow the contours of the Mississippi, generalizations are difficult, but lakeside is approximately north, riverside is approximately south, uptown (i.e., upriver) is west-ish, and downtown tends to be east or

southeast. Natives and longtime residents understand this perfectly, just as they understand that the west bank of the river is actually south of the city.

20. Rasmussen Statement to Criminal Investigation 2; Schlosser and Gebbia 31.

21. Schlosser and Gebbia 11.

22. Schlosser and Gebbia 12.

23. Schlosser and Gebbia 12–13.

24. Lind "Fire Bares Grisly Face" A6b.

25. Brecht "The Upstairs Lounge Fire" 63; Butler.

26. Brecht "The Upstairs Lounge Fire" 62–63.

27. Butler.

28. Schlosser and Gebbia 16–17.

29. Lind "Fire Bares Grisly Face" A6b.

30. Lind "Fire Bares Grisly Face" A6b.

31. Schlosser and Gebbia 17.

32. Schlosser and Gebbia 21–27.

33. Schlosser and Gebbia 24.

34. Schlosser and Gebbia 28.

35. In his statements, Buddy refers to Adam as his "roommate" rather than his lover, although it was common knowledge that they considered themselves a committed couple. The use of the word "roommate" for lover occurs in several other records, reflecting a more cautious, hesitant time, when even people like Buddy, who were out of the closet, tended to use "inoffensive" language when dealing with strangers, particularly authority figures.

36. Rasmussen to Criminal Investigation 1–3; Schlosser and Gebbia 28–31.

37. Schlosser and Gebbia 31–33.

38. Schlosser and Gebbia 33–34.

39. Schlosser and Gebbia 35.

40. Schlosser and Gebbia 35–36.

41. Schlosser and Gebbia 36–38.

42. Speaking for the majority as he publicly announced the decision in *Lawrence v. Texas*, Justice Anthony Kennedy said, "The petitioners are entitled to respect for their private lives. The State cannot demean their existence or control their destiny by making their private sexual conduct a crime" (cited in Toobin 222).

43. Treadway "It's Not Illegal" 14.

44. "False Confessions."

45. Schlosser and Gebbia 42–44.

46. Schlosser and Gebbia 44.

47. "Chief Feels Fire Arson" 1.

48. Willey 19.

49. "Chief Feels Fire Arson" 1; Segura "Devastating French Quarter Fire" 3.

50. The main variations in the descriptions

have to do with his height, which is estimated as being anywhere between 5'2" to 5'10", depending upon the witness.

51. Schlosser and Gebbia 48–49.
52. Schlosser and Gebbia 49.
53. Schlosser and Gebbia 49–51.
54. Schlosser and Gebbia 51.
55. In the report, his first name is spelled in the more usual way: Roger.
56. Schlosser and Gebbia 55–56.
57. Schlosser and Gebbia 55.
58. Schlosser and Gebbia 55–56.
59. Schlosser and Gebbia 55.
60. A strip of paving, turf or landscaping that separates opposing lanes of traffic is called the median strip in most of the nation, but is called the neutral ground in New Orleans.
61. Schlosser and Gebbia 56.
62. The NOPD General Case Report provides contradictory information, giving the date of July 6 on page 55, and July 7 on page 58. The records from Charity Hospital made available to both police and fire marshal investigators indicate that Rodger Nunez was discharged on July 7.
63. Schlosser and Gebbia 58.
64. Davis Fire Marshal Statement 1.
65. Adams; Butler; Hyde and Roth 28–29; Lind, Thomas and Philbin "29 Dead" A6; Schlosser and Gebbia 56.
66. Schlosser and Gebbia 58.
67. "Chief Feels Fire Arson" 1.
68. Schlosser and Gebbia 62.
69. Johnston 1.
70. Hyde, Roth and Fischer 11.
71. Hyde, Roth and Fischer 6.
72. NOFD Investigation Report (Supplement) 6.
73. Townsend 205–206.
74. NOFD Investigation Report.
75. Glenn Green is described in the case report as Scarborough's "friend, later learned to be his roommate" (Schlosser and Gebbia 60).
76. Scarborough 4.

Chapter 6

1. Schlosser and Gebbia spell this name as Gerry.
2. Schlosser and Gebbia 24–25; Hyde and Roth, 13, 19–20; Nunez 10.
3. Hyde, Roth and Fischer 20.
4. Hyde, Roth and Fischer 20.
5. Schlosser and Gebbia 55.

6. Schlosser and Gebbia 58; Hyde and Roth 22.
7. Hyde, Roth and Fischer 22.
8. Schlosser and Gebbia 59–63.
9. Hyde, Roth and Fischer 22, 29; Nunez Statement 8.
10. Hyde, Roth and Fischer 23–24; Scarborough 1–2; Schlosser and Gebbia 60–61.
11. Nunez B of I; Nunez Statement 1.
12. His school records have not been found, but his name does not appear on the list of students who have received high school diplomas from the state of Louisiana. Additionally, he enlisted in the army in August of 1964. Assuming a normal progression through both primary and secondary school, August of 1964 would have been during the summer preceding his senior year in high school.
13. Nunez Statement 1.
14. Townsend 211–213.
15. Nunez State Police Record.
16. Townsend 213–214.
17. Raybourne.
18. Nunez, Elaine Statement 1.
19. Guidry Second Statement 8.
20. Davis Statement to Arson Investigation 2; Guidry First Statement 4; Nunez Statement 7.
21. Davis Statement to Arson Investigation 2–3.
22. Guidry First Statement 1–3.
23. Davis Statement to Arson Investigation 3.
24. Butler; Adams; Hyde, Roth and Fischer 28–29; Lind, Thomas and Philbin "29 Dead" A6; Schlosser and Gebbia 56.
25. "Vice Charges Okayed by DA" sec. 2: 22; "Charges Accepted in Morals Case" sec. 2: 41; "Police Charge Sex Offenses" sec. 2: 22.
26. Garrison wrote about his investigation and prosecution of Shaw in the book *On the Trail of the Assassins: My Investigation and the Prosecution of the Murder of President Kennedy.* Garrison's conspiracy theory received respectful treatment in Oliver Stone's film *JFK* and in books such as Joan Mellen's *A Farewell to Justice: JFK's Assassination and the Case That Should Have Changed History.* Other people find Garrison's case dubious. See such books as James Kirkwood's *American Grotesque* and Patricia Lambert's *False Witness.*
27. Davis Statement to Criminal Investigation 1–2.
28. Davis Statement to Arson Investigation 4–6.

29. Davis Statement to Arson Investigation 3–4; Schlosser and Gebbia 58.

30. Davis Statement to Arson Investigation 4–5.

31. Rasmussen Statement to Arson Investigation 2; Rasmussen Statement to Criminal Investigation 1–2.

32. Guidry First Statement 3.

33. Hyde, Roth and Fischer 25–26; Rasmussen Statement to Arson Investigation 1–2.

34. Guidry Second Statement 1–2, 6–7; Hyde, Roth and Fischer 25–26.

35. Hyde, Roth and Fischer 26–27.

36. Hyde, Roth and Fischer 30.

37. Nunez Statement 1, 13.

38. Nunez Statement 5–6.

39. Nunez Statement 12.

40. Hyde, Roth and Fischer 30.

41. Hyde, Roth and Fischer 36.

42. Ronayne 245–247.

43. Ronayne 244; United States v. Scheffer.

44. "PSE History."

45. "PSE History"; Ronayne 273.

46. M'Lellen 6.

47. Forest 2; Ledet 1.

48. Forest 9–10.

49. Forest 4.

50. Ledet 1–2.

51. Massaci.

52. Townsend 320–321.

53. Raybourne.

54. Adams; Marcell; Townsend 304 – 307.

55. Townsend 306.

56. Marcell.

57. Nunez, Elaine Statement 1.

58. Lupin; Nunez, Elaine Statement 1.

59. Minimum wage increased slightly to $2 per hour in 1974. His disability check was half of what he would have earned as a full-time, unskilled worker.

60. Nunez, Elaine Statement 2.

61. Forest 4; Nunez, Elaine Statement 2.

62. Nunez, Elaine Statement 2.

63. Lupin.

64. Forest 5–6.

65. Rasmussen Statement to Criminal Investigation 1; Schlosser and Gebbia 60.

66. Forest 9.

67. Nunez, Elaine Statement 1–2.

68. Bullard 2.

69. Winn personal email.

70. Fein personal email.

71. Raybourne.

72. Forest 5.

73. Schlosser and Gebbia 46.

74. Ussery 3.

75. Edwards.

76. Adams; Butler; Marcell; Raybourne; Winn personal email.

Chapter 7

1. Marcy Marcell was born Marco Sperandeo, but after identifying as transgender, she adopted her former drag name.

2. Batson personal interview; Killgore.

3. NOPD Pledges to Prevent Anita Groups Confrontation" 7.

4. Batson "New Orleans"; "NOPD Pledges to Prevent Anita Groups Confrontation" 7.

5. Citron "Anti-Anita Forces Hold Protest" 14.

6. Citron "Anita Sings" 14.

7. Wickman "A Colorful History."

8. Breton interview: Breton journal; Perry and Swicegood 101; Segura "Cleric Says Oppression Problem for Homosexuals" 7; Batson personal interview; Butler; Killgore; Pizanie; Winn telephone interview.

9. For example, Johnny Townsend reports that Stewart Butler watched several people go out the side door and ultimately used that door himself (Townsend 308); however, in a 2009 interview for this book, Stewart Butler said that neither he nor anybody else used the side door. Similarly, when Toni Pizanie was interviewed for this book in 2009, she claimed to have attended the St. Mark's memorial service, and she told the same story to friends on numerous occasions. However, in 2003, she published an article in which she said she had not been present (Pizanie "Sappho Psalms: Why?"). Pizanie died in 2010 and cannot clarify.

10. Perry Interview.

11. Toni Pizanie believed the woman who made the statement was Charlene Schneider, who would later own the lesbian bar Charlene's. Stewart Butler, who attended the memorial service, does not recall it being Charlene, but says that "it would certainly have been in her character." Paul Killgore and Troy Perry both say they saw the woman clearly, and that it was definitely not Charlene. Charlene herself is dead, and cannot comment.

12. Breton interview.

13. Perez and Palmquist 92.

14. Not to be confused with the Human Rights Campaign (also known as HRC), a national gay rights organization currently in operation and based in Washington, D.C.

15. "Politics" 4.

16. Treadway "50s Climate of Hostility Gone" 21.

17. Treadway "A Walk on the Gay Side" 8.

18. *Degrees of Equality.*

19. Raybourne.

20. Though Nagin suspended the sensitivity training, he continued to appoint representatives of the LGBT community to the city's HRC; Larry Bagneris, one such representative, was instrumental in getting the city's cooperation in the placement of the memorial plaque commemorating the fire.

21. Pizanie personal interview.

22. "Aid Asked for Fire Survivors" 9.

23. "Fund Tops $1,400" 1; "Fund Nudges $5,000" 22; "Memorial Fund Tops $7,200" 19; "Memorial Fund Passes $10,000" 13, "Fund Passes $15,500" 4; "Fund Exceeds $16,500" 9; "Memorial Fund Coming to an End" 24.

24. Perry telephone interview.

25. Records, National New Orleans Memorial Fund.

26. Townsend 131–133.

27. "Yesterday's Dreams, Today's Ghosts" 12, 16.

28. Records, National New Orleans Memorial Fund.

29. Referring to the 1973's status quo as "Don't Ask, Don't Tell" is a bit of an anachronism; the military policy instituted under President Clinton, and the term that describes it, would not come into existence for another twenty years.

30. Dubos telephone interview; "How the Media Saw It" 6; Perry and Swicegood 87–88.

31. There are six passages that are normally cited as biblical condemnation of homosexuality. They are: Genesis 19:5; Leviticus 18:22 and 20:13; Romans 1:26–27; I Corinthians 6:9; I Timothy 1:9–10. There is no such passage in Revelations.

32. Wilson "Race Note Seen in Prison Rapes" 1; "Volz Airs Plan to Halt Rapes" 3.

33. "Plea for Prison Access Refused" 13.

34. "Lady Baronessa" 6.

35. DuBos telephone interview.

36. Treadway "A Walk on the Gay Side" 8.

37. "APA: Gay No Mental Disorder" 43.

38. Treadway "Homosexuals Disagree on Behavior's 'Sickness'" 2.

39. "APA Council Passes Resolution"; Herek.

40. CA SB 1172, regarding sexual orientation change efforts, reads, in part, "This bill would prohibit a mental health provider, as defined, from engaging in sexual orientation change efforts, as defined, with a patient under 18 years of age. The bill would provide that any sexual orientation change efforts attempted on a patient under 18 years of age by a mental health provider shall be considered unprofessional conduct and shall subject the provider to discipline by the provider's licensing entity."

41. In yet another sign of how the 1970s differ from the early twenty-first century, the psychiatrists and the clergy Treadway interviewed were all men. It is perhaps for this reason that the series never addresses lesbianism, except when Treadway quotes Celeste Newbrough.

42. Though the psychiatric and mental health professions, as a whole, have long since abandoned the idea that conversion is effective, necessary, or even desirable, a minority still pursues conversion as a goal. In writing about this issue, Dan Savage has argued that supporters of such therapy represent an ameliorated homophobia, but homophobia nonetheless. Savage believes that by arguing that homosexuality doesn't have to exist, conversion proponents implicitly argue that gays have no right to exist (Savage 18). Evidence of this point of view surfaces in arguments against marriage equality and other laws designed to protect GLBT people, with Republican House Speaker John Boehner, for example, arguing that anti-discrimination laws should be reserved to protect people for "immutable" characteristics, and anti-marriage equality activist Janet Shaw Crouse saying that same-sex marriage isn't necessary because people can choose whether or not to be homosexual (Montopoli; Crouse; see also Blomberg).

43. Treadway "Psychiatric and Clerical Views" 18.

44. "The Law" 5.

45. Treadway "It's Not Illegal" 14.

46. Treadway "It's Not Illegal" 14.

47. Wian and Pearson.

48. James.

49. Treadway "50s Climate" 21.

50. Lee "The Way Back" 15; Patterson "Biased Reporting" 8.

51. All six biblical passages cited as condemnation of homosexuality refer to sex between two men. The possibility of sexual activity between women is never referenced. Biblically speaking, lesbianism does not exist.

52. "School to Appeal Gay Student Issue" 13.

53. Patterson "Gays and Christians" 8; Somme "'Judging' Gays" 10.
54. Kaufman TVF 16; Walker 13.
55. Ussery "Police Crackdown" 3.
56. The practice is not extinct. In 2003 a biography was published of an American writer who enjoyed a national reputation in the first half of the twentieth century. He also enjoyed sexual activity with both men and women. His biographer, who asked not to be identified in this context, has said that she was pressured by her publisher to remove references to the homosexual affairs. References to affairs with women were allowed to remain.
57. Cuthbert E1–2.
58. Cuthbert E1–2.
59. Brecht personal interview; Finch A1, 8; Thompson B1, 8.
60. Brecht personal interview; Pizanie personal interview; O'Brien E1–2.
61. In Nazi Germany, for example, known homosexuals were imprisoned in camps and made to wear a pink triangle.
62. Butler personal interview; Killgore personal interview; Marcell personal interview; Pizanie personal interview.
63. "Ambush Mag Presents 40th Anniversary"; Dias and Downs; Perez.
64. Pizanie Interview.
65. Ross.
66. Buckley; Boulard 32–33; Restak C01.
67. Lindsey.
68. The Catholic church has never altered its position on homosexuality, and Pope Benedict XVI, formerly Cardinal Joseph Ratzinger, only softened the prohibition against condom use in 2010, announcing that while condoms should still not be used for contraception, they would be allowed for use in preventing the spread of HIV. Even then, he said that condom use was not appropriate for all people, but only for selected, smaller groups, such as male prostitutes, a group which apparently enjoys a powerful lobby in the Vatican (Bolcer).

3. Redman.
4. Samuels.
5. "Raw Data."
6. Ironically, Marcus Bachmann himself fits the stereotype of the lisping, effeminate gay man, leading to rumors that he himself is a self-hating, closeted homosexual. See Mullen; see also Cottle.
7. Goldberg.
8. "APA Council Passes Resolution."
9. Herek.
10. CA SB 1172, regarding sexual orientation change efforts, reads, in part, "This bill would prohibit a mental health provider, as defined, from engaging in sexual orientation change efforts, as defined, with a patient under 18 years of age. The bill would provide that any sexual orientation change efforts attempted on a patient under 18 years of age by a mental health provider shall be considered unprofessional conduct and shall subject the provider to discipline by the provider's licensing entity."
11. Cavaliere.
12. The National Coalition for the Homeless estimates that LGBT youth are more than twice as likely to be homeless as teens from the general population, citing family conflict as a primary reason. LGBT youth are also more likely to have been the victims of sexual abuse.
13. For all its critical acclaim, the 2005 film *Brokeback Mountain* was in many ways a throwback to the "tortured homosexual" genre of the '60s and '70s. Similarly, the 2013 film *Side Effects* resurrected another film stereotype from that era: the "diabolical lesbian."
14. Dailey; Sprigg.
15. "Information on Divorce Rates"; Luscombe; Wilcox.
16. Winn; Carrel.
17. Brecht telephone interview; Mozingo.
18. Mozingo.

Afterword

1. Grant.
2. Douglas-Brown; Kinkaid.

Bibliography

Adams, Regina. Personal interview. July 1, 2009.

"Aid Asked for Fire Survivors." *The Advocate* 116 (July 18, 1973): 9. Print.

"Ambush Mag Presents 40thAnniversary Upstairs Lounge Fire Memorial Weekend June 20–24." n.d. NOLApride.org. Web. June 26, 2013.

Anderson, Ed, and Liza Frazier. "House Panel Alters Duke Welfare Bill." *The Times–Picayune.* Friday, May 4, 1991, A14. Print.

Anderson, Royd. *The Upstairs Lounge Fire.* Lake Oaks Studio, 2013. DVD.

"APA Council of Representatives Passes Resolution on So-Called Reparative Therapy." University of California, Davis. 14 August 1997. Web. November 23, 2012.

"APA: Gay No Mental Disorder." *The Times–Picayune.* Sunday, December 16, 1973, sec. 1: 43. Print.

Arceneaux, Rev. Richard C., Jr. "Gay Is Unnatural." *The Times–Picayune.* Wednesday, October 3, 1973, sec. 1: 12. Print.

"As the Fire Violations Pile Up." *The Times–Picayune.* Sunday, July 15, 1973, sec. 1: 14. Print.

Ball, Millie. "Anita Arrives Amid Tight Security." *The Times–Picayune.* Saturday, June 18, 1977, sec. 1: 14. Print.

_____."Edwards Tours Rault Building." *The Times–Picayune.* Friday, December 1, 1972, sec. 1: 1, 10. Print.

_____. "'I'd Rather My Child Be Dead Than Homo.'" *The Times–Picayune.* Sunday, June 19, 1977, sec. 1: 3. Print.

Barker, Pepper. "Up Stairs 'a family.'" Letter to Editor. *The States-Item.* Thursday, July 5, 1973, A10. Print.

Batson, Roberts. "New Orleans." *GLBTQ Social Sciences.* 2004. Web. January 23, 2013.

_____. Personal email. August 4, 2011.

_____. Personal interview. December 21, 2009.

_____. "Roberts Batson." *OutHistory.* 12 April 2009. Web. January 23, 2013.

Beaulieu, Lovell. "No Incidents at Anita Protest." *The Times–Picayune.* Sunday, June 19, 1977, sec. 1: 3. Print.

"'Beer Bust' Erupts into Fiery Trap." *San Gabriel Valley Daily Tribune.* Monday, June 25, 1973, sec.1: 1, 2. Print.

Billings, Rev. David. Personal email. August 20, 2009.

Black Mama, White Mama. Dir. Eddie Romero. Perf. Margaret Markhov and Pam Grier. Soul Cinema, 1973. Film.

"Blaze Victims' Memorial Set." *The Times–Picayune.* Saturday, June 30, 1973, sec. 1:11. Print.

"Blaze Victims' Names Sought." *The Times–Picayune.* Tuesday, June 26, 1973, sec. 1: 3. Print.

Blomberg, Daniel. "Legal Statement from Alliance Defense Fund." 24 August 2010. Web. January 26, 2013. *Awaken Manhattan.*

Bouden, Mrs. Barbara. "Fire Reveals Bias."

Letter to the Editor. *The Times–Picayune.* Friday, June 29, 1973, sec. 1: 12. Print.

Boulard, Gary. "The Man Behind the Mask." *The Advocate: The National Gay and Lesbian Newsmagazine* (May 2, 1995): 29–35. Print.

Brecht, Rev. Dexter. Personal interview. June 2, 2009.

_____. Telephone interview. August 5, 2009.

_____. "The Upstairs Lounge Fire." *Love, Bourbon Street: Reflections of New Orleans.* Eds. Greg Herren and Paul J. Willis. New York: Alyson Books, 2006, 61–65. Print.

Brener, Milton. *The Garrison Case: A Study in the Abuse of Power.* New York: C.N. Potter, 1969. Print.

Breton, Rev. Paul. Telephone interview. March 3, 2010.

_____. Unpublished journal. This consists of news clippings, handbills and programs from some of the memorial services, transcripts of letters and telegrams, as well as personal observations by the Reverend Breton, who loaned this journal to the author. Print.

Buckley, William F., Jr. "Crucial Steps in Combating the AIDS Epidemic; Identify All the Carriers." *The New York Times.* 18 March 1986. Web. February 17, 2013.

Bullard, Jacqueline. Statement to the Arson Investigation Division of the Louisiana State Fire Marshal. March 11, 1975. Print.

Butler, Stewart. Personal interview. July 2, 2009.

Byrd, Phillip. Personal email. February 13, 2013.

Carrel, Jack. Personal interview. July 9, 2009.

Carter, David. *Stonewall: The Riots That Sparked the Gay Revolution.* New York: St. Martin's Griffin, 2004. Print.

Cavaliere, Victoria. "New Jersey Bans Gay Conversion Therapy." *Chicago Tribune News.* 19 August 2013. Web. August 28, 2013.

"Charges Accepted in Morals Case." *The Times–Picayune.* Thursday, October 9, 1958, sec. 1: 22. Print.

"Charred Rubble Sifted for Clues." *The States-Item.* Tuesday, June 26, 1973, A1, 3. Print.

"Chief Feels Fire Arson: Believes Flammable Used at Up Stairs." *The Times–Picayune.* Monday, July 16, 1973, sec 1: 1, 24. Print.

"Church Strives Following Fire." *The Times–Picayune.* Saturday, February 16, 1974, sec. 2: 4. Print.

Citron, Alan. "Anita Sings 'Among Friends.'" *The Times–Picayune.* Saturday, June 18, 1977, sec. 1: 14. Print.

_____. "Anti-Anita Forces Hold Silent Protest." *The Times–Picayune.* Saturday, June 18, 1977, sec. 1: 1, 14. Print.

_____. "'Out of the Closets, Into Streets' Is Gay Protest Rally Cry." *The Times–Picayune.* Sunday, June 19, 1977, sec. 1: 3. Print.

"Condolences to Victims' Families Offered by Archbishop Hannan." *The Times–Picayune.* Thursday, November 30, 1972, sec. 1: 3. Print.

Cottle, Michelle. "Bachmann Rumor Grows Louder. *The Daily Beast.* 16 July 2011. Web. November 20, 2012.

"Craighead, Courtney." Obituary. *The Times–Picayune.* Friday, 24 June 2005. Web. April 16, 2009.

Cross, Richard Robert. Statement to the Arson Investigation Division of the Louisiana State Fire Marshal. October 23, 1973. Print.

Crouse, Janet Shaw. "Five Myths About Same Sex Marriage." *Townhall.* 9 March 2010.Web. January 27, 2013.

Cuthbert, David. "Where There Was Smoke." *The Times–Picayune.* Saturday, June 20, 1998. E1–2. Print.

Dailey, Timothy J. "Ten Facts About Same-Sex Marriage." *Truenews.org.* n.d. Web. November 21, 2012.

"Davis." Obituary. *The Times–Picayune.* Sunday, June 3, 1984, sec. 1: 22. Print.

Davis, Eugene C. Dektor PSE in Reference to the Fire at the Up Stairs Lounge. Bastrop Police Department, Bastrop, Louisiana. October 14, 1973. Print.

_____. Proceedings of the Orleans Parish Grand Jury. June 28, 1967. Web. September 7, 2011.

_____. Statement to the Arson Investigation Division of the Louisiana State Fire Marshal. October 1, 1973. Print.

_____. Statement to the Criminal Investigation Division of the New Orleans Police Department, Homicide Unit. July 9, 1973. Print.

Degrees of Equality: A National Study Examining Workplace Climate for LGBT Workers. Human Rights Campaign Foundation. September 2009. Web. July 24, 2011.

Dias, Elizabeth, and Jim Downs. "The Horror Upstairs." 1 July 2001. Web. June 21, 2013.

Douglas-Brown, Laura. "Police Release Copies of Complaints Against Officers in Eagle Raid." *Southern Voice.* 15 September 2009. Web. September 16, 2009.

DuBos, Clancy. "Blood, Moans: Charity Scene." *The Times–Picayune.* Monday, June 25, 1973, sec. 1: 1–2. Print.

_____. Telephone interview. February 18, 2013.

Dufrene, Francis. Telephone interview. June 1, 2013.

Duplantis, Steven. Personal interview. August 1, 2013.

Eaton, John P. "Cancelled Passages Aboard Titanic." *Encyclopedia Titanica.* 29 June 2010. Web.

Edwards, Aaron, L.A.C. Personal interview. July 21, 2010.

Ellis, Scott S. *Madame Vieux Carré: The French Quarter in the Twentieth Century.* Jackson: University Press of Mississippi, 2010. Print.

E[stevan], Bruha, and Richard Hargrove. "Editorial." *The New Orleans Causeway* 1. 2 (December 1973): 5. Print.

Esteve, Phil. Statement to the Arson Investigation Division of the Louisiana State Fire Marshal. June 27, 1973. Print.

"False Confessions." *The Innocence Project.* 3 March 2012. Web.

"Fatal Fire Probe Continues." *The Times–Picayune.* Thursday, June 28, 1973, sec. 1: 5. Print.

Fein, Skylar. Personal email. July 17, 2009.

_____. Personal interview. June 4, 2009.

_____. "Remember the Upstairs Lounge: Skylar Fein at Prospect.1." Contemporary Arts Center, New Orleans, November 2008 – January 2009.

Finch, Susan. "Fire of '73: Tragedy United Gays." *The Times–Picayune.* Thursday, June 24, 1993, A 1, 8. Print.

"Fire Fund Gives $13,800." *The Advocate* 143 (July 31, 1974): 8. Print.

"First Gay Dollars Reach New Orleans Fire Victims." *The Advocate* 131 (February 13, 1974): 2, 11. Print.

"Five-Story Dive Kicks Off Marriott Hotel's Opening." *The Times–Picayune.* Friday, July 21, 1972, sec. 1: 3. Print.

Forest, Ralph. Statement to the Arson Investigation Division of the Louisiana State Fire Marshal. November 19, 1974. Print.

France, David. *How to Survive a Plague.* Public Square Films, 2012. DVD.

Frazer, Tom. "Sons of Fire Victim Sent Home—Unaware of Father's Death." *The States-Item.* Tuesday, June 26, 1973, A3. Print.

"Fund Exceeds $16,500." *The Advocate* 128 (January 2, 1974): 9. Print.

"Fund Nudges $5,000 Mark." *The Advocate* 118 (August 15, 1973): 22. Print.

"Fund Passes $15,500." *The Advocate* 124 (November 7, 1973): 4. Print.

"Fund Tops $1,400 in 9 Days." *The Advocate* 117 (August 1, 1973): 1. Print.

Garrison, Jim. *On the Trail of the Assassins: My Investigation and the Prosecution of the Murder of President Kennedy.* New York: Sheridan Square Press, 1988. Print.

Gill, John. Telephone interview. March 2, 2010.

Goldberg, Michelle. "Marcus Bachmann's Gay 'Cure.'" The Daily Beast. 10 July 2011. Web. November 20, 2012.

Gosnell, Jean. Statement to the Arson Investigation Division of the Louisiana State Fire Marshal. December 30, 1973. Print.

Grady, Bill. "Pro-Bryant Group Small." *The Times–Picayune.* Sunday, June 19, 1977, sec. 1: 3. Print.

Grant, Jon E. "Substance Abuse Treatment for Lesbian, Gay, Bisexual, Transgender Individuals." n.d. Web. November 20, 2012.

Gregg, Katherine. "Update: Carcieri, Gay Rights Meet on Burial Rights Veto." *Projo*

7 to 7 News Blog. Providence Journal. 7 November 2009. Web. July 16, 2010.

Guidry, Mark Allen. First Statement to the Arson Investigation Division of the Louisiana State Fire Marshal. July 2, 1973. Print.

_____. Second Statement to the Arson Investigation Division of the Louisiana State Fire Marshal. July 23, 1973. Print.

Hanley, Ryan. "Tourism: A City on Life Support." Dying City Series: Part 1. Inferior Publishing 1: 1. Web. July 26, 2011.

Hannan, Archbishop Philip M. "The Archbishop Speaks: Strength to Overcome." *The Clarion Herald* 10: 45 (January 11, 1973): 1. Print.

Hargrove, Richard M. "Another Aspect of Sunday's Tragedy." Letter to Editor. *The States-Item.* Saturday, June 30, 1973, A6. Print.

Harris, Tom. "How ESP Works: ESP Research." n.d. Web. September 17, 2011.

"Hate Attitude Noted By Cleric: Sniper Became Militant in Navy." *The Times-Picayune.* Wednesday, January 10, 1973, sec. 1: 1, 19. Print.

"Hate Crimes." The FBI: Federal Bureau of Investigation. n.d. Web. March 1, 2012.

Hendrix, Carey. Personal interview. October 3, 2011.

Herek, Gregory M. "The APA Resolution on Appropriate Therapeutic Responses to Sexual Orientation." University of California, Davis. 1997. Web. November 23, 2012.

Hernon, Peter. *A Terrible Thunder: The Story of the New Orleans Sniper.* New Orleans: Garret County Press, 2001. Print.

Hiller, Tony, and Peter Simons. "United We Stand." Perf. The Brotherhood of Man. Deram, 1970. Perf. Sonny and Cher. Kapp Records, 1971.

"History of the MCC." *Metropolitan Community Churches.* MCC. Fall 2004. Web. July 7, 2010.

"'Homophobia' Causes Told." *The Times-Picayune.* Saturday, February 8, 1975, sec. 1: 15. Print.

Houston, Julia. "Neighborhood Population: New Orleans French Quarter." Web. July 26, 2011.

"How the Media Saw It." *Vieux Carré Courier* X. 8 (June 29–July 5, 1973): 6. Print.

"HRC to Attack Gay Problems." *The Times-Picayune.* Wednesday, August 8, 1973, sec. 1: 17. Print.

"Hurt By Label." *The Times-Picayune.* Wednesday, July 4, 1973, sec. 1: 10. Print.

Hyde, Edward S., William M. Roth and John M. Fischer. Case Report of the Arson Investigation Division of the Louisiana State Fire Marshal. Orleans Parish Case File Number 464–73 6–24–73. July 22, 1975. Print.

"Information on Divorce Rates." *Divorce Rate.org.* n.d. Web. November 23, 2012.

"Inquiries Continue for Quarter Fire." *The Daily Record.* Tuesday, June 26, 1973, sec. 1: 1, 8. Print.

Jacob, Mrs. C.W. "Sympathy, Apology." Letter to Editor. *The Times-Picayune.* Monday, July 2, 1973, sec. 1: 8. Print.

James, Susan Donaldson. "Boy Scouts Vote to End Ban on Gay Scouts; Gay Adults Still Barred." ABC News. 23 May 2013. Web. June 26, 2013.

Johnston, Mark. "Methenamine Pill Test." *Beaulieu of America Technical Services Newsletter* 9. 3 (March 2009): 1. Web. July 20, 2010.

Kaiser, Charles. *The Gay Metropolis.* New York: Harcourt Brace, 1997. Print.

_____. Personal email. August 4, 2010.

Katz, Allan. "Flammable Substance Suspected: Probe of Up Stairs Fire Incomplete." *The Times-Picayune.* Sunday, July 15, 1973. Print.

_____. "Labeling the Dead: An Impossible Job?" *The States-Item.* Monday, June 25, 1973. A6b. Print.

Kaufman, Bill. "Networks 'Coming Out' with Gay Comedy Roles." *The Times-Picayune.* Sunday, August 29, 1976, TVF: 16. Print.

Killgore, Paul. Personal Interview. August 9, 2009.

Kincaid, Timothy. "Yet Another 'Reason' for the Atlanta Bar Raid." *Box Turtle Bulletin.* 14 September 2009. Web. September 15, 2009.

Kirk, Michael. "People Do Care." Letter to

Editor. *The States-Item.* Thursday, July 5, 1973, A10. Print.

Kirkwood, James. *American Grotesque: An Account of the Clay Shaw–Jim Garrison Kennedy Assassination Trial in New Orleans.* New York: Simon & Schuster, 1970. Print.

"Lady Baronessa." *The Times–Picayune.* Monday, May 14, 1973, sec. 4: 6. Print.

Lafourcade, Emile, Jr. "Multiple Rites Arranged for Three Police Victims." *The Times–Picayune.* Tuesday, January 9, 1973, sec. 1: 5. Print.

_____. "Sniper Rife Same Used in Other Crimes." *The Times–Picayune.* Wednesday, January 10, 1973, sec 1: 1. Print.

Lambert, Patricia. *False Witness.* New York: M. Evans, 1998. Print.

"Landrieu Leaves After Fire News." *The Times–Picayune.* Thursday, January 11, 1973, sec. 1: 1. Print.

LaPlace, John. "Endless Lines of Blood Donors Flock to Charity." *The Times–Picayune.* Monday, January 8, 1973, sec. 1: 2. Print.

_____. "Scene of French Quarter Fire Is Called Dante's 'Inferno,' Hitler's Incinerators." *The Times–Picayune.* Monday, June 25, 1973, sec. 1: 1–2. Print.

_____, and Ed Anderson. "Arson Possibility Is Raised." *The Times–Picayune.* Monday, June 25, 1973, sec. 1: 1, 3. Print.

"The Law." *The New Orleans Causeway* 1. 1 (August 6, 1973): 5. Print.

Lee, Vincent. "Gay Leaders Plan Aid for Victims of Bar Fire." *The Times–Picayune.* Wednesday, June 27, 1973, sec. 1: 14. Print.

_____. "The Way Back: Behavior Therapy Is Key to Program." *The Times–Picayune.* Saturday, February 3, 1973, sec. 1: 15. Print.

_____, and Emile Lafourcade, Jr. "Girl in Yellow Screaming and Then She Fell." *The Times–Picayune.* Thursday, November 30, 1973, sec. 1: 1, 5. Print.

Lewis, Don. "Tragedy Fund Is Established." *The Times–Picayune.* Saturday, January 13, 1973, sec. 1: 1, 2. Print.

"LGBT Homeless." *The National Coalition of the Homeless.* 21 February 2012. Web. November 21, 2012.

Lind, Angus. "Fire Bares the Grisly Face of Death." *The States-Item.* Monday, June 25, 1973, A6b. Print.

_____, Lanny Thomas, and Walt Philbin. "29 Dead in Quarter Holocaust." *The States-Item.* Monday, June 25, 1973, A1, 6. Print.

Linde, Dennis. "Burning Love." Perf. Elvis Presley. RCA, 1972. Single.

Lindsey, Robert. "AIDS Among Clergy Presents Challenges to Catholic Church." *The New York Times.* 2 February 1987. Web. February 17, 2013.

Locascio, Frank J., Jr. Letter to Mr. William M. Roth, Jr., and Mr. John M. Fischer, relative to the fire at the Up Stairs Lounge. June 26, 1980. Print.

Louisiana State Fire Marshal Case File 464–73. The Upstairs Lounge Fire. June 24, 1973. Print. Held by the Louisiana State Archives, Baton Rouge, Louisiana.

"Louisianans in Indiana Express Grief and Shock." *The Times–Picayune.* Friday, December 1, 1973, sec. 1: 6. Print.

Lugalia, Terry. "Households, Families and Children: A 30-Year Perspective." Bureau of the Census. 1992. Web. April 29, 2013.

Lupin, Ralph, M.D., Asst. Coroner. Autopsy Report: Rodger Dale Nunez. Orleans Parish Coroner's Office. November 16, 1974. Print.

Luscombe, Belinda. "Are Marriage Statistics Divorced From Reality." *Time Magazine.* 24. May 2010. Web. November 21, 2012.

Lynch, Bill. "Fire Regulations Ignored, Even in Capitol High-Rise." *The States-Item.* Friday, June 29, 1973, A9. Print.

Magill, Rich. *Exposing Hatred: A Report on the Victimization of Lesbian and Gay People in New Orleans, Louisiana.* Mayor's Advisory Committee on Lesbian and Gay Issues. New Orleans, Louisiana, 1991. Print.

Marcell, Marcy. Personal interview. June 29, 2009.

"Margaret Sanger (1879–1966)." *Women Working, 1800–1930.* Harvard University Library Open Collections Program. n.d. Web. July 1, 2013.

Massaci, Jim Jr. Telephone interview. August 6, 2009.

"Mayor Offers Sympathy, Prayers, Thanks in Fire." *The Times–Picayune*. Monday, December 1, 1972, sec. 1: 11. Print.

McCarthy Brendan. "Sweeping NOPD Reform Strategy Outlined In Federal Consent Decree." *The Times–Picayune*. Wednesday, 25 July 2012. Web. July 26, 2012.

Mellen, Joan. *A Farewell to Justice: JFK's Assassination and the Case that Should Have Changed History*. Washington, D.C.: Potomac Press, 2005. Print.

"Memorial Fund Coming to an End." *The Advocate* 145 (August 28, 1974): 24. Print.

"Memorial Fund Passes $10,000." *The Advocate* 120 (September 12, 1973): 13. Print.

"Memorial Fund Tops $7,200." *The Advocate* 119 (August 29, 1973): 19. Print.

"Michele Bachmann in Her Own Words: 'Gays Are Part of Satan.'" *Gawker*. 7 July 2007. Web. November 20, 2012.

M'Lellen, Joseph. "Literary Secret No Longer That." *The Times–Picayune*. Thursday, October 18, 1973, sec. 2: 6. Print.

Monroe, Albert. Statement to the Arson Investigation Division of the Louisiana State Fire Marshal. July 2, 1073. Print.

Montopoli, Brian. "Why GOP Leader Opposes Hate Crimes Protection." *CBS News*. 13. October 2009. Web. January 27, 2013.

Mozingo, Rev. Keith. Personal interview. July 25, 2012.

Mullen, Mike. "Marcus Bachman: Gay or Straight." City Pages Blog. 5 July 2011. Web. November 20, 2012.

Murphy, Edward. "Fire Traps." Letter to the Editor. *The States-Item*. Thursday, July 5, 1973, A10. Print.

Nauth, Zack. "Lawmakers: Duke Flunked Freshman Term." *The Times–Picayune*. Sunday, July 16, 1989, B1. Print.

"New Burn Unit Used At Charity: Quarter Blaze Victims Forced Opening." *The Times–Picayune*. Thursday, June 28, 1973, sec. 7: 16. Print.

New Orleans Fire Department Fire Prevention Division: Inspection and/or Investigation Report(s). October 9, 1970;

October 19, 1970; October 29, 1970; December 4, 1970; March 11, 1971. Print.

_____. Investigation Report of Fire. June 24, 1973. Print.

_____. Investigation Report of Fire: Fatality List. June 24, 1973. Print.

_____. Investigation Report of Fire: Supplemental Information. n.d. Print.

Newhouse, Eric. "Bar Not Inspected in 2 Years." *The Times–Picayune*. Sunday, July 1, 1973, sec. 1: 4. Print.

_____. "Smokie." This story was written for the Associated Press News Service. It reportedly ran in several cities nationwide, but not in any Louisiana newspapers. A transcript of the story is in the Breton Journal.

_____. "32 Perished in Up Stairs Bar Fire Year Ago Today." *The Times–Picayune*. Monday, June 24, 1974, sec. 1: 11. Print.

"N.O. Mourning Is Proclaimed." *The Times–Picayune*. Wednesday, January 10, 1973, sec. 1: 9. Print.

Nolan, Bruce, and Chris Segura. "Memorial for the Fire Has Forgiveness Theme." *The Times Picayune*. Tuesday, June 26, 1973, sec. 1: 3. Print.

"NOPD Pledges to Prevent Anita Groups Confrontation." *The Times–Picayune*. Friday, June 17, 1977, sec. 2: 7. Print.

Nunez, Elaine Wharton Basset. Statement to the Arson Investigation Division of the Louisiana State Fire Marshal. December 9, 1974. Print.

Nunez, Rodger. Bureau of Identification Photograph 164–505. New Orleans Police Department. December 14, 1972. Print.

_____. Dektor PSE Administered in Reference to the Fire at the Up Stairs Lounge. Abbeville Sheriff's Office, Abbeville, Louisiana. October 9, 1973. Print.

_____. State Police Record No. 814 225. State of Louisiana: Department of Public Safety, Division of State Police. Print.

_____. Statement to the Arson Investigation Division of the Louisiana State Fire Marshal. September 18, 1973. Print.

O'Brien, Keith. "Final Witness: Plaque Commemorates the Losses and Legacy of Upstairs Lounge Fire." *The Times–*

Picayune. Wednesday, July 2, 2003, E1–2. Print.

Pagano, Toni. See Pizanie, Toni Pagano.

P[arker], J[ustin]. "The Post Office." *The New Orleans Causeway* 1. 2 (December, 1973): 2. Print.

"Passing the Buck on Fire Prevention." *The States-Item*. Friday, June 29, 1973, A8. Print.

Patterson, James H. "Biased Reporting." *The Times–Picayune*. Thursday, February 8, 1973, sec. 1: 8. Print.

_____. "Gays and Christians." *The Times–Picayune*. Wednesday, June 12, 1974, sec. 1: 8. Print.

_____. "Series 'Anti-Gay.'" *The Times–Picayune*. Friday, September 21, 1973, sec 1: 14. Print.

Pela, Robert. "The Legend of Lizzie." *The Advocate*. 30 July 1992. Web. August 4, 2011.

Perez, Frank. "After UpStairs Lounge fire, Gay and Straight New Orleans Changed." NOLA.com. 22 June 2013. Web. June 25, 2013.

_____, and Jeffrey Palmquist. *In Exile: The History and Lore Surrounding New Orleans Gay Culture and Its Oldest Gay Bar*. Hurlford, Scotland: L.L. Publications, 2012. Print.

Perry, Rev. Troy D., as told to Charles L. Lucas. *The Lord Is My Shepherd, and He Knows I'm Gay*. New York: Bantam, 1972. Print.

_____. Telephone interview. January 4, 2010.

_____, with Thomas L.P. Swicegood. *Don't Be Afraid Anymore*. New York: St. Martin's Press, 1990. Print.

Philbin, Walt. "First the Horror—Then the Leap." *The States-Item*. Monday, June 15, 1973, A6b. Print.

Pizanie, Toni Pagano. Personal interview. June 1, 2009.

_____. "Sappho Psalm: Why." *Ambush* 21. 1 (2003). Web. November 15, 2013.

"Plea for Prison Access Refused." *The Times–Picayune*. Thursday, April 12, 1973, sec. 5: 13. Print.

"Police Charge Sex Offenses: Arrests Follow Quizzing of Runaway Boy." *The Times–*

Picayune. Tuesday, October 21, 1958, sec. 2: 22. Print.

"Politics." *The New Orleans Causeway* 1: 1 (August 6, 1973): 4. Print.

"Position Taken on Sex Claims." *The Times–Picayune*. Saturday, February 10, 1973, sec. 1: 20. Print.

"Premonition." *Encyclopedia Titanica*. n.d. Web. June 29, 2010.

"PSE History." Dektor Corporation. n.d. Web. July 30, 2010.

"Quarter Bar Owner is Found Slain at Home." *The Times–Picayune*. Friday, June 1, 1984, sec. 1: 17. Print.

Rasmussen, Douglas M (Buddy). Statement to the Arson Investigation Division of the Louisiana State Fire Marshal. July 18, 1973. Print.

_____. Statement to the Criminal Investigation Unit of the New Orleans Police Department. June 25, 1973. Print.

Ratzinger, Joseph. "Letter to the Bishops of the Catholic Church on the Pastoral Care of Homosexual Persons." 1 October 1986. Web. July 24, 2011.

"Rault Tragedy Claims Sixth Victim." *The Times–Picayune*. Thursday, January 11, 1973, sec. 1: 6. Print.

"Raw Data: Excerpts of Santorum's AP Interview." *Fox News*. 22 April 2003. Web. November 20, 2012.

Raybourne, Lawrence. Telephone interview. August 7, 2009.

Records, National New Orleans Memorial Fund. ONE National Archives. Los Angeles. Print.

Redman, Daniel. "Dead Law Walking: Why Are New York Cops Arresting Gay People on Charges Ruled Unconstitutional 26 Years Ago?" *Slate*. 20 October 2009. Web. October 21, 2009.

"Remembering Edwin Edwards' Infamous 'Live Boy' Statement." *The Midwest Democracy Project*. Web. August 6, 2011.

Restak, Richard. "Worry About Survival of Society First: Then AIDS Victims' Civil Rights." *The Washington Post*. Sunday, September 8, 1985. Outlook: C01. Print.

Rexford, Milton. "My Favorite Darrin." n.d. Web. August 4, 2011.

Richards, Lewis S. "The 29 Fire." Letter to

Editor. *The Daily Record*. Thursday, June 28, 1963, sec. 1: 2. Print.

Richardson, Rev. William P., Jr. Letter to the Congregation of St. George's. June 28, 1973. Print.

Rikard, Dorothy. Statement to the Arson Investigation Division of the Louisiana State Fire Marshal. March 17, 1975. Print.

Romagosa, Father Elmo L. "Shepherd Tends to His Flock." *The Clarion Herald* 10. 45 (January 11, 1973): 1, 3. Print.

Ronayne, John A. "Admissibility of Testing by the Psychological Stress Evaluator." *Pace Law Review* 9. 243 (1989): 242–273. Print.

"Ronson Flame Accessories." Ronson. n.d. July 16, 2010.

Ross, Alex. "Love on the March." *The New Yorker*. 12 November 2012. Web. November 18. 2012.

Rushton, Bill. "After the Fire Up Stairs." *Vieux Carré Courier* X. 8 (June 29–July5, 1973): 1, 4–6. Print.

_____. "Fire Three: Who the Victims Were." *Vieux Carré Courier* X. 8 (July 13–19, 1973): 6–7. Print.

_____. "Forgetting the Fire: Who Won't Speak Out." *Vieux Carré Courier* X. 8 (July 6–12, 1973): 1, 6. Print.

Rutland, William R. "No Thieves' Hangout." *The States-Item*. Thursday, July 5, 1973, A10. Print.

Samuels, Diana. "East Baton Rouge Sherriff's Office 'Made Mistakes' in Arrests of Gay Men at Baton Rouge Parks." *The Times–Picayune*. 29 July 2013. Web. August 28, 2013.

Savage, Dan. *The Kid: What Happened After My Boyfriend and I Decided to Get Pregnant*. New York: Plume, 2000. Print.

Savant, Cynthia Ann (Cee Cee). Statement to the Arson Investigation Division of the Louisiana state Fire Marshal. August 1, 1974. Print.

Scarborough, Michael. Statement to the Arson Investigation Division of the Louisiana State Fire Marshal. July 16, 1973. Print.

Schlosser, Charles, and Sam Gebbia. New Orleans Police Department General Case

Report. Item No. F-21149–73. August 30, 1973. Print.

"School to Appeal Gay Student Issue." *The Times–Picayune*. Monday, January 21, 1974, sec. 1: 13. Print.

Sears, James T. *Rebels, Rubyfruit, and Rhinestones: Queering Space in the Stonewall South*. New Brunswick: Rutgers University Press, 2001. Print.

Segura, Chris. "Cleric Says Oppression Problem for Homosexuals: Memorial Service Held for Fire Victims." *The Times–Picayune*. Monday, July 2, 1973, sec. 2: 7. Print.

_____. "Devastating French Quarter Fire Probed by 3 Agencies." *The Times–Picayune*. Tuesday, June 26, 1973, sec. 1: 1, 3. Print.

_____. "Incident Begins in Chaos and Produces Confusion." *The Times–Picayune*. Tuesday, January 9, 1973, sec. 1: 6. Print.

_____. "100 Policemen Fire at Sniper." *The Times–Picayune*. Monday, January 8, 1973, sec. 1: 6. Print.

_____. "Positive Identifications Made for 9 Fire Victims." *The Times–Picayune*. Wednesday, June 27, 1973, sec. 1: 3. Print.

Shiltz, Randy. *And the Band Played On: Politics, People, and the AIDS Epidemic*, 20th Anniv. ed. New York: St. Martin's Press, 2007. Print.

"Six More Victims of Fire Identified, Coroner Says." *The Times–Picayune*. Friday, June 29, 1973, sec. 1: 9. Print.

Somme, Etienne. "The Homosexual Question." *The Times–Picayune*. Sunday, October 7, 1973, sec. 2: 2. Print.

_____. "'Judging' Gays." *The Times–Picayune*. Sunday, June 9, 1974, sec. 1: 10. Print.

"Souls Laundered." *The Times–Picayune*. Friday, October 12, 1973, sec. 1: 14. Print.

Sprigg, Peter. "Homosexual Parent Survey: Summary of Findings." *Family Research Council*. n.d. Web. November 21, 2012.

"Survivor Discovers Her True Friends." *The Advocate* 143 (July 31, 1974): 8. Print.

Swindall, Sharon. "Bar Fire Kills at least 28." *The Daily Record*. Monday, June 25, 1973, sec. 1: 1, 6. Print.

_____. "Rookie Fireman Describes Fire."

The Daily Record. Thursday, June 28, 1973, sec. 1: 1. Print.

_____. "Tourist Recalls Nightmare." *The Daily Record.* Wednesday, June 27, 1973, sec. 1: 7. Print.

Tavernise, Sabrina. "Married Couples Are No Longer a Majority, Census finds." *The New York Times.* 26 May 2011. Web. April 29, 2013.

"30th Bar Blaze Victim Dies: Eight Remain Unidentified." *The States-Item.* Friday, June 29, 1973, A3. Print.

Thomas, Lanny. "Fun, Drinks, Song, with Death at the Piano." *The States-Item.* Monday, June 25, 1973, A6b. Print.

_____. "Have Labels Overshadowed 29 Deaths." *The States-Item.* Thursday, June 28, 1973, A16. Print.

Thompson, Mark L. "32 Killed in Fire Remembered in Quarter Church." *The Times–Picayune.* Friday, June 2, 1995, B1, 8. Print.

"Toll of Blaze Here Now Is 32." *The Times–Picayune.* Friday, July 13, 1973, sec. 1: 22. Print.

Toobin, Jeffrey. *The Nine: Inside the Secret World of the Supreme Court.* New York: Random House, 2007. Print.

Townsend, Johnny. *Let the Faggots Burn.* BookLocker.com, 2011. Print.

Treadway, Joan. "Copter Pilot Rescues Eight." *The Times–Picayune.* Thursday, November 30, 1972, sec. 1: 16. Print.

_____. "50s 'Climate of Hostility' to Gays Gone—What Now?" *The Times–Picayune.* Sunday, September 16, 1973, sec. 1: 21. Print.

_____. "Gay Community Surfaces in Tragedy of N.O. Fire." *The Times–Picayune.* Tuesday, September 11, 1973, sec. 1: 13. Print.

_____. "Homosexuals Disagree on Behavior's 'Sickness.'" *The Times–Picayune.* Thursday, September 13, 1973, sec. 4: 2. Print.

_____. "It's Not Illegal to Be Gay—Certain Acts Are Criminal." *The Times–Picayune.* Saturday, September 15, 1973, sec. 1: 14. Print.

_____. "Psychiatric and Clerical Views—A Wide Spectrum." *The Times–Picayune.* Friday, September 14, 1973, sec. 2: 18. Print.

_____. "A Walk on the Gay Side: Independent Route Taken for Personal Objectives." *The Times–Picayune.* Wednesday, September 12, 1973, sec. 2: 8. Print.

Tresch, George. Telephone interview. July 5, 2012.

"200 Attend Service for Lounge Victims." *The States-Item.* Monday, July 2, 1973, A3. Print.

"2 Suspects Are Found in Quarter Slayings." *The Times–Picayune.* Friday, September 2, 1988, B4. Print.

United States v. Scheffer. Legal Information Institute: Cornell University Law School. n.d. Web. March 4, 2012.

"Upstairs Lounge Fire Network News Coverage." Youtube. n.d. Web. July 25, 2011.

Ussery, Bob. "Police Crackdown on Gays in Park Is 'Due to Calls.'" *The Times–Picayune.* Tuesday, August 17, 1976, sec. 2: 3. Print.

_____. "Wallender Is Now Facing Tough California Charge." *The Times–Picayune.* Friday, November 16, 1973, Sec. 1: 1, 3. Print.

"VCC Blaned for French Quarter Firetraps." *The States-Item.* Thursday, June 28, 1973, A3. Print.

"Vice Charges Okayed by DA: Obscenity, 8 Other Morals Cases Accepted." *The Times–Picayune.* Wednesday, October 8, 1958, sec. 2: 22. Print.

Vieux Carré Commission. *Regulations and Procedures.* New Orleans, Louisiana, 2001. Print.

"Volz Airs Plan to Halt Rapes." *The Times–Picayune.* Saturday, March 24, 1973, sec. 2: 3. Print.

Walker, Greta. "Publisher: Gay Men Have More Buying Power." *The Times–Picayune.* Sunday, August 22, 1976, sec. 4: 13. Print.

"'We Knew Them as People' Pastor Tells Gay Mourners." *The States-Item.* Tuesday, June 26, 1973, A3. Print.

Weiss, Kenn. "Fire Safety Check to Start in Quarter: Fontaine Believes Arson Caused Fire." *The Times–Picayune.* Saturday, June 30, 1973, sec. 1: 1. Print.

Weldon, Nancy. "Counseling Given in Gay Marriages." *The Times–Picayune*. Sunday, March 9, 1975, sec. 1: 40. Print.

"We'll Know Next Time: Memorial Fund Coming To An End." *The Advocate* 145 (August 28, 1974): 24. Print.

Whittaker, Steven (pseud.). Personal email. June 28, 2013.

_____. Telephone interview. June 27, 2013.

["Who Is the Gay People's Coalition"]. *The New Orleans Causeway*. 1: 1 (August 6, 1973): 2. Print.

Wian, Casey, and Michael Pearson. "Boy Scout Leaders Put Off Vote On Gay Membership." 6 February 2013. Web. February 14, 2013.

Wickman, Forrest. "A Colorful History: How the Rainbow Became a Symbol of Gay Pride." *Slate*. Tuesday, 5 June 2012. Web. February 21, 2013.

Wilcox, W. Bradford. "The Evolution of Divorce." *National Affairs*. Fall 2009. Web. November 21, 2012.

Willey, A. Elwood. "The Upstairs Lounge Fire: New Orleans Louisiana." *NFPA Journal* 68. 1 (January 1974) 16–20. Print.

Wilson, Austin. "Race Note Seen in Prison Rapes." *The Times–Picayune*. Friday, March 24, 1973, sec. 5: 1.

Winn, Rev. Carole Cotton. Personal email. August 18, 2009.

_____. Telephone interview. August 17, 2009.

Wolff, Tim. *The Sons of Tenessee Williams*. First Run Features, 2011. DVD.

"Yesterday's Dreams, Today's Ghosts." *The Advocate* 133 (March 13, 1974): 12, 16 Print.

Index

Numbers in **bold italics** indicate pages with photographs.